History
of
Pioneer Kentucky

Robert S. Cotterill
Member of the Filson Club, of the Kentucky State
Historical Society and of the Bradford Memorial
and Historical Association; Professor of
History, Western Maryland College

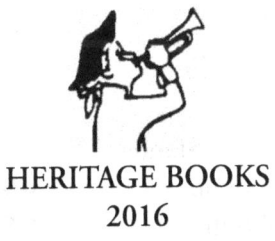

HERITAGE BOOKS
2016

HERITAGE BOOKS
AN IMPRINT OF HERITAGE BOOKS, INC.

Books, CDs, and more—Worldwide

For our listing of thousands of titles see our website
at
www.HeritageBooks.com

A Facsimile Reprint
Published 2016 by
HERITAGE BOOKS, INC.
Publishing Division
5810 Ruatan Street
Berwyn Heights, Md. 20740

Copyright © 1917 R. S. Cotterill

Originally published
Johnson & Hardin
Cincinnati
1917

— Publisher's Notice —
In reprints such as this, it is often not possible to remove blemishes from the original. We feel the contents of this book warrant its reissue despite these blemishes and hope you will agree and read it with pleasure.

International Standard Book Numbers
Paperbound: 978-0-7884-0754-3
Clothbound: 978-0-7884-6410-2

TO MY WIFE

PREFACE

THE HISTORY OF PIONEER KENTUCKY is submitted to the reader with many misgivings on the part of its author. As the work has progressed he has come to realize more and more clearly the greatness of the undertaking and his own deficiencies as a historian. Seven years ago, when this little book was begun, he had, if the truth be told, but scant suspicion of either. Perhaps the only good thing that can be said of it is, that the author has searched diligently for the truth and told it without prejudice when he found it.

The preparation of the book has gone forward in the midst of constant duties as a teacher, and this fact has affected the plan of the work. It was a State history that was first in mind. But the fleetness of time and the rarity of opportunities for research soon made it necessary to limit the period under investigation. It is the author's hope to carry on the history of the State in succeeding volumes as leisure, and the public, permits.

Most of the material used has been obtained from the Draper Collection now housed in the Historical Library at the University of Wisconsin, and from the Durrett Collection now distributed in the Library of the University of Chicago. Much of this material, especially in the Draper Collection, is in manuscript, uncalendared and practically inaccessible save after most patient searching. No claim is made of having exhausted this; a thorough investiga-

PREFACE.

tion would require constant effort over a long period of time, and this the writer was not able to make.

The author tenders his warmest thanks to his present and former pupils for their constant aid and encouragement. Except for the untiring efforts of Miss Bessie Conkwright the book would hardly have seen the light of day. For the faithful assistance of Miss Eloise Somerlatt in revision and proof-reading the author is entirely unable to express an adequate appreciation.

CONTENTS

	PAGE
THE DEBATABLE LAND	1
BACKGROUND OF KENTUCKY HISTORY	16
PREHISTORIC KENTUCKY	30
EXPLORATION OF KENTUCKY	42
THE SURVEYORS	58
TRANSYLVANIA	71
TRANSYLVANIA AND VIRGINIA	94
KENTUCKY COUNTY	108
THE GREAT INVASION	129
GROWTH AND EXPANSION	150
THE YEAR OF SORROWS	177
THE STRUGGLE FOR AUTONOMY	198
ECONOMIC AND SOCIAL	229

History of Pioneer Kentucky

THE DEBATABLE LAND

BY THE middle of the eighteenth century, the English colonies in America had grown, by means of wars, treachery and natural increase, from a few isolated settlements to twelve virile states. In the same age, the French, impelled by religion and lust of power, had extended their claims and sometimes their authority over a region many times larger than the mother country. But the Alleghany Mountains barred the western advance of the English, while the French had not the power, though not lacking the inclination, to settle the long reaches separating their villages on the St. Lawrence, the Mississippi and the Gulf. There was left between the Mississippi and the Alleghanies a vast region claimed by both nations and occupied by neither. Through this flowed a broad river which the French, from its appearance and their own ignorance, named La Belle Riviere. South of this river lay in unbroken wildness, a land which had not yet suffered the habitation of a white man. Both French and English claimed it, the Indian fought for it, and no one possessed it. It was, indeed, a Debatable Land.

It was not, however, an unknown country. If it could be said of early Kentucky, as of ancient Athens, that it was as great as it reputation, it would have lacked little of perfection. Although inhabited by no tribe, hardly a warrior of the Ohio Indians but had visited it on war parties or on hunting trips. To the traders that came to them from Virginia and the other colonies, they described Kentucky in language at once vague and beautiful. Its eastern limits, as all men knew, were the borders of Virginia, but its other boundaries were yet to be determined. On the north they rested on the Ohio; the Tennessee or even the Mississippi was assigned as the western terminal. But to the south it stretched away, vague and indefinite, over the river valleys and through the blue haze of the mountains. That it stopped short of the Cherokees, was all the curiosity of the trader could elicit and the jealousy of the red man would disclose. The Indian Kentucky, in fact, had its center at the old Indian trading post at Indian Fields, near Red River, and the name was applied without nice distinctions to all the country around. The traders carried to their homes innumerable stories of the country, and the reports they spread of its beauty assuredly did not grow less in the telling.

In very truth, there could not have been found in all the land a paradise more perfect for the hunter. From the eastern mountains to the Mississippi, the earth was covered by a forest almost unbroken of deciduous and evergreen trees.[1] There was little underbrush and no swamps. So luxuriantly and so closely intermingled grew the trees, the Indians could report without exaggeration that the sun's rays never reached the earth in the Kentucky country. Here in the valleys grew the great oaks, the hickory, the ash and the walnut. Along the water courses the sycamore grew white and tall; the foothills were covered by the beech and the poplar, standing round and straight and beautiful as Ionic pillars. The

---

[1] Filson, *Description of Kentucky*, p. 22.

maple and the sugar-tree abounded everywhere. In the mountains, the pine, the cedar and the hazel predominated. In the shadows of the statelier trees were those of a humbler appearance. The coffee-tree and the cucumber-tree were familiar to the early Kentuckians, but are entirely unknown to their descendants. The pawpaw and mulberry are yet familiar names. The sugar-tree, the walnut, the pawpaw, the hickory and the mulberry produced fruit which formed no small part of the primitive bill of fare. So extensive were the forests that not even a century of characteristic destruction at the hands of the people has sufficed to entirely denude the state. The paucity of undergrowth, added to the size and orderly ranks of the trees, gave to the Kentucky forest a peculiar charm in the eyes of the hunter, the hermit, and the pioneer. Irregular Indian and buffalo trails wound through the forests from north to south and from east to west; in our time these remain, sometimes macadamized and forming a modern road, but oftener existing as sunken paths through the valleys or as gulleys over the hills.[2]

But there was one section of Kentucky whereon no forests grew. An area of six thousand square miles lying immediately south of the Falls of the Ohio was destitute of trees, though over-abounding in grass.[3] The name "Barrens" given it by the settler has been replaced by the more appropriate and less euphonious "Pennyrile." This region lay, a vast oasis, in a desert of woodland. The simple pioneers, slow to believe in the fertility of any soil untenanted by the trees, fastened upon it a name that is now hardly a memory. The dearth of forest, however,

---

[2] The old buffalo road from Upper Blue Licks to Lower Blue Licks is still visible in many places.
[3] Shaler, *History of Kentucky*, p. 28.

was owing not to the poverty of the soil but to the cunning of red hunters. The Indians had early cleared away the trees from the land in order that the growing grass might tempt thither the buffaloes that roamed the prairies of Illinois and the west. Whether persuaded by this or by other causes, the buffaloes came in numbers large enough to excite the wonder, the admiration and sometimes the fear of the settler. The belief in a great desert existing somewhere in the heart of America was a part of the creed of all orthodox men in colonial days. It held in the popular imagination the place of the El Dorado of two centuries before; everyone believed in it and it was marked down in every map. It required, then, very little provocation for an explorer to discover a desert. When the first travelers in Kentucky looked out upon the "Barrens," they were not slow to persuade themselves that they saw before them the Great American Desert and to name it accordingly. The desert character of the "Barrens" has long since been exploded, but it is interesting to observe that the idea of a great central desert in America is not yet extinct. Since the settlement of Kentucky, the desert has moved gradually westward, until at the present time it rests at the base of the Rocky Moutains in much diminished awfulness.

But is was not alone as a woodland that Kentucky excited the curiosity or the desire of the hunter. The earth there, so said the Indians, was carpeted with cane even as the land of Virginia with the grass. To the men of the Yadkin and Shenandoah this was passing strange, and not a few of them were drawn to Kentucky to view the novel spectacle.[4] Nor had the Indians reported falsely: the

---

[4] Simon Kenton was led to Kentucky by the desire of finding the famous canelands. Collins, *History of Kentucky*, Vol. II, p. 443.

northern region of Kentucky lying along the Ohio was covered with the evergreen crop. Herein the cane grew wild and rank. At its greatest height it reached twelve feet and never fell below three. At times the stalk attained a diameter of two inches, and never were paths able to be made through the brakes save with the utmost difficulty. It was in these cane-brakes that the Indians fought their fiercest battles and prepared their deadliest ambushes. When the settlement of Kentucky began, it was in the cane-brakes that the settlers were most often ensnared. As Kentucky was divided into barrens and woodland, so was it divided—sharply—into hill and plain. The entire eastern region—one-third of the present state—was a "vein of mountains" running from northeast to southwest and half a hundred miles in breadth. Their Indian name, "Ouasiotos,"[5] has long been replaced by the Cumberland. They were in no case lofty nor difficult of passage, but from their eastern slope presented an appearance so gloomy that ofttimes the hunter had not the courage to attempt their real difficulties. But once safely over their ranges, a traveler might feel well repaid for his past privations by the prospect before him of central Kentucky. This was a region of rolling plain, covered with the now famous bluegrass and dotted closely with stately trees. Herein then, as now, lay the heart of Kentucky. The Indians saw in it their favorite hunting ground and the eastern hunters sought it as their heart's desire; the first and firmest settlements were planted on its rivers, and it early demanded, and has since retained, the hegemony of the state. Along the Ohio and the Mississippi the plains fell slowly away to the prairie. A broken chain of hills ran through at

---

[5] The name is so spelled on Evan's map of 1755.

the north from east to west which, although of considerable elevation in some places, never approached the dignity of mountains.

Not the least beautiful nor the least useful of the features of Kentucky were the rivers. There need be no error in writing of these, since they remain in appearance, as in use, practically the same as in the days of Pontiac. There are the same shoals in their beds and the same jungles along their banks. Their currents are crossed not by bridges but by ferry boats which, even if not as old as those of pioneer build, are yet of very similar structure and utility. One of these rivers, rising in the eastern mountains, after many wearisome detours flows into the Ohio near its mouth. Among the Indians it was called the Shawnee River, but Dr. Walker renamed it the Cumberland [6] in honor of the Duke of Cumberland to whose character the "amazing crookedness" of the stream bore a startling resemblance. Twin sister of the Cumberland is the Tennessee, which after beginning in east Tennessee makes many weird detours in that State and Alabama before turning to the Ohio. It was the Cherokee River in the same sense that the Mediterranean was a Roman sea.[7] Somewhat to the east of these were the Green and the Salt rivers. The latter of these in early times was called Pigeon River. The licking was known to the Indians as the Nepernine and to the early settlers as the Great Salt Creek.[8] It owes its present name to the multitude of salt "licks" along its banks. The Big Sandy River of today was the Totteroy or Chatteraway of the Indians. But

---

[6] Walker's "Journal" in Johnston, *First Exploration of Kentucky*.
[7] Treaty of Fort Stanwix in *Documentary History of New York*, Vol. I, p. 587.
[8] Lewis Evan's map, 1755.

the largest, the most beautiful, and the best known was the river now called the Kentucky. Among the Indians themselves it was a favorite stream, and the fertile plains through which it flowed were the favorite hunting ground of the red men. In the facile limestone soil its current had cut a deep bed and the banks in pioneer time, and even now, were clothed with the stately forest. Its wide reputation among the Indian tribes is evidenced by the numerous names it possessed. It was variously called Cuttawa, Catawba, Catawa, Chenoka, Chenoa and Millewakane.[9] From this last the indefatigable Dr. Walker evolved a name of his own, "Milley." Among the early settlers it was for some time known as the Louisa or Levisa River through a mistaken identification with another stream to which Dr. Walker had given that name.[10] The tributaries and headwaters of the Kentucky rivers interlocked in a most remarkable manner. A map of Kentucky seemed a mere network of rivers. All rose in the Cumberland Mountains and all flowed into the Ohio. Portages were short and easy. The rivers were all alike distinguished by winding courses and multiple shoals.

The bluegrass of Kentucky grew from a soil that rested lightly upon deep strata of limestone. This was a rock easily affected by the action of water. As a result many of the rivers had cut deep beds for themselves and some had even sunk from view, existing for much of their courses as underground streams. The same causes had produced caverns and caves over the land in almost endless variety. Of these the most noted was Mammoth Cave on Green River. It was an object of awe to the Indians and, since its discovery by the white men, has ranked as one of the

---

[9] Johnston, *First Explorations of Kentucky*, p. 63 (note).
[10] A tributary of the Kanawha.

Seven Wonders of the world. At its dark mouth the superstitious Indian paused in veneration as the devout Greek before the Lake of Avernus. Generations gone, their mound-building ancestors had used the caves for a much more practical purpose in making them their dwelling places. Exploration has revealed in the caves many vestiges of their past life—their pottery, their clothing and their arms. It was, in fact, from their dwelling in the caves of Kentucky that the Cherokees gained their distinctive name among their Indian neighbors.

More tempting to the buffaloes than the long grasses of the barrens were the numerous salt "licks" that were scattered over the land. These were springs of salt water[11] and derive their name from the fact that the game thronged thither to lick the surrounding ground so deeply impregnated with the salt. They were the great congregating places of all the wild animals: one observer reported that he saw ten thousand at the Lower Blue Licks at one time. It is undoubtedly true that they thronged to the licks in enormous numbers and literally trampled each other under foot in their eagerness to reach the salt. The ground surrounding the various licks are for many acres veritable reservoirs of buried bones. All paths led to the licks. Beasts of prey found it more profitable to await at the licks their intended victim than to hunt them down in the forest. Nor did the settlers neglect the methods of the beasts, whose instincts they in so large measure possessed; the licks furnished them the meat and the means of preserving it. The licks were scattered all over the land but were more numerous along the rivers—one of which owes

---

[11] Prof. Shaler asserts in his *History of Kentucky* that the salt springs are an indication that at one time the surface of Kentucky was below sea level, pp. 40, 41.

its name to their proximity. The two best known, perhaps, were the Upper and Lower Blue Licks on the Licking. Both are now extinct. Drennon's Lick and Boone's on the Kentucky and Bullitt's on Salt River were, and are, springs of great power. The latter was the great salt manufacturing center in the pioneer days of Kentucky. Big Bone Lick in northern Kentucky was not so much a spring as a sepulcher. To the Indians it was from time immemorial the "place of the big bones." [12] When the first pioneers reached the Lick they found bones lying around it in great quantities and of gigantic size. They were the melancholy relics of a vanished race of mastodons. These animals must have exceeded by many times the size of elephants and indubitably flourished when the earth was young. The Indians when questioned about them asserted stolidly that the bones had lain in that position since the beginning of years.

The game to be found in Kentucky was of such quality and quantity as to render the land the favorite hunting ground of both northern and southern Indians.[13] The buffaloes abounded at the licks and on the plain. They fed and moved in large herds at fixed periods and by regular roads. As they traveled the forests year after year from one lick to another, they made deeply marked roads through the country. On account of their huge size and the delicious savor of their cooked flesh they were esteemed by the Indians above all other game. The deer were not less numerous than the buffaloes and were hunted by both red men and white for the flesh and the skins. Bears were numerous, and with the panther, the wildcat and the wolf, were frequently encountered at the licks or in the

---

[12] Lewis Evan's map of Kentucky, 1755.
[13] Filson, *Description of Kentucky*, p. 27.

mountains. Wild ducks and geese were abundant on the rivers and were "amazingly" numerous on the Ohio. Turkeys, pheasants, partridges and parroquets were common, while the Indians asserted and the white man believed that there was native to the land a woodcock whose bill was pure ivory! Great owls there were, too, we are told, which made surprising noises. In the rivers were buffalo-fish and cat-fish whose weight often reached one hundred pounds. There were trout of thirty-pound weight, but no shad or herring. Beavers and otters were found in not a few streams.

The English race in America owes to the Iroquois Indians a debt which it has but tardily acknowledged and never paid.[14] Living among the lakes of New York they formed for the colonies a conscious shield which the French, try as they might, could not successfully pierce. Had Champlain, instead of arousing their enmity, secured their allegiance, the war for Independence might have been fought against the fleur-de-lis rather than the blended cross. Nor was their power confined to their habitation; like their Roman prototype, they conquered widely and ruthlessly. By 1750 there was not a tribe east of the Mississippi failing to acknowledge their pre-eminence, and but few that failed to bow to their power. They brooked no rivals; many a rivaling tribe conquered was compelled to take the name "women," under which stigma they could initiate nothing of importance either at home or in the field save by express permission of their masters, the Iroquois. The *pax Iroquois* was of incalculable benefit to the English. Penn settled among, christianized and despoiled the Susquehannas, who dared not fight against the

---

[14] Fiske, *Discovery of America*, Vol. I, Chap. I.

will of the Iroquois; the Tuscaroras of North Carolina suffered without revenge a myriad of injuries from the white men until it pleased their overlords to let them take the warpath. Finally, when the human tide of settlers poured over the Alleghanies into the valley of Kentucky, it was into a country almost void of men. It was the hunting ground of the dreaded Six Nations; their savage mandate had gone forth that no one should dwell therein. The fear of the Iroquois and the dread of their wrath had kept the land inviolate. Short hunting parties stole in and out of the state, but of fixed habitation there was little, and, at the time of settlement, none. So the early Kentuckians had no obstinate Indian tribes to subdue, but merely straggling parties to encounter or friendly Iroquois to cajole. When the Iroquois finally were compelled to choose between the Englishman and the colonist, the exploration was too far advanced to be checked.

There were, in truth, in 1750 but three places in Kentucky where the red men dwelt. These were the extreme west of Kentucky, where the Chickasaws lived in savage independence on the cliffs of the Mississippi; a small section of ground opposite the mouth of the Scioto River, occupied by a Shawnese town; and an isolated town in central Kentucky. The record of the last of these is at once the most interesting and the least known. In 1745, Chartier, a French trader, met and traded with the Shawnese Indians at the Falls of the Ohio.[15] Setting out from the Falls in company with a predatory band of Indians, his company soon encountered two traders whom they despoiled of their goods, amounting to about £1600 in value. Continuing their journey southward, they set-

---

[15] Draper, MSS. *Life of Boone*, Vol. II, p. 169.

tled on a small stream that was afterwards named Lulbegrud Creek.[16] Here they laid out a town to which they gave the name Eskippakithiki. Though the town has long since disappeared, the present name, Indian Old Fields, preserves the memory of the ancient post.[17] Dwelling in the heart of the bluegrass region and at a distance from both kinsman and foe, the exiled Shawnese prospered and grew apace. But after two or three years the warriors of the Six Nations learned of the trespassers on their hunting grounds. From that hour the life of the Shawnese was one of danger and fear; the Iroquois harassed them incessantly. The northern Shawnese meanwhile sent reiterated requests for their wandering brethren to return to the tribe, but they were reluctant to leave Kentucky. Finally, worn out by Iroquois attacks, the exiles began their journey out of the land. Numbering four hundred and fifty, they traveled down the Lulbegrud, the Red, the Kentucky, and the Ohio, to the Tennessee. Ascending the Tennessee to Bear Creek they met and wantonly attacked the Chickasaws. That warlike tribe speedily punished and expelled the intruders, who fled to the Creeks of the south. In 1748 the remnant of the tribe took up anew the journey to the Ohio Shawnese. They tarried for awhile on the Cumberland River in Tennessee until attacked by the unforgiving Chickasaws. Reduced to two hundred and fifty they set out again down the Cumberland, having their women and children in canoes and the warriors traveling on guard along the bank. They reached the Ohio, but on account of the heavy rains were unable to ascend it. Stopping at the Wabash they were

---

[16] Lulbegrud Creek was so named by Boone.
[17] The site of the old town is some fifteen miles from the present town of Winchester.

persuaded to join the Indians at Kaskaskia. After a stay here of two years they were, in 1762, taken home by the Ohio Shawnese. Eskippakithiki at one time was a town of considerable size. It was a market and a neutral meeting place for the northern and southern Indians. In the period of its prosperity and after its abandonment, it was visited frequently by white traders, among whom the rollicking John Finley was conspicuous. It was at Eskippakithiki that the venerable Shawnese chieftain, Black Hoof, was born. He accompanied the tribe on all its wanderings, and years afterwards when Kentucky was settled and himself an old man, he revisited his old home, identified its landmarks and related its history.

The Ohio Shawnese dwelling along the banks of the Scioto River possessed at its mouth on the Ohio a capital of a hundred houses. A portion of this was destroyed some years before the exploration of Kentucky by a furious storm that raised the Scioto and the Ohio far above their accustomed beds.[18] The dispossessed Shawnese took courage to cross the Ohio and establish anew their dwelling places on the Kentucky shore. The new town was, in modern parlance, merely a suburb of the old and the same name Shannoah was common to both. The Kentucky town contained forty houses and the combined strength of the two was about two hundred and fifty men.

The Chickasaws of the region bordering on the Mississippi could hardly be called inhabitants of Kentucky; to the early Kentuckians the name embraced the land east of the Cherokee or Tennessee River.[19] The Chickasaws were comparatively few in number, never having more than a

---
[18] Gist's "Journal" in Johnston, *First Exploration of Kentucky.*
[19] Treaty of Fort Stanwix, in *Documentary History of New York,* Vol. I, p. 587.

few hundred fighting men, but their numerical weakness was more than overbalanced by their native fierceness and daring. Happily, their arms were never turned against the infant settlements; secure behind their river they ignored and were ignored by the settlers. Not until Clarke, in violation of all rights of friendship and fairness, attempted to place a fort [20] in the midst of their homes did they lift their hands. In the early annals of Kentucky there is much mention of the Shawnese, the Wyandots and the Cherokees, but the name of the Chickasaws rarely finds a place in its history.

To the impartial observer it would seem that two hundred and fifty miles of separating forests and mountains would have sufficed to prevent the quarrels and even the contests of the red nations. But no obstacle seemed able to restrain the Shawnese on the north of Kentucky and the Cherokees on the south, and in consequence of this Kentucky was crossed and recrossed by well-marked war roads by which the warriors of either nation sallied forth for slaughter or revenge. These roads, like the paths of the desert, were marked white with the bones of the dead. Beginning at Shannoah on the Ohio, the greatest of all these roads ran south across the headwaters of the Great Salt Lick Creek and the Kentucky and through the passes of the Ouasiotos to the Cherokee country.

Along this road went year after year Shawnese against Cherokee, and Cherokee against Shawnese, unceasingly. From many regions this was the "common road to the Cuttawa country." [21] Boone built his Wilderness Road for fifty miles along this highway of contention. Another war road ran from Shannoah to the Great Buffalo Lick and thence

---

[20] Fort Jefferson.
[21] Lewis Evan's Map.

west to the Falls of the Ohio, passing Big Bone Lick in its course. From Big Bone Lick a warpath ran to the great war road and joined it on the crossing of the north fork of the Kentucky; thence it ran northeast to the Totteroy and down it to the Ohio. The continuation of this road northward extended to the northwest territory and even to the Great Lakes.

Much effort has been expended and great ingenuity displayed in the various attempts to determine the origin and meaning of the name Kentucky. The honor of giving a name to the State has been readily assigned to each tribe that has in the past threatened the country and molested its people. Common sense would suggest that the name of a country might originate with its owners, or at least its conquerors, and the truth seems to be that although Kentucky was known by different names to the various tribes that desired and tormented it, the dominant and lasting name was Iroquois. The Kentakee of the Six Nations was easily corrupted into "Kentuckee" by the traders whose spelling was conditioned on a by no means subtle perception of sounds. Nor has the meaning of the word escaped the imaginative powers of the etymologist. The school children are taught that it signifies the "head of the river;" it has been said to mean "a cane land," a "middle land" and even a "dark and bloody ground." But the Iroquois Kentakee was in simple English, "meadow land" [22] and was a term peculiarly appropriate to central Kentucky to which region the name was at first limited. For a score of years the land was called indifferently "Louisa" or "Kentucke." How the latter name prevailed and gradually extended to all sections of the State is rather a matter for the psychologist than the historian.

---

[22] Brown, *Political Beginnings of Kentucky*, p. 10 (note).

BACKGROUND OF KENTUCKY HISTORY.

IT WOULD have been well for the pioneers of Kentucky had the policy of the Iroquois served to destroy the people whose country their strength sufficed to subdue. But the various tribes that had claimed or possessed Kentucky had been but prohibited from the land; they remained on the borders of the country, constantly striking at each other across the length and breadth of it, and prepared for all their internecine wars to unite against any prospective occupant thereon. So it came to pass that when the first settlers came into Kentucky, their entrance was opposed, their settlements endangered, and their progress delayed by Indians who were no more occupants of the land than they. Therefore, for the better understanding of the history of Kentucky it is necessary to consider the location and organization of these border Indians and the source and character of the immigration which wrested Kentucky from their hands.

Kentucky from its very position was an object of attack to both northern and southern Indians. The Cherokees from their homes in Georgia and Tennessee had an easy, though long, entrance to the land over the Cuttawa war road. The northern Indians [1] from their greater proximity were even more to be feared. These northern Indians usually acted together in a loose confederation under the leadership of the Shawnese.[2] This fierce and unforgiving people had its homes principally along the valleys of the

---

[1] Dodge, *Red Men of the Ohio Valley*, Chap. I.
[2] Croghan in 1765 estimated their number at 300.

Scioto River. They were by no means destitute of towns, and at least two, under the names of Piqua and Chillicothe, attained considerable size and widespread notoriety. The Shawnese were not a savage or a nomadic people. They lived in the land of their fathers and could boast of, and apologize for, more than the ordinary advancement of an Indian tribe. They cultivated with success the rich valleys of the Scioto; their abundant corn crops aroused the cupidity of their white neighbor and became in time of war the first and principal object of attack. They dwelt in substantial houses and, after the settlement of Kentucky by the white man, came to possess considerable property in horses and slaves. Up to the last half of the seventeenth century they had dwelt on the banks of the Cumberland River in western Kentucky, and had given their name to that stream. In 1682 they fell under the sway of the widely conquering Iroquois and remained so until the downfall of the latter. They were divided into many sections in different parts of the country, until finally in 1760 the whole people was united along the Scioto. The Shawnese, notwithstanding their nominal vassalage to the Iroquois, were of a warlike and enterprising nature. Ninety per cent. of the battles and outrages of early Kentucky might, with justice, be laid at their door. Their chieftains were as a rule men of distinction and often of great ability. The warriors though bloodthirsty in battle did not often avenge themselves on captives or prisoners.

The Delawares had by 1750 diminished greatly in numbers, valor and renown. They claimed and were acknowledged to be the most ancient of the aborigines. They, like the Shawnese, were now under the power of the Iroquois and had even been forced by the haughty confederacy to designate themselves "women." They had been removed by the Iroquois from their primitive homes in Delaware and Pennsylvania to the lands north of the Ohio. There they were settled on the banks of the Muskingum and Tuscarawa rivers; in the solitudes of their new environment they gradually came to possess many of their old-time virtues, and at the time of the American Revolution their chiefs exerted great influence in the affairs of the northern Indians. They were, in general, inclined to peace with the white man and only infrequently were induced by the fiercer Shawnese to unite with them in their bloody forays on the Kentucky settlements. Their warriors numbered some six hundred and fifty and had, united to the usual bravery and cunning of the Indian, a very unusual sense of justice and fairness.

The Wyandots [3] were nominally Christians and lived along the banks of the Sandusky River. They were originally of Iroquois stock and were called Hurons by the French. They were the bravest of the brave. In their expeditions against foes of whatever color or nation they abandoned themselves to the wildest atrocities. They were characterized by a perseverance and tenacity of purpose rarely encountered among savages. They alone of the Indians preferred open fighting to ambuscade and possessed the ability to continue a battle even when heavily punished. The ordinary Indian war party while not lacking in courage was not steadfast in fighting if its own loss was of any considerable extent; the Wyandots fought to the last man and would not retreat. While they less frequently took part in the forays into Kentucky they never entered the State without leaving a trail of blood and lamentation.[4] They were unconquered by the Iroquois and,

---

[3] Simon Girty was an honored member of the Wyandots.
[4] Estill's defeat and the slaughter at Upper and Lower Blue Licks were due to the Wyandots.

though with heavy losses, had brought to an abrupt and inglorious close the conquering march of that people towards the west.

The Shawnese were the principal people that molested Kentucky from the north, and the Wyandots and the Delawares were their chief abettors. A few other tribes, however, are worthy of notice. The Miamis dwelt along the Miami and the Maumee rivers. Their ancient name was Twigtee or Tawixti.[5] They, like the other Indians, waged war with the Iroquois and were not finally worsed by them until 1702. The Mingoes were a mongrel tribe of Indians made up chiefly of refugees and outcasts from other tribes; their main strength came from the Senecas of New York. They were a savage and vicious race but some of their leaders were men of much magnanimity. They dwelt in eastern Ohio. All these differing tribes lived lives of constant strife among themselves, yet on many occasions they showed themselves capable of laying aside their contentions and acting in close alliance. With the exception of the Wyandots they were all nominally tributary to the Iroquois. But the burden of their vassalage rested lightly upon them; in most essentials they were free. They numbered, perhaps, some fifty thousand souls.

From the south, Kentucky enjoyed comparative immunity from Indian attack. In fact the only tribe whom interest or propinquity impelled to warfare with the first Kentuckians was the Cherokees. This tribe, when immigration was first directed to Kentucky, had its principal towns in eastern Tennessee. They had originally extended much farther north over the Alleghany region, but had gradually been driven south by the Iroquois and Shawnese.

---

[5] Croghan assigns 250 warriors each to the Wyandots and Twigtees. Croghan's "Journal," *Early Western Travels* (ed. Thwaites).

They were of Iroquois stock and called themselves Ani-Yunwiya.[6] Among themselves they were divided into three main divisions. Each of these divisions spoke a differing dialect of the same language. Though as a people the Cherokees were confined to Tennessee and Georgia, they asserted a claim to all Kentucky as well. Moreover, they sold their claim at various prices and at different times.[7] While they made no attempt to occupy Kentucky, they were continually fighting for it and on its soil. The Shawnese were their great enemies, and the two rivals struggled without ceasing along the whole length of Cuttawa road. Yet for the most part the Cherokees respected their treaties and agreements with the white men. Occasionally they were induced by the Shawnese to bury their ancestral enmity and aid in destroying the Kentucky settlers, but it must not be forgotten that the white men in their relation with both northern and southern Indians were often the aggressors. For the rest, the Cherokees, like most other Indian peoples, lived in fixed habitations and subsisted from the fruits of the field. They numbered about 2,500 warriors in 1750. They fled before the power, and sometimes acknowledged the suzerainty of the Iroquois.

Among the standard American delusions, that one in which Kentucky is represented as a child of Virginia deservedly holds a prominent position. A close study, indeed, of the older commonwealth will result in great benefit, inasmuch as it will not fail to disclose how thoroughly Kentucky was *not* Virginian in origin, in customs or in ideals. Virginia's part in Kentucky's history will be found to con-

---

[6] Mooney, "Myths of the Cherokees," in *Nineteenth Report of the American Bureau of Ethnology.*
[7] Notably to Henderson.

sist not so much in a contribution of settlers as in an opportune abandonment of a very shadowy claim to sovereignty. Inasmuch as the aspirations and the movements of a people are for the most part a direct result of their economic environment, it becomes necessary to consider the industrial conditions of those sections from which the population of Kentucky was supposed to be drawn. For the peculiar economic development of Virginia, thanks must be given to the intricate workings of the organ popularly designated as the brain of James I. To the casual reader, the settlement of Virginia appears less a trading venture than an exploitation of this monarch's weird theories of government. He purposed to apply to the distant solitudes of America the same principles that Philip II had fastened upon the populous provinces of Holland; the very lives of the colonists were to be regulated by the royal hand. But three thousand miles of stormy sea separated the government and the governed; the early control of England narrowed itself down to a careful framing of laws, the execution of which was prudently entrusted to divine Providence. For this reason the early Virginians were blessed with abundant laws and few restraints.

The laws of King James would indicate that he was by no means prodigal with the lands whose possession he enjoyed through explorations and divine right. By a gift of fifty acres of land covered with forest and reeking with malaria, the London Company proposed to compensate the settler for a lost home, a perilous voyage and the prospect of an early grave.[8] Moreover for each colonist he succeeded, preferably by fair means, in bringing to the new world, an additional fifty acres was bestowed. The land laws of Virginia, as of Massachusetts, had for their

---

[8] Bruce, *Economic History of Virginia*. *Passim*.

object a system of small farms. But the laws of New England were framed by a home government; the early regulations of Virginia were made and administered from across the sea. In consequence, while the New England laws were for the most part obeyed, those of Virginia were easily evaded. The absence of a strong home government and the presence of an obliging land office, contributed equally to establishing in Virginia a plantation system and a landed aristocracy. A large number of the plantations of Tidewater Virginia were built up of tracts taken out in the name of immigrants who had no existence save in the fertile imagination of the planter by whom their passage was supposed to be paid. Ancestors and acquaintances long dead, and even horses and cows, lent their names toward securing additional land. Instances are not lacking of enterprising settlers copying from neighboring cemeteries the names of a generation dead and certifying them as bona fide immigrants.

In this way was the plantation system established in Virginia; it was perpetuated by the cultivation of tobacco and the consequent use of slave labor. The succeeding generations were content to hold their possessions intact, and so far from increasing their estates they counted themselves fortunate to placate their creditors; for the large estates, cultivated extensively and by slave labor, became to their owners not a source of profit but of positive loss. Nor was this condition the result entirely of the kind of labor or the manner of cultivation; it was largely the result of incapable landlords. Probably never has history exhibited such prominent examples of incompetency and degeneracy as in colonial Virginia. For one hundred and seventy-five years the State was politically and economically at the feet of its aristocracy and in all that time it added not one respectable item to history. Year after year the planters fell more hopelessly in debt to their London creditors.[9] The principle of primogeniture and the prevalence of indentured servants filled the land with "poor white trash" whom the very slaves despised. The descendants of this class, whom conscience or the lack of opportunity prevented from acquiring land, were as distinguished for their shiftlessness as for their poverty. They sank lower and lower each generation; by 1750 they had lost all initiative and were living in such misery as to attract the attention of contemporary writers. They were separated from the aristocracy by caste distinctions and joined to them by a mutual depravity. The settlement of a new land by any of these was about as probable as a descent of the Iguorrotes on the planet Venus.

In Pennsylvania, as in New England, the small-farm system prevailed and for similar reasons. There was no land-monopolizing tendency as in Virginia and as a consequence no such sharp division into classes. Great wealth was as rare as extreme poverty. Slave labor had little part in the economic life; the labor on each farm was done by the owner. Germans, Dutch, Swedes, and Scotch-Irish (who were neither Scotch nor Irish), were attracted to its domain by its lack of religious dissensions, security from Indian warfare, and, particularly, by its incentives to industry and opportunities for prospering. Its population was heterogeneous and its people varied. The people were thrifty and keenly alive to all chances for bettering their worldly condition. In time when the country became more thickly settled and the best lands taken up, the character

---

[9] Bassett, *Virginia Planter and London Merchant*, American Historical Association Report, 1901, Vol. I.

and condition of the settlers enabled them readily to migrate to other regions.

One of the most important of the migrations from this region followed southward the great valley which lies between the Blue Ridge and the Alleghanies and is watered by the Shenandoah. The low ranges of the Blue Ridge had formed an impenetrable barrier to the shiftless peasantry and effete aristocracy of the Tidewater Virginia, so that at the time of the Pennsylvania migration the valley was practically uninhabited. Into this poured the wave of immigration from the north as a mighty river seeking a new channel. Many remained in the valley and established there the economic system of Pennsylvania as distinguished from that of Virginia.[10] These pioneers were *in* but not *of* Virginia. They remained essentially Pennsylvanian in thought and custom and had no part in the social and political life of the State. Such of her population as Kentucky drew from Virginia came from this section and not from the preponderant Tidewater. Kentucky, then, was the child of Virginia in the same sense that the Plymouth colony was a child of the Dutch republic.

But not all the Pennsylvanians settled in the Shenandoah Valley; many went still farther southward beyond the limits of the State into North Carolina. Here along the Yadkin and the Catawba lived a community that differed from the aristocracy of the eastern section of the State in the same degree that the valley men of Virginia differed from the Tidewater planters. Slaves were few, small farms were the rule, and everybody worked in the fields. But the soil along the Yadkin was far inferior to that along the Shenandoah and poverty was widespread. Each man,

---

[10] Wayland, *German Element in the Shenandoah Valley. Passim.*

for the most part, united in himself the occupations of farming, hunting and mechanic. They were a rough people and had little respect for authority; the government was too far remote to be dreaded or even felt. But it would have, indeed, been difficult to find a more virile people than they. They were none the less independent because of their poverty; their intelligence was as keen as their illiteracy was widespread. They were far from peaceful in their private lives and their fearlessness in battle equalled that of the fiercest Wyandot. Driven to hunting for subsistence, oftentimes, on account of the barrenness of their farms, they were accustomed to distant and prolonged travels which missed exploration only in name. They were peculiarly fitted above any body of men in English America for the exploration and settling of a new and hazardous country.

When the tide of immigration began to flow into Kentucky, it was from the Shenandoah Valley, the backwoods of Pennsylvania and the frontiers of Carolina, that the mass of settlers came. Despite the absence of Indian inhabitants, the occupation of Kentucky was a task demanding men of the strongest caliber. The settlers must need be men of the most rugged mold, prompt in action and enduring in defeat. There was a work to be done that no weakling could do. In the men of the Yadkin and the Shenandoah there was found a type capable of doing the work. So clearly did their fitness display itself in the history of early Kentucky that we are prone to designate them, in the phrase, that Filson applied to Boone, as "instruments ordained to settle the wilderness." Had the settlement of Kentucky depended on the achievements of Tidewater Virginians, it would be at this moment a kingdom of red Indians and a pasture for wild buffaloes.

In the settlement of a new land there are, in general, three motives that impel the emigrant. These motives are desire for riches, a wish to escape persecution at home, and a love for adventure.

But the men of Pennsylvania, of Carolina, and of the Shenandoah Valley had experienced nothing in the line of persecution beyond an occasional quarrel with the Quakers in Pennsylvania, or the forcible seizure of some property for tax. Indeed, the temperament of these men was such that in any instance of persecution they were likely to be the aggressors rather than the sufferers. Nor was the economic condition in their homes at all to be deplored. They were poor, but not paupers; they held in their own hands the means, if not the material, of permanent prosperity. As for the Yadkin men, though their farms were small they were not exhausted and would have richly repaid steady cultivation. But steady cultivation above all things they could not in the nature of things receive. The necessity, as well as the love of hunting, frequently called the farmer away when his presence was most necessary at home. Sporadic Indian attacks added another element of uncertainty to farming. But the same conditions prevailed or were thought to prevail in Kentucky, except that the land was more fertile. So a removal to Kentucky by these men could have added neither greater steadiness nor security to their labor. The condition of the valley men and the Pennsylvanians was even better than that of the Yadkin settlers. Their farms were more fertile and their settlements more compact. They were thus less frequently called on to supplement by the spoils of hunting, the fruits of agriculture. Their location exposed them less to Indian attack. In all three sections free land could still be easily obtained. Only to a very little extent had the people become crowded.

Notwithstanding this, the abundance of free land in Kentucky and the prospect of acquiring a new home at little or no cost, must have been a decided influence in attracting immigrants. This influence was stronger when the country became more settled and better known.

By far the strongest motive in the early settlement of Kentucky and at the beginning practically the only one, was the love of adventure. The Alleghany Mountains were as great an incentive to the imagination of the frontiersman as they were an impediment to his movements. What lay beyond the blue haze of their ranges was a matter of much mystery and pleasing speculation. From time to time itinerant peddlers or traders wandered into the valley and related wondrous stories of their adventures beyond the mountains. At harvest times, on hunting trips, or around the huge fireplaces in the dead of winter Kentucky was the chief subject of conversation. When game became scarce around their homes the farmer-hunters could but cast longing looks towards Kentucky where, if there was any truth in report, was a kingdom of game of all kinds, from the wild turkey to the buffalo. The wide solitudes of Kentucky bore a special charm for those of the settlers who disliked the presence of many neighbors. To the pioneers the thought of wandering unrestrained through the silent forest, of sleeping under open skies and of living for indefinite time without human companionship, was so far from being terrifying that it was their ideal of existence. They were the true hermits. Nor did the probability of an encounter with the Indians detract from the charm of the western country. The attitude of the settlers towards the Indians was by no means so sentimental as that of many of their descendants today. Their opinion and their treatment of them is suggested by the name which they applied to them. In their eyes all Indians, male and female, were "varmints." An Indian to them was very much the same as a snake or weasel to ourselves. And the early Kentuckians were not peculiar in this respect; an overwhelming majority of the English race in America held the same opinion. The French and Spanish settlers did not hesitate to intermarry and intermingle with the Indians. But the English race, notwithstanding the celebrated union of Rolfe and Pocahontas, held itself aloof. Where the French proselyted and the Spanish exterminated, the English were content to despise. Though the Indian sometimes inspired them with pity and often with fear the most constant feeling was one of unmitigated loathing. The killing of an Indian was considered, if not a passport to paradise, at least an act highly commendable in itself. Evidently to men possessing such ideals, Indian fighting in Kentucky was a great attraction.

However pleasant might be the speculations in regard to Kentucky, physical entrance into it was by no means easy. There were, indeed, but two practicable routes from the east; one was the Ohio River at the north and the other the Cumberland Gap at the extreme southeast. The Ohio River which skirts the entire northern boundary of Kentucky is formed in western Pennsylvania by the junction of the Alleghany and the Monongahela. Its name is a contraction and a corruption of the word Youghiogheny. The Allegheny and its tributaries drain the northwestern portion of Pennsylvania and even a small section of New York. The Monongahela, flowing from the opposite direction, drains the southwestern portion of Pennsylvania and much of what is now West Virginia. These two rivers unite at Pittsburg, which became at an early date the chief point of departure for those seeking Kentucky from the north. The distance from Pittsburg to Maysville is almost four hundred miles and it required many weeks to make the trip. Nevertheless, after the first few years this became the chief route into the land.

In the extreme southeast corner of Kentucky lay Cumberland Gap. Here Kentucky forms a corner with Virginia on the boundary of Tennessee; here, too, the Cumberland Mountains have narrowed to a single range between two valleys. In the eastern valley rises the Powell branch of the Tennessee and in the western valley is found the beginning of the Cumberland. For a considerable distance the courses of the two rivers are parallel and separated only by the single ridge of the Cumberland. This ridge is continuous and difficult of crossing save at one place where there is a pass or gap. Passing through this, the Cumberland, the immigrant had but to follow the windings of the Cumberland River until it bursts through the Pine Mountains, when he would find himself well into the interior of Kentucky. This was the route taken by the earlier immigrants who were drawn almost exclusively from the Shenandoah and Yadkin River regions.

There was a third route, though but little used; it was to follow the Greenbrier River through the mountains until it reached the Ohio. The wild and forbidding country through which this passed practically prohibited its use.

PREHISTORIC KENTUCKY.

THERE are many traditions to indicate, and a few shreds of evidence to prove, that in the far past Kentucky supported an advanced and extensive civilization. Nor was it a civilization whose greatness or decline has, like the Roman, left its influence largely written on succeeding ages. It has vanished wholly; the Kentuckians of today owe nothing of good or evil to its existence and have no link to connect them with its remains. Yet as this civilization existed on the same soil as we, it becomes the duty, if not the pleasure, of the historian of Kentucky to investigate the remains and describe, if he may, its history.

The Delawares, whom the Indians of every tribe addressed in reverence of their antiquity as "grandfathers,"[1] were accustomed to relate as an ancient and authentic tradition that eastern North America was at one time occupied and possessed by a white people. The Indian name for these was Allegewi.[2] They were no savages or nomads but a nation of fixed habitation and great culture. Whence they had come or when, are points upon which the traditions are silent. But the traditions of the Delawares, the Sacs, the Shawnese and even other tribes attest the fact of their presence, their civilization and their power. In the dim past, continue the traditions, the savage Iroquois emerged from the great western country[3] and began to hew their conquering way to their present abode. The Delawares at the same time began their migration to the

---
[1] The Iroquois, however, would address them only as "nephews."
[2] The Allegewi left their name on the Allegheny Mountains and River.
[3] Heckwelder, *Indian Nations*, Chap. I.

east but took a route much south of the Iroquois. Both tribes were confronted and halted on the banks of the Mississippi [4] by the strange Allegewi. But though the Iroquois forced their way resistlessly across, the weaker Delawares were treacherously assailed in mid-stream and all but destroyed by their foes. The Iroquois and Delawares soon formed an alliance and began a merciless war against their common enemy. The Allegewi in a number of terrific battles were driven southward and finally stood desperately at bay in their favorite land, Kentucky. Here they built huge mounds for fortifications, for burial places, and for temples. How long their last stand respited the Allegewi no one knows, but finally at the falls of the Ohio they staked their lives and fortunes on the issue of one great battle and lost. Their people were expelled and their civilization forgotten.

Each reader of these traditions may give or withhold his belief according to his character. A candid mind, however, will fail to find in them anything of the improbable with the possible exception of the "white" color. The fact of a primitive alliance of the Delawares and the Iroquois is a well attested one. And the eastward migration of the Iroquois, if not the Delawares, is an event so well known as to require no proof. No legend or tradition, moreover, if depicting the internecine strife of the Indians, need be considered wild or improbable. But in the absence of corroborative evidence an impartial seeker after truth would be slow to accept, on the authority of a savage tradition, the idea of a white race and a great civilization in a country of red barbarism.

---

[4] Rafinesque. Brinton, in his *Walam Olum*, says this was the Ohio. The Delawares called the Ohio the Allegewi-Sipu.

When the Indians related these traditions to the first settlers, they observed that when the waters of the Ohio became low an island would be formed at the falls whereon the doubting white men might find evidence of the truth of their relation. When the waters fell the island was found to be covered with innumerable bones.[5] These, said the Indians, were the skeletons of the Allegewi who had perished here in the last battle; it, of course, gave no explanation who the Allegewi were, what their color, or whence their origin. Indians of all tribes more than once expressed their astonishment that white men could dwell in the Kentucky land where, they asserted, the ghosts and the specters of the dead nations roamed eternally. They professed to believe that Kentucky was a land of blood and spirits wherein it was unholy for any man, white or red, to dwell.

Inasmuch as the Indians had obvious reasons for wishing to create in the white men a horror and dread of Kentucky, their statements in regard to its haunted character must be received, and were, at a considerable discount.

The Cherokees of Georgia were called in their own language Ani-Yunwiya, "real people"; and Ani-Ketuwaghi, "people of Kitwuha," an ancient settlement.[6] They were also called in the Mobilian trade language Tsalagi, "people of the caves;" they were known to the Six Nations as Oyatageron, "inhabitants of the cave country," and by the Catawbas they were called Manterau, "coming out of the ground." But the Delaware Allegewi literally means "cave people." And considering the indubitable fact that the Cherokees were known far and wide as the cave dwellers, the conclusion seems certain that by "Allegewi"

---

[5] Young, *Prehistoric Men of Kentucky*, p. 4.
[6] The name Kitwuha was commonly corrupted to Cuttawa.

the Delawares meant the Cherokees. Furthermore the traditions of the Cherokees in regard to their migration from the north agree in every essential point with the Delaware's tradition of the Allegewi.[7] The Wyandots identified the Cherokees as Allegewi and affirmed that the latter were driven south from their fortification in the Ohio valley by the Iroquois. The Cherokees, or Allegewi, were near kinsmen of the Iroquois and the truth perhaps may be that "in ancient times as in the historic period they were always the southern vanguard of the Iroquoian race, always primarily a mountain people, but with their flank resting upon the Ohio and its great tributaries, following the trend of the Blue Ridge and the Cumberland as they slowly gave way before the pressure from the north until they were finally cut off from the parent stock by the wedge of Algonquian invasion, but always, whether in the north or south, keeping their distinctive titles among the tribes as the people of the cave country."

The Delaware traditions have it that the war of the Iroquois and the Tallegewi or Allegewi continued during the reigns or leadership of five successive chiefs.[8] There was a succession, furthermore, of twenty-five chiefs from the conquest of the Allegewi to the coming of white men. It would be impossible to express in years the time represented by the rule of these chieftains, but that the expulsion of the Allegewi occurred in a time far past is shown clearly by the many dialectic differences that came to distinguish the Cherokees from the parent Iroquois.

The traditions of all tribes agree in attributing to the Allegewi the mounds that were scattered all over Kentucky

---

[7] Mooney, "Myths of the Cherokees," in *Nineteenth Report of American Bureau of Ethnology.*
[8] Brinton, "Walam Olum," in *Lenape and their Legends.*

and the Ohio valley. Inasmuch as the character of a people may often be, in a great measure, ascertained or at least conjectured from their remains, a study of the mounds should throw light on the mound builders and aid in determining whether they were Indians or a white race that has perished from the earth.

A consideration of the mounds erected in ancient Kentucky shows that they were built of different forms and for varying purposes. Many have been cut down and the evidence thereby secured proves indubitably that they were erected for burial places. Others show by their size and contour that they were intended to be used for fortifications in a great and extensive warfare. By far the majority of the mounds used for burial places were built in a conical form with an altitude of eight or ten feet, but sometimes reaching as high as forty. Within these were found the bones of men and women buried centuries ago. Nor was the style of burying at all uniform. A mound cut down at Mt. Sterling contained, although it was of considerable extent, but a single skeleton buried at the center. Around the skeleton, nearer the outer edge of the mound, were found many remains of primitive art of so much importance in character and amount as to justify the conclusion that the mound was the mausoleum of a great chief.[9] The Moberly mound in Madison County, contained six skeletons, around whom were found many remains of primitive weapons conclusively showing that it was the grave of warriors. Indeed, in the femur of one skeleton was still remaining, deeply imbedded, the spearhead that must have caused death. A very peculiar mound was that known as the Lindsay mound in Union

---

[9] Young, *Prehistoric Men of Kentucky*, p. 31.

County. Here there was no burial at the center but the skeletons were found placed each with the head towards the center and the feet out, "similar to the spokes of a wheel." Moreover, within the mound were found many tiers of skeletons, the lowest of which was accompanied by no pottery or other remains. This was conjectured to be the burial place of the common people as distinguished from that of the chiefs or leaders. Numerous over the State are the mounds of pyramidal forms. They are rarely found containing bones, and generally are closely connected with other remains of a warlike nature. Perhaps the most remarkable of this class was that in Ballard County;[10] its base contained fifteen acres and it was but a few feet in height. Smaller mounds were scattered over its surface. Occasionally the mounds were made in the form of animals as, for instance, the great bear effigy in Greenup County.

As the author of the *Prehistoric Men of Kentucky* has said, the pioneers knew little, and cared less, for the ancient mounds that they encountered in Kentucky. Indeed, in the early days while the land was yet unrobbed of its forests, the majority of the mounds escaped detection. After the ground began to be cleared and the soil cultivated, the settlers noticed the mounds and inquired their origin. The Indians said that they knew nothing of them; that they were erected by a people earlier than they. The emergencies of a pioneer life forbade the settler to turn his attention to archaeological research. So the mounds, as any other land, were soon converted into cornfields, and plowshare in a few years levelled their elevation and destroyed their contents. Thus perished what, perhaps,

---

[10] Collins, *History of Kentucky*, Vol. II, p. 39.

could have thrown great light on the entire question of the mounds, their purpose, and their builders.

Yet the burial mounds were not the only remains of the ancient inhabitants of the land. Even more striking, though not so numerous, were the fortifications they built during the course of that great war in which they defended and lost Kentucky. In Hickman County still exists the ancient work known as O'Byam's Fort.[11] It is located on a bluff whose southern end drops vertically almost fifty feet. There was a sloping ascent from its northern end, but it was blocked at the summit by a wall and ditch. This wall measures some eighteen feet, and is discontinued at the steep southern end. It has many times been pronounced the best chosen position for defense in the entire region; its selection plainly shows that its builders, whether Indian or others, possessed great talent for military things.

Indeed, even a casual investigation of these ancient forts can not fail to show the unusual cunning displayed in the selection of their sites. Practically all are located on steep bluffs where some sides are fortified by nature; considerable art is displayed in the protection of the sides exposed to attack. These features are all to be seen at their best in fortifications scattered all over the land and notable in the fort on Green River near Bowling Green in Caldwell County, in Larue County and in Hardin County. The similarity of these show that they were probably all erected by the same people and their very existence indicates defensive warfare. Perhaps the most wonderful of the forts of these olden times is the one on Indian Fort Mountain in Madison County. The mountain rises pre-

---

[11] Cyrus Thomas, in *Twelfth Annual Report of the American Bureau of Ethnology.*

cipitously from the plain to an elevated height; it is practically unscalable at all points save the east. Here a long ridge of nearly a mile gradually sinks to the plain and gives a means of ascent from the valley to the summit of the mountain. But at the point where this ridge enters the top of the mountain the ancient people constructed, and there still exists, a huge stone wall three hundred and eighty-seven feet long. This wall, built on a steep slope, is sixty feet high on its outer side and five on the inner. As is shown by the nature of many of the stones, they must have been quarried in the valley and carried thence to the summit. Some of these are of five hundred pounds weight. The top is level and contains four or five hundred acres. At several places on the other and precipitate sides, walls were erected, evidently because the builders believed these points pregnable to attack. Furthermore, on the top of the cliffs in various places may still be seen the stones heaped up in ages past to be hurled down on the enemy below. The fort, by reason of its size and strength, must have served as the great rallying place for a harassed nation.[12]

In the burial mounds, the fortifications and the caves of the land, have been found various remains that reveal the dress, the occupation and the civilization of the mound builders.[13] Their clothing was made of tanned skins, of combed cloth and feathers, and of a cloth made of flax and the bark of trees. And in the preparation of the cloth they evidently had the knowledge of many dyes. They wore moccasins made of bark cloth, and the number of moccasins found prove the universal custom of wearing them. They had the use of coarse needles made of bone,

---
[12] Young, *Prehistoric Men of Kentucky*, p. 75.
[13] *Ibid.*, p. 100.

and of thread rudely made of hide, the bark or the wild hemp. Copper spools were in use. As a weapon they used a battle-axe weighing from one to thirty pounds, a battle-axe blade formed of flint and measuring five by three inches, and the bow and arrow. The arrowheads were probably in many cases dipped in poison. The spear and the flint knives were also in use. In his home life the mound builder used the stone axe for felling the trees, pestles and mortar in the preparation of corn, meats and nuts for food. The number found of these would indicate that the domestic life of their makers was more advanced than the ordinary Indian people. The pottery remains are likewise extensive and show great originality and considerable art. The manufactured fishhooks from bone and fashioned pipes of all sizes and designs from sandstone and steatite. Finally, by the remains, we can perceive that they worshipped idols of a peculiarly atrocious appearance.

The mound builders have been considered in the light of Delaware tradition and their identity with the Cherokees has been suggested. It has been endeavored by a consideration of the mounds, the forts, and the articles of dress, domestic life and military, to arrive at some facts by which their civilization and identity might be determined. It now remains to hazard an opinion and, if may be, present the proof that the mound builders were not a peculiar or a vanished race but were red Indians calling themselves Kituwhagi and called by the English the Cherokees.

From the standpoint of tradition, as already set forth, the testimony is overwhelming that the mound builders were called Allegewi, and the Allegewi were the same people as the Cherokees. The unusual and striking agreement of the many tribal traditions on this point must in the absence of controverting testimony, be received as an evidence of its truth, notwithstanding the notorious unreliability of Indian legends. Then, if an examination of the remains discloses no opposing evidence, it may fairly be assumed that the identity of the two people was real. But nothing in the character of these remains would suggest that they are the remains of another race than the Indians.[14] It is a fact, undoubtedly true, that the Indians of North America built mounds even in the historic period. They are not the exclusive product of Kentucky but are scattered all over the country. Furthermore, they are dissimilar one to another in many respects, indicating that they were erected not by a united people but by a people broken up into many separate tribes. There could have been no work involved in their construction that the Indians could not do, nor a culture that the Indians did not possess. Though some are of considerable size, their proportions are as a rule so greatly exaggerated by writers as to suggest that Baron Munchausen may have fathered the theory of their origin and the report of their size. The Indians were not without knowledge of such simple geometrical figures as the square, circle, octagon, etc., which are used in the design of the mounds. Nor is the assertion of the Indians that they knew nothing of the Kentucky mounds of any moment; the greatness of Indian ignorance, on even recent events is of such a character that if it were accepted as historical evidence the universe would quickly be reduced to void. The methods of burial in the mounds were peculiarly Indian. Finally, when the white men reached America they found the Indians engaged in erecting and

---

[14] Thomas, "Mound Explorations," in the *Tenth Annual Report of the Bureau of Ethnology.*

utilizing the mounds; many of those excavated have been found to contain articles of European manufacture.

In the case of the fortifications, the conclusion must perforce be the same. These, too, are scattered over the country, and not limited to Kentucky. Their number and position indicate, not a warfare between two great nations, but an internecine strife. The skill shown in the selection of their sites and the labor used in their building are such as the Indians were fully capable of displaying. In historic times, if there is any value in the testimony of white men, they were engaged in work of similar magnitude and for similar purposes. Notwithstanding many theories to the contrary, the American Indians were not nomads; they had as a rule fixed habitations to which they invariably returned, no matter how far they had wandered afield.

The finding of the mortars and pestles, the cloth, the needles and thread, prove that the mound builders were people of agricultural pursuits, of skill in weaving, and ingenuity in fabricating tools. Yet all the southern Indians were the same. The evidence is overwhelming that the Cherokees lived on the fruits of the field and were considerably advanced in the arts of agriculture. They wore clothes made from home-spun flax, and that they understood the use of tools is shown by their possessing and utilizing mines of copper. The pottery of the mound builders differs in no essential from the pottery of the various Indian tribes and savage chieftains, from Hudson Bay to Florida, pledged their solemn treaties in calumets that were unchanged from the time of the battle of Sandy Island.

It is pleasing, and perhaps profitable, to the imagination, to picture olden Kentucky as a gloomy land peopled by the ghosts of the ancient dead, the superstitious Indians visiting it only in reverence, the very trees redolent of mystery. But though less pleasant to imagine, it is safer to believe that the desolation of the country was more due to the fear of an Iroquois tomahawk than to veneration of a fallen empire or dread of a spectral foe.

EXPLORATION OF KENTUCKY.

THE process of determining who was the first man to explore Kentucky is as unprofitable as it is difficult. The mere entering or crossing the land can not, unless the visit bore fruit, be considered as a part of State history, however much it interested or lamented the visitor. Without doubt, it was no unusual occurrence for a trader, a hunter, or even a missionary, to be led by zeal or accident into the Kentucky country. Indeed, if we may trust to legend or its colleague, early history, Kentucky, even before 1750, had a score of explorers whose adventures were as marvelous as those recorded by Dean Swift or by Marco Polo. Many of these left records of their travels. But these records, except as showing the sameness of colonial sufferings and displaying the imaginative capacity of the writers, bear no more relation to Kentucky history than do the precepts of the Zend-Avesta. The real history of Kentucky may be said to begin with the expedition of Dr. Thomas Walker in 1750.

The Americans in 1750 possessed many desires and few opportunities for acquiring great fortunes. Morever, then, as now, the far off and distant enterprises were those that possessed the greatest attractions. The men of the coast region found far greater pleasure in estimating the profits to be derived from western speculation than in turning the attention to the routine of business at home. Indeed, the plan of acquiring and exploiting transmontane lands seems to have been a favorite before all others with the then seekers of riches. From time to time their wishes and desires took practical shape in the forming of land companies for the utilizing of vacant and unsettled lands in the west. In the years 1748 and 1749 two such companies [1] were formed which, although failing of their main object, are of considerable interest from their relation to Kentucky history. In 1748 Hanbury, a London merchant, Thomas Lee, president of the Virginia Council, Robert Dinwiddie, later governor of Virginia, Lawrence and Augustine Washington, and others, formed the Ohio Company. They received by royal permission five hundred thousand acres of land between the Kentucky and the Monongahela rivers, and the privilege of settling it at their own risk. Their land was to be located in the western wilderness on both banks of the Ohio. In 1749 the Loyal Land Company was formed and given eight hundred thousand acres to be located indefinitely in the west, north of 36° 30'.

The Loyal Land Company, though the last to be organized, was the first to begin work. In the winter of 1749 they commissioned Dr. Thomas Walker of Albemarle County, Virginia, to explore the western country and report concerning its character. Dr. Walker began his journey in March, 1750, nowithstanding the bad season. With five companions [2] he set out for the southwest and entered Kentucky by way of Cumberland Gap. Had his movements been determined by a complete knowledge of the country he was seeking, he could not possibly have chosen a worse region for exploration. He named the gap through which he passed the Cumberland, and gave the same name to the Shawnee River which he discovered a little later. On April 23d, the little company had reached

---

[1] Johnson, *First Exploration of Kentucky*, Introduction.
[2] Powell, Tomlinson, Chew, Lawless and Hughes. The party was well mounted and took along two extra horses for baggage.

a point on the Cumberland River some four miles below the present Barbousville. Here three men were left while Dr. Walker and the others pressed on in search of a better country. They soon returned in disappointment and found their companions had erected some cabins in their absence.[3] The united company pressed on westward until on May 11th they reached a river, which from its banks of shelving rock they named Rockcastle. To the five tributaries of this stream were given the names of Walker's companions; he, himself, modestly refrained from thus handing down his name to posterity. On Rockcastle River they made a four days' stop to make shoes for themselves. On May 22d, they reached the Kentucky River which Dr. Walker named the Milley. Then sore in body and spirit they turned their faces towards Virginia. They had entered the land the middle of April and left it the middle of June; they had succeeded in traversing the worst possible section of the country and in viewing it at the most unpromising time of the year. They had caught not a glimpse of the Bluegrass. By chance, or lack of enterprise, they failed utterly to find the region they sought. No wonder, then, if when they reached Virginia they spread reports that were far from complimentary to Kentucky.

Much more fortunate was the Ohio Company in the choosing of an explorer, or the selection of his route. Their choice fell on Christopher Gist,[4] a Yadkin man and a tried explorer. He was instructed to explore the western country as far as the Falls of the Ohio and to locate the Company's grant. Gist, in company with a negro servant, began his journey from Old Town on the Potomac, the

---
[3] These may fairly be called the first cabins in Kentucky. The remnants of the old chimney is still standing.
[4] He was a near neighbor to Boone.

last day of October, 1750. He proceeded to Shannopin Town, the present Pittsburg, then through Ohio until he reached the Scioto River. He descended the Scioto to the Shawnee town, Shannoah, at its mouth, which he reached January 30, 1751. In order to ascertain the strength of the northern Indians, he made from Shannoah a wide detour of one hundred and fifty miles to the Twigtee towns. Returning to Shannoah he crossed over into Kentucky, March 12th. He visited Big Bone Lick and secured for his employers a mastodon's tooth weighing five pounds. A few days later he reached and crossed the Licking at the Lower Blue Licks. An accommodating Indian had volunteered the information [5] that he was now within fifteen miles of the Falls of the Ohio, and that the surrounding country was infested by French and Indians. Whether to the Indian mind fifteen and one hundred and fifty are synonymous terms or whether the information was given in bad faith, Gist, at least, gave up all thoughts of visiting the Falls and turned his attention and his course to the south. He penetrated the Bluegrass, crossed the Kentucky and the Red rivers and from the summit of Pilot Knob, in what is now Powell County, looked over the wide plain of central Kentucky. After spending some time in viewing and exploring the land, he crossed the Cumberland Mountains and returned to Virginia by Pound Gap and later proceeded to his old home on the Yadkin.[6]

The expeditions of Gist and Walker were similar, in that both had traversed a country desolate of men. But Walker had spent his entire time floundering through the

---

[5] This information had been given him by an Indian at Shannoah.
[6] Two years later, Dinwiddie, Lieutenant-Governor of Virginia, suspecting the French activities along the Ohio, called upon Gist to guide Washington on an investigating journey.

thickets and defiles of the mountains, while Gist had penetrated to the heart of Kentucky. The Virginian had seen only the worst of Kentucky; the Carolinian had traversed the best. To Walker, the land was rough, infertile, abounding in venomous snakes and beasts of prey; to Gist, it was a country of plains and a region of magnificent game. Walker's report was such as to discourage his employers and friends from further efforts to settle the land; the story of Gist incited the Ohio Company to fresh efforts and inflamed the already ardent spirits of his Yadkin neighbors. However, the intervention of the French and Indian war put an end to the activities of both companies and left Kentucky without a visitor almost for fifteen years.

Two years after the journeys of Walker and Gist, Lewis Evans of Philadelphia, made a map of Kentucky from information he had acquired from the two and from traders. This map was published by Benjamin Franklin and was republished in 1755. Considering the prevailing ignorance of the western country and the astounding unreliability of the traders' information, the map is surprising in its accuracy and extent. Although the English settlers of that day were by no means given to the reading of many books, it is highly probable that the Evans map fell into the hands of many restless spirits and excited their desire, while it increased their knowledge of Kentucky. But the only actual explorers of whom we have a record of visiting Kentucky in all that troubled time, were John Finley in 1752, and James McBride two years later.[7] Finley was a frontier trader, trading back and forth with the Ohio Indians. From them he gathered such reports of Kentucky as to arouse in him a desire to visit it. In

---

[7] Draper, MSS. *Life of Boone*, Vol. II, p. 164.

1752, with three or four companions, he came down the Ohio in canoes to the Falls. Returning, he fell in with a band of Shawnese at Big Bone Lick. They carried him a prisoner to their post, Eskippakithiki, in central Kentucky. Here he was kept, probably not unwillingly, until January, 1753, when foreseeing trouble among the various tribes there assembled, he made his escape and returned home, destined to do much at a later time for the settlement of Kentucky.

There is little evidence that McBride really visited Kentucky. The story was that he, with several companions, came down the Ohio in canoes and landed at the mouth of the Kentucky.[8] He cut the date and his initials on a tree. Nothing is known of his subsequent career, and for many years he was believed to be the first explorer of Kentucky, until the investigations of later historians revealed the error.

The great French and Indian war, beginning in 1754, absorbed the interest and resources of the English. For nine years it was waged furiously over the wide expanse of America, from Quebec to Lookout Mountain. The French carried with them into the war their Indian neighbors of the northwest, and all but succeeded in detaching the Iroquois from their long alliance. While the war was in progress, and the Indians kept the field, there was little prospect of white visitors in Kentucky. And even when the war was ended and the French in yielding their dominions had pledged their late allies to peace, the compact was but indifferently observed on both sides. The Indians were far from liking their new masters; they and the forest-loving French had many things in common, but

---

[8] Filson, *Description of Kentucky*, p. 7.

they differed from the English as the east from the west. Each race lived in constant suspicion of the other, and, as is usual, a suspicion of injury brought on the injury itself. For these reasons the exploration of Kentucky, which had ceased during the war, was slow to be renewed when the war was ended.

But it was not alone the attitude of the Indians that prevented, or at least retarded, exploration. Immediately after the war was ended by the treaty of Paris, the King of England issued a proclamation forbidding his "loving subjects" from settling or even possessing the lands west of the mountains. His proclaimed object was to keep the territory for the use of the Indians perpetually. But the English colonists had views far different from these and treated the King's decree with the same quality of reverence that they had shown to the earlier Navigation Acts. Even the commissioners chosen for drawing the line that should separate the two races deliberately disregarded their instructions, and instead of making the Kanawha the western limit of Virginia, they surveyed and induced the Iroquois to approve a line running down the Ohio and terminating at the Tennessee.[9] This opened up Kentucky to the colonists, or at least gave them access to it as far as governmental permission was able to effect it.

It is necessary to consider one other event that bade well to close Kentucky permanently to the English. This was the war of Pontiac. Pontiac was a chief of the Ottawas and one of the many Indians who brooded sullenly over the changed relations of white men and red after the treaty of Paris. But while others were only ready to complain, Pontiac speedily prepared to oppose. He se-

---

[9] **Sir William Johnson** and **John Stuart**, two royal Commissioners of Indian Affairs, had charge of the work.

cretly and rapidly fanned the flames of Indian discontent, bound the jealous tribes together in a cohesive fighting mass, made and matured his plans with transcendent skill, and finally struck at the hated English such a swift and terrible blow that only three forts of a multitude escaped the well-plotted destruction.[10] Even the Senecas joined him in his efforts. For the moment, the English power in America had more to dread at the hands of the desperate Indians than ever from Frenchmen or Spaniards. But the qualities that had enabled the English to build up their power in the desert and the forest stood them in good stead now. They rallied and fought with unyielding tenacity and merciless power. After two years of such atrocities as perhaps America had never before witnessed, Bouquet penetrated the Indian territory with a force as wild, as ferocious, and as subtle as the Indians themselves and forced the reluctant tribes to peace. It does not require a seer to conjecture, nor a prophet to predict that in this time Kentucky was by no means a Mecca for white explorers.

When the trouble was settled, one by one the explorers began to turn their course anew to Kentucky. In 1765 Colonel George Croghan[11] passed down the Ohio and traveled some little way into Kentucky.[12] Like Gist fifteen years before, he visited and wondered at the remains around Big Bone Lick. A year later Captain Harry Gordon descended the Ohio from Fort Pitt and left in his journal some observations in regard to the Falls. Finally, in 1767,

---

[10] This war is most vividly and accurately described by Parkman, in his *Conspiracy of Pontiac*.
[11] Thwaites, *Early Western Travels*, Vol. I.
[12] As an example of the vague geographical ideas current, it is interesting to note that Croghan, in landing at a certain stream, was uncertain whether he had reached the Kentucky or the Holstein.

John Finley ventured again into central Kentucky and no doubt visited again the Indian Eskippakithiki whither he had been carried in 1752. This visit of Finley was to bear much fruit, for he, like Gist, was a Yadkin man, and on his return home he related his adventures with doubtless such embellishments as presented themselves to his Celtic fancy.

In May, 1769, the long-restrained movement of the Yadkin people to the Kentucky country began. John Stewart, Daniel Boone, Joseph Holden, James Mooney and William Cool, all farmers of the Yadkin community, banded themselves together to go in search of that famous but elusive country that the Iroquois called Kentucky.[13] As the leader and guide of the company there went along the rollicking, roisterly, red-headed Irishman, John Finley. Finley, who was at different seasons peddler, trader, farmer, hunter and explorer, had visited Kentucky at least twice before, and on each occasion had brought back with him manifold tales of what he had experienced there. He had made the acquaintance of Boone on the Braddock expedition and had greatly aroused the spirits of that ardent hunter by his reports of Kentucky and the game. The desire then kindled in Boone for seeing Kentucky had grown greater with the passing of years. He had already made one attempt to reach the land. In 1767 he had penetrated far into the interior of the Cumberlands, but failed to find the level land which Finley had described. While he was wandering through the mountains, Finley was actually encamped in central Kentucky; and when the latter reached the Yadkin and the two compared notes they were not long in resolving that another expedi-

---

[13] Draper, MSS. *Life of Boone*, Vol. II, p. 173.

tion should get under way for the land that Finley had visited and both desired. The fact that it was spring and the season was at hand when hard work would be demanded by the farms made the plan for immediate departure a most welcome one to the men among whose virtues that of farm work was certainly not included. So on May 1, 1769, almost twenty years after Dr. Thomas Walker had entered Kentucky, the men took up their march for Cumberland Gap, with Finley in the lead, pledging himself to lead them to central Kentucky by the most direct route. They passed through the gap and pressed determinedly on through the mountains. On the seventh of June Finley made good his promises by bringing them to the top of a mountain overlooking Red River[14] and pointing out the beautiful plain stretching out indefinitely to the west. According to Boone's own account the little party was enraptured with the prospect; they pitched their camp on Red River and abandoned themselves to joys of unlimited hunting. Seemingly there was no end to the game. Boone had hunted over the Alleghany region from Pennsylvania to Florida, but had never found anything to compare to this. The men, and especially Finley, knew the reputation of the land for bloodshed and for carnage. But not even a sign of Indians was now to be seen in the land. So the men continued their hunting in all confidence while the days passed by as a dream. Summer came and went, and autumn passed, but still the hunters had no thoughts of returning. They gradually moved their camp westward until they reached the Kentucky, for they all wished to view the beautiful land. So with their camp as a common

---

[14] Z. F. Smith in his *History of Kentucky*, locates this camp at the junction of Clark, Powell and Estill counties. Without doubt Finley had piloted the party to Eskippakithiki.

meeting place the party hunted and explored the land from the Kentucky to Dick's River. Nor was pleasure their only incentive to hunting; the furs and the skins of the slain animals would sell for a high price on the Yadkin and the members of the party hoped by the spoils of the chase to more than repay themselves for their neglected farms.

So secure did they feel against Indian attack that they began to separate into two's and three's for greater convenience in hunting. On December 22d two of the party, Boone and Stewart, were suddenly set upon by a band of Shawnese near the old town Eskippakithiki. They soon found that the Indians were more eager for plunder than for bloodshed. Boone and Stewart were compelled to lead their captors to the hunting camp. Here the Indians found great quantities of skins which had been collected during the long hunt and these they proceeded to appropriate with a satisfaction highly civilized. The business completed, they released Boone and Stewart, leaving them enough food for their journey home and the exceedingly practical advice, "never to come back or the wasps and yellow jackets would sting them." They also relieved the hunters of all the horses they could find. But Boone and Stewart had no thought of walking home and, with empty hands, facing their insistent families. They hastened to pursue the Indians and managed to recover five horses. The Indians in their turn pursued Boone and Stewart and speedily recaptured them. The two were kept in close confinement for seven days by the exasperated Indians, but they finally succeeded in escaping and made the best of their way back to the camp. They found the camp deserted, and setting out with all speed for home they soon overtook their companions who had become alarmed and decided to leave the country. Boone was more than pleased to find with them his brother Squire, who, with a companion, Alexander Neely, had come out into the "wilderness" and had stumbled on the party in the absence of Boone and Stewart.

Stewart, Neely and the two Boones [15] resolved to remain in Kentucky and resume the hunting, but the others made all haste home. After their late experience with the Shawnese it would seem that the hunters ought to have learned caution, but it was not long before the desire for game overcame all prudence, and they began hunting in pairs. In a few days Boone and Stewart again fell in with the Indians and only Boone escaped. A short time afterwards Neely disappeared,[16] and the two brothers were left alone in the land. Not at all dismayed by the loss of Stewart and Neely they kept steadily at their hunting. The roving Shawnese were either ignorant or indifferent to the presence of the two hunters, for after the loss of their companions they were not again molested by the Indians. But a lack of ammunition threatened to bring to an abrupt close an expedition that human opposition had not been able to check. In this emergency it was decided that the younger brother should revisit the Yadkin and secure a supply of ammunition; he was, moreover, to bring back if possible some horses on which they might convey to their homes the spoils they had secured. So at the beginning of May, 1770, one year after he had left his "peaceful habitation" on the Yadkin, Daniel Boone was left alone in the Kentucky country. Three months were consumed by Squire Boone on his overland journey.

---

[15] Finley went to Pennsylvania, and here disappears from history.
[16] The skeleton of Neely was found long afterwards in a hollow tree.

Yet, though alone in the wilderness, Daniel was anything but unhappy. After the loneliness of the first few days had passed he found more pleasure even than before in his hunting and exploring. He roamed far enough northward to get a view of the Ohio River and penetrated to the Salt and Green rivers in the southwest. Many times he was alarmed by the indications of Indians, but never failed to avoid them. Moving with incessant caution, changing his camp every night, and sleeping in the densest canebrakes, he for three months performed the unique feat of roaming undetected in a country infested by hostile people. Squire Boone returned in July and the two met at their old camp on the twenty-seventh of the month. Warned by increasing signs of the Indians, they abandoned central Kentucky and traveled to the Cumberland River. Here they found game in such abundance that their ammunition was again shortly exhausted and Squire Boone, in the autumn of 1770, again made the trip to the Yadkin for another supply. Daniel remain behind, evidently in no hurry to return to his neglected farm and family.

But the two Boones after all had not been alone in Kentucky. In the spring of 1770 a company of forty men, gathered from the Holstein, the Clinch and the New River regions, set out across the mountains and through Cumberland Gap for the Kentucky hunting grounds. In Wayne County, six miles from the present Monticello, the party pitched camp and scattered in different directions in pursuit of the abundant game. Every five weeks, so they agreed, they were to meet and deposit their spoils at the common camp. But the adventurous spirits of the men soon nullified the arrangement. Ten of the men constructed rude boats and loading them with skins traveled down the Cumberland, the Ohio, and the Mississippi to the Spanish Natchez, whence after selling their spoils they returned home; others for various reasons recrossed the mountains and a few perished. A band of nine led by James Knox, had previous to this, separated from the others and pushed on toward central Kentucky. Not far from Laurel River they encountered a band of Cherokees; the leader of the Indians was recognized through a slight deformity by one of the white men and was saluted as "Captain Dick." The flattered chieftain directed the party to his own river, Dick's River, where they might find abundant game, kill and go home. The white men obeyed the first two injunctions as implicitly as they neglected the last. They spent some time on Dick's River and gradually moved westward to the Green River. Here they erected a "skin house" on Caney Creek and speedily set about filling it. They were apparently alone in the country. Their surprise, then, can be conjectured when one day while encamped they heard not far away in the forest a voice raised in what was probably meant to be song. Cautiously approaching they saw a white man stretched full length on the ground singing with the full strength of a pair of lungs which had evidently been fashioned for other purposes. It was Daniel Boone,[17] who with rare recklessness was giving himself up to the pleasure of his own music in entire forgetfulness of Indians and all things hostile. Squire Boone, who had returned from his second trip to the Yadkin, soon joined the party. The meeting occurred in February, 1771, and they all hunted together until March, when the two brothers finally set out for home after an absence of two years. They reached Cumberland Gap with their pack horses laden with pelfries.

---

[17] Draper, MSS. *Life of Boone*, Vol. III, p. 64.

Here the Cherokees met them and with grim humor relieved them of their burden. So the two brothers after two years of hardship and danger, having collected a small fortune twice and lost it, returned home empty handed to their families.

Knox and his companions joined by twelve others, some of whom were their late comrades on the Cumberland, continued their hunting along the Green River until the capture of two of the party caused the others to hastily abandon the locality. Returning after two months they found their dogs gone wild and their "skin house" despoiled. One of the party, named Bledsoe, with a unique capacity for forceful and expressive English, carved on a convenient tree the laconic inscription, "2300 deer skins lost. Ruination, by God." The hunters persevered in establishing another depot only to have it plundered by the Cherokees, who seemed to regard the despoiling of other people's property as a part of their manifest destiny. This latter disaster lent sudden popularity to the idea of a return home, and late in 1772 the hunters returned to their own people, to be greeeted as the "Long Hunters," and to contribute by their stories to the increasing desire for Kentucky.

Twenty-two years had passed since Dr. Walker had traveled through the mountains of Kentucky. In this time many people had passed the mountains and had roamed with delight through the heart of Kentucky; yet at the close of the period there was not a single habitation nor a solitary white man in the land. But the period had been a time of exploration rather than of settlement; the men who had been in the land had come thither for game. With this idea they had taken every risk and had endured every hardship. But in their wandering throughout the land they insensibly fell under the spell of the beauty that had thrice lured John Finley from his home. When they compared the abundant game, the fertile soil, the level land, and the beautiful rivers with the region of their home, they could but form the desire to enter into and possess the land. And so it came to pass that the Boones and the Long Hunters, notwithstanding they had suffered much in their hunting and had been ultimately robbed of the profit of it, on returning home began straightway to make plans for settling the land. Nor they alone: the stories of the country and their adventures therein had aroused the entire Yadkin people. All other thoughts and plans were put aside; their farms and even their hunting were allowed to suffer while the community made ready for the new promised land. At the opening of 1773 the Yadkin people resembled for all the world a mighty river held momentarily in check by the dam of the Cumberlands.

THE SURVEYORS.

KENTUCKY, however, was not ready for settlement. After the Boones and the Long Hunters had left the land there came in as a prelude to settlement, men of a more prosaic and practical profession than the picturesque hunters and adventurers who preceded them. These were the surveyors. Sent by the State of Virginia, they traveled up and down Kentucky, surveying the lands for record and laying out imaginary towns and cities in almost every valley. They were practical men and were concerned primarily with the land and its fertility. The beautiful forests, the wide plains, and the abounding game meant little or nothing to them. They formed, as it were, the skirmish line of the army of actual settlers that from 1775 came into Kentucky.

Mention has already been made of the benevolent decree issued by the King of England in 1763. It set apart for the Indians and the royal fur trade all the western region gained by the treaty of Paris. But the colonials who had fought the French and Indians and had been promised bounty lands therefor, desired to have them located nowhere so much as in this western wilderness. Moreover, the sympathies of all classes in America were with the old soldiers. Long practice had rendered them adepts at disregarding royal regulations. They speedily and unanimously decided that the King's decree was properly to be interpreted merely as a document to soothe the ruffled feelings of the Indians, but was by no means to be taken seriously as a guide for Anglo-Saxon conduct. The patroons of New York, the burgesses of Virginia, and the peasants of the Yadkin turned to the west with a promptness highly suggestive of colonial capacity for ignoring the kingly will. Washington sent confidential agents at once to survey for him the best lands they could find. Governor Dunmore dispatched official surveyors to cement Virginia's shadowy claim to the land, and the King's own commissioner at Fort Stanwix in 1768, in express disobedience of the King, induced the Iroquois first to claim and then to cede to the King the entire region between the Ohio and the Tennessee. In this arrangement the King sullenly acquiesced.

In May, 1773, a party of surveyors, headed by Captain Bullitt and including James Harrod, were sent out by Governor Dunmore to survey in Kentucky the bounty lands for Virginia soldiers. Bullitt began his journey from Fort Pitt and descended the Ohio in canoes. At the mouth of the Kanawha they met a company whose leading spirits were the three McAfee brothers, James, George and Robert. These had come from Botecourt County, Virginia, across the mountains to the Kanawha and there meeting Hancock Taylor and others by agreement, they had all come on down the river to the Ohio. Here at the mouth of the Kanawha, Bullitt separated from the others and journeyed into the interior of the Ohio country to visit the Miamis who, it was feared, might have a natural reluctance to see the Iroquois cede away the Kentucky lands claimed by themselves. He reached Old Chillicothe unnoticed and demanded a conference with the surprised red men. In this conference, after many metaphors[1] and no little juggling with the facts, he induced the Miamis to consent in consideration of prospective presents, to the

---

[1] His speech is given in full in Marshall, *History of Kentucky*, Vol. I, p. 34.

occupation of Kentucky by the white men. Much pleased with himself, he returned to the Ohio and rejoined his companions at Limestone Creek.[2] His journey had consumed thirteen days.

The united company spent several days in the vicinity of Limestone Creek.[3] They surveyed several tracts of land and laid off a section in town lots. Moving gradually down the Ohio, they discovered and named Bracken and Wilper's creeks after two of the party. At the mouth of the latter creek, Robert McAfee parted from his companions for an exploring expedition. He journeyed southward until he came to the Licking and down it to the forks.[4] Here, after making some surveys, he abandoned the river and again journed overland to the Ohio. Finding his company gone past he hastily built a canoe and overtook them at the mouth of the Licking. Here Douglass, a surveyor, was left behind to make surveys while the others drifted on down the Ohio. At the mouth of the Big Miami, Hite with six men joined them and the entire party began to give their attention to finding Big Bone Lick of which they had heard much both from Indian and white man. In the night they passed Big Bone Creek without knowing it and only discovered their mistake when they were ten miles below. Marching back they found the Lick and spent the Fourth of July there. They used the ribs of the mastodons for tent poles and the heads for chairs. They observed with wonder and awe the mighty skeletons that lay strewn around the spring, and the swarming thousands of animals that came there to drink. Here, on July 7th, the McAfee party left Bul-

---

[2] This was the site of the future Maysville, which in colonial days bore the name Limestone.
[3] The McAfee "Journals" in the *Woods-McAfee Memorial*.
[4] The site of the modern Falmouth.

litt and his company, and moving down the Ohio soon reached the mouth of the Kentucky. They rowed up the river twenty miles until they came to a salt lick where they went ashore to get a closer view of the game thronging around. Here they came upon one of their late companions who, profiting by the information received from a Delaware Indian at Big Bone Lick, had followed an Indian trail to this place and quietly preempted the best location, much to the indignation of the McAfees. Nevertheless they called the lick Drennon's, for the man.

After a week's delay at Drennon's Lick the company moved on up the Kentucky, surveying as they went. Following a buffalo trail they crossed the river where Leestown was later built and turning to the west soon found themselves on Salt River, which they promptly christened Crooked Creek. July 31st, after having surveyed some fifteen thousand acres of land, the party began their journey home.[5] They crossed Dick's and the Kentucky rivers, and crossing the mountains after great hardships passed through Cumberland Gap and thence home.

Meanwhile Bullitt and his men had moved down the Ohio the day after McAfee, and had encamped at the Falls. For six weeks between this place and Salt River the men, having been joined by the three surveyors of the McAfee party, were busily engaged in surveying and locating new land. In August Bullitt himself surveyed the tract where Louisville now stands and marked it off in town lots. The men were charmed with the appearance and fertility of the region; they resolved to return home and prepare for a permanent settlement in the land. Fortune, however, prevented the carrying out of their resolution.

---

[5] Taylor, Bracken and Drennon joined Bullitt at the Falls.

The surveyors and the adventurers that had made up the companies of Bullitt and McAfee had been fortunate in entering Kentucky and successful in traversing it;[6] a far different fate was in store for the men from the south. The reports of the Boones and the Long Hunters had not failed of results. The Yadkin men were preparing to move on to Kentucky. With the elder Boone as their leader, they collected in September, 1773, six families of neighbors and began the journey to Kentucky. It was not a party of hunters or surveyors; it was a migration of settlers. Women and children were along; the pack horses were laden heavily with the baggage to be used in their new homes. Their cattle were driven before them, even as when the Massachusetts' congregation overflowed into the valley of the Connecticut. In Powell's Valley Boone was joined by forty men. The company, now swelled to formidable power, moved on and encamped at Cumberland Gap on the brink of Kentucky. But it so happened that in the rear of the main body were a few [7] with whom Boone wished to communicate. He dispatched his son James with two men to meet them and secure flour. On his return with several companions, young Boone missed the trail and was compelled to encamp for the night some three miles from his father. At daybreak the camp was surprised by the Shawnese and all slain except one laborer and a negro slave. Boone and his men on hearing the firing hastened up, but was too late for all but the melancholy task of burying the dead. As a consequence of this inauspicious beginning, the majority, of which Boone was *not* one, were clamorous to return to safer fields. The

---

[6] It was in 1773 that Kenton came down the Ohio seeking the cane lands. Draper, MSS. *Life of Boone,* Vol. III, p. 108.

[7] These were the Bryans into which family Boone had married.

long growing desire for Kentucky had received a rude check. The entire band retreated forty miles into the Clinch Valley and passed the winter there. So failed the first concerted effort of the Yadkin people to settle Kentucky. An Indian war was soon to demand their energies.

With the coming of spring the rush of surveyors to Kentucky began anew. The people, or at least the officials, of Virginia did not consider that in losing their royal charter they had also lost the rights therein granted. To their minds the Old Dominion continued to extend to the indefinite west, widening its domain as its length was increased. Fincastle County, as the westernmost organized section of Virginia, claimed and asserted jurisdiction over the transmontane west. Of this county Colonel William Preston was official surveyor and under him as deputies were John Floyd, James Douglass and Hancock Taylor.[8] In May, 1774, Preston sent all three to Kentucky to continue the locating of the bounty lands. Floyd made his first surveys in eastern Kentucky and extended his labors over the central and the northern parts as far west as the Falls. Douglass began on Licking River and later moved into the same region as Floyd. Taylor confined his efforts to the Kentucky River region, and in the midst of his work was wounded by the prowling Shawnese and found a speedy grave in Madison County.

Of much more importance than any of these was the well-nigh successful attempt of James Harrod[9] to found a settlement in central Kentucky. In May, Harrod at the head of thirty-one men came from his home in Virginia down the Monongahela River to the Ohio and down that

---
[8] Douglass and Taylor had both been members of the Bullitt-McAfee party.
[9] Harrod had been a valued companion of Bullitt in 1773.

stream to the mouth of the Kentucky. This they then ascended to Oregon Creek; they journeyed across to Salt River, whence they proceeded to where Harrodsburg now stands.[10] Within two weeks Isaac Hite joined them with eleven men. Rendezvousing near the Big Spring, east of Harrodsburg, the men proceeded with great alacrity to locate and select by lot places suitable for building cabins. The vicinities of Danville, Boiling Springs, Big Spring, and Harrodsburg were surveyed and appropriated. Harrodsburg, then called Harrodstown, was named and laid off as a town, each man receiving two lots, one of one-half acres and the other of ten acres. Some land was cleared and a corn crop raised by an enterprising settler. Yet the company did not escape unscathed the ubiquitous Indians; a few men while separated from the others were ambuscaded and one killed. Two of the others set out straightway for home and a fourth man [11] alone reached camp and told the news.

Notice has already been taken of the French and Indian War and of the conspiracy of Pontiac in their relation to the exploration of Kentucky. The crushing of Pontiac had left the northern Indians nominally subdued. But their surrender was a sullen one and the white frontiersmen found the condition of peace much more terrible than war, for the red men saw with lowering brow the steady, lawless, irresistible march of the English to the west. Nor was this all; the passions engendered by a half century of conflict raged wildly in both red man and white. Forays and reprisals were frequent on either side. Complaint and upbraidings speedily followed. White men living on the frontier forgot their heritage and gave themselves up

---

[10] Collins, *History of Kentucky*, Vol. II, p. 517.
[11] John Harmon.

to the wildest passions. A hunter on the Kanawha having a favorite dog stolen straightway suspected an Indian and murdered both him and his squaw; many an event fully as trifling served to bring the exasperated savage to the warpath.[12] Wherever white men met red in this piping time of peace there followed quarrels and blows, the slaying of women and children, the burning of cabins, and the sacking of Indian villages. It was evident, even to the most peaceful, that the Indian war must be fought anew.

Politics insinuated itself into the question and complicated it. The Indians faced the frontiers of both Pennsylvania and Virginia. But their relations with the two were far from similar. With the Pennsylvanians they were sincerely and justly at peace,[13] for the Quakers were scrupulous in their dealings with them. But Virginia from the beginning recognized or respected no rights inherent under a red skin. The Virginia men, moreover, were filled with a lust for new land. They were constantly encroaching, always moving forward. They cared little for abtract justice and nothing at all for concrete Indian rights. So the Indians regarded the Pennsylvanians tranquilly, but the Virginians with bitter hatred. From Fort Pitt as her most western post Pennsylvania was accustomed to carry on her dealings with the well-disposed Indians. But early in the spring of 1774 Virginia, whose object it seemed was avowedly to bring on another war with the Indians, forcibly seized Fort Pitt and asserted a claim to the surrounding country.[14] Governor Dunmore appointed Con-

---

[12] Magill, *History of Kentucky.*
[13] St. Clair to Penn, May 29, 1774. *American Archives,* Vol. I, p. 286.
[14] Dunmore to Penn, March 3, 1774. *American Archives,* Vol. I, p. 252.

nolly, a wild, intemperate Irishman, as commandant there. The Indians, already well experienced in the ways of the Virginians, were quick to take alarm. They could expect no justice if Virginia was to be their neighbor. Their apprehensions were justified. Connolly, and probably Dunmore, were speculating heavily in Kentucky land and Connolly in person owned great tracts around the Falls. He left no stone unturned to provoke the Shawnese to war. In April he sent a circular letter [15] to all settlers along the Ohio that the Shawnese were not trustworthy and that they could look out for themselves. The frontiersmen took this as a declaration of war. A certain Captain Cresap with a band of frontiersmen at once began hostilities by attacking and defeating several canoes of Indians on the Ohio. A more savage deed was that of Greathouse in ambuscading and murdering a band of friendly Indians some forty miles above Wheeling. Among the slain were members of the family of Logan, the great Mingo chief, who promptly took the war trail and secured thirteen scalps before his anger was appeased. He carried the entire Mingo tribe into the war with him and the entire northern region gradually united for the inevitable war. Cornstalk, the Shawnese chief, was their leader.

Meanwhile Connolly by repeated injuries did his best to keep the Indians aroused and the Virginia frontiersmen were constantly writing to Governor Dunmore that war was necessary, inevitable, and already begun. The wily Governor made quick use of the pretext. Loudly censuring the conduct of the Indians, he ordered two large forces to be levied for service against the enemy; one, commanded

---

[15] Connolly's Proclamation of April 7, 1774. *American Archives*, Vol. I, p. 278.

by himself, to proceed by way of Fort Pitt and the Ohio, and the other under General Lewis to march overland and meet him north of the Ohio.

But Kentucky at this time contained many surveyors sent there by the Governor's own command, and Harrod was already laying the foundations for a permanent settlement at a town which bears his name. These men would fall the first victims in an Indian war, and Dunmore had no thought of sacrificing them. So through Preston and his subordinate, Russell, Boone was commissioned [16] to once more cross Kentucky and warn the white men of the coming conflict. Boone was to have one companion and he chose Michael Stoner. The two began their journey from the Clinch Valley and lost no time in penetrating into Kentucky.[17] They reached Harrodstown in the midst of the building activity. Boone, notwithstanding his mission, seemed to take great interest in the new settlement and secured half of a double cabin for himself. After a little delay the two messengers passed on to the Falls and explained their errand to the men at work. Then, followed by the alarmed surveyors, they once more crossed the valley and reached home by way of Cumberland Gap sixty-eight days after they had left it. They had traveled over eight hundred miles on their journey.

The surveyors and settlers after abandoning Kentucky, joined General Lewis at Point Pleasant. Lewis expected to meet Dunmore at this place,[18] but the wily Cornstalk had with instinctive genius planned to destroy each force in detail. Leading his Shawnese, Delaware, Wyandot

---
[16] Draper, MSS. *Life of Boone*, Vol. III, p. 126.
[17] On this trip Boone passed over the site of the future Boonesborough.
[18] Thwaites and Kellogg, *Lord Dunmore's War*, p. 287.

and Mingo warriors stealthily through the forest, he crossed the Ohio and fell like a thunderbolt on the unsuspecting English. But English perseverance was too much for Indian valor, and after an all day's battle the beaten chieftain was compelled to draw back in the shadows of the northern forests. Dunmore, marching from Fort Pitt, soon reached the Indian country and dictated terms of peace to the dispirited warriors.[19] By their treaty the red men pledged themselves not to cross to the south of the Ohio except for trade, and to do no harm to white men coming down the river. Enough has been written to show that the war was provoked more by white men than by red, but once begun the Indian had fought it valiantly and to utter exhaustion. In consideration of their cause for war and their valor in conducting it, a Kentuckian may be pardoned for failing to censure their violation of the treaty that closed it. The war is known to history as Lord Dunmore's War, a name given to it in commemoration of its chief provoker.

But the Kentucky country had been drained of its men by the conflict. Not a soul was within its borders or among its forests. Here and there were melancholy reminders of vanished hopes, trees blazed by explorers, stakes driven by surveyors; at Harrodstown a few desolate cabins, and in Madison County a new-made grave. The land had once more returned to solitude and quiet.

In the meantime, while the explorers and surveyors had been traversing Kentucky, and even while the campaign was being carried on against the Ohio Indians, the tide of eastern immigration was moving steadily and resist-

---

[19] Logan remained defiant and on this occasion burst out in the passionate speech that has immortalized his name.

lessly toward the Kentucky country. From the Shenandoah Valley in Virginia, a well-defined movement was under way westward into the smaller mountain valleys wherever fertile or habitable country could be found. This advance in the course of its slow groping way finally reached and came to a halt in the valleys of the Tennessee River and its tributaries, in what is now the eastern part of the State of Tennessee. This transmontane country was vaguely known to the Tidewater population and it was for many years a matter of conjecture whether it was in the limits of Virginia or of North Carolina. The people of western Virginia took the former view and were soon engaged in finding homes along the Wataga, the Clinch, the Powell and the Holstein. It was in 1769 that William Bean led the first Virginians to the Wataga River. Joined shortly by many others, his settlement became known as the Wataga settlement. In 1771 the Indian trader Carter settled on the Holstein River, and being joined by his neighbors from Abingdon, Virginia, his settlement became known as the Carter Valley settlement. Carter, a few years later, played a part in helping Henderson secure his path grant to Kentucky. The approach of the Revolution drove many Carolinians across the mountains to settle along the Clinch, the Powell and the Nolichucky. Separated by long distances from the governments of Virginia and North Carolina the Wataga and Carter Valley settlements united in 1772 in the Wataga Association for local government. The other settlements shortly came into the association, which modeled its laws after those of Virginia and aspired to independence. John Carter was a leading spirit in the movement.

In 1775 the Wataga Association was "farthest west," and when the emigration began anew westward to Kentucky, Powell's Valley served as the point of departure. It was the gathering point for men from all sections who were seeking the western lands, and Henderson, when he came to negotiate with the Cherokees for the ill-fated Transylvania found the Wataga River the most convenient point for his conference with the red men.

TRANSYLVANIA.

THE year 1775 was a troubled one for the English-speaking people in America. The mother country and her child had been separated now for over half a century. For a long time their different paths had been apart only in place, not in spirit; now even the consciousness of kind was departing. The first colonists had deemed themselves Englishmen sojourning in a strange land. However distant they wandered, or long, they never lost nor sought to lose the memory of their English birthright. But now a new generation had grown up that knew not England. They had no memories of its fields, acquaintance with its customs, or affection for its name. Their home was America and their hearts were there. In the process of becoming colonial they had ceased to be English. So it came to pass, without the intention of either, that out of this difference in sympathy that followed the separation of place, many misunderstandings arose and flourished. Actions of the mother country that would have been received as a matter of course fifty years before, became, in 1775, considered as symptoms of conscious tyranny. Colonial aspirations which would have found ready sympathy in the England of William of Orange, or even the second James, occasioned only distrust and suspicion in 1775. Suspicion had taken the place of co-operation; antagonism, of friendship; hostility, of peace. So, in 1775, without real cause, but as the result of petit measures on each side, two great peoples were on the brink of war. Both were suffering from high indignation and wounded vanity. Stamp Acts, Boston Port Bills, Committees of Correspondence and Continental Congresses swiftly followed.

As war grew more and more inevitable, both English and Americans began to make overtures for the aid of the Indians. The English influence, thanks to Sir John Johnson in New York, and the remembrance the Indians of the Ohio had of their Virginia neighbors, finally prevailed. The Indians became in fact allies of the English; from Detroit in Canada a vigilant English ruler directed their movements and mitigated, wherever possible, their atrocities.[1] It seemed a most inopportune time for the settlement of Kentucky or any western land. Nevertheless, it was this time above all others that the colonists chose for western expansion. In the troubled state of affairs at home there was a prospect that in the remote west they would be allowed to attain that which the colonial mind considered the greatest of blessings, self-government.

The memory of Richard Henderson has for more than a century suffered from the ambition of some writers, the hatred of others, and the ignorance of all. Like many other notable figures in American history, he was born in and early emigrated from Virginia. From his utterances in later life it is safe to suppose that his removal from Virginia was so early as to leave him without affection for it, or that his short life there was sufficient to inspire a violent dislike.[2] The elder Henderson, with the boy Richard and the remainder of his family, settled in the Yadkin region of North Carolina. The industry even more than the ability of the father may be inferred from the fact that he became sheriff

---

[1] A perusal of the Haldemand papers is sufficient to dissipate the idea that the English deliberately encouraged the Indians in their atrocities.

[2] Henderson's "Journal" contains many innuendoes at things Virginian.

in that turbulent community where peace officers were required to be constantly on duty. Richard, becoming older, acted as his assistant, and as a corollary took up the study of law. The legal libraries extant at that time in the Yadkin were not burdensome, either in quality or extent. Nevertheless, when the time came for him to be admitted to the bar, he successfully passed an examination as rigid as the Chief Justice [3] could make it. At the bar he speedily distinguished himself and was ultimately chosen by Governor Tryon as Justice of the Superior Court. This position he held for a full term of six years, retiring from the bench in 1774.[4] Henderson was a man of extraordinary ability and of greater ambition. From a home of poverty and a youth of illiteracy he had risen by native ability to be a leader among his people. He had tasted power and enjoyed it. Moreover, in his character was that large magnetism that made him popular with all classes and made men look to him instinctively as a leader. Popular, ambitious and conscious of his ability, it was natural that after retiring from the bench he should be far from content with the life of a rural barrister. He turned his thoughts to Kentucky.

The surveyors who had been forced by Dunmore's war to abandon Kentucky had not been silent concerning the land they had left. On the Point Pleasant campaign Kentucky had been a subject as exciting as the war itself.[5] Back in the "settlements" men began again to plan for land companies. Patrick Henry [6] sent a messenger to sound the Cherokees in regard to a sale of their Kentucky lands, but

---

[3] Berry.
[4] Draper, MSS. *Life of Boone*, Vol. III, p. 165.
[5] *Autobiography of Daniel Trabue.*
[6] Deposition of Patrick Henry, *Calendar of Virginia State Papers*, Vol. I, p. 289.

the approach of the Revolution interrupted the negotiations by offering a more brilliant outlet for his peculiar talents. Boone had not gone on the campaign with Lewis, but had remained in reluctant command of the three forts in the Clinch Valley. He suggested to Henderson that he purchase the Cherokee title to Kentucky and establish a colony there. The suggestion came to not unwilling ears. On the twenty-seventh of August, 1774, Henderson, John Williams, Thomas Hart, Nathaniel Hart, James Luttrell and Williams Johnston formed themselves into the Louisa Company for the purpose of renting or purchasing the land from the Indians on the Mississippi.[7] Whatever vices may be imputed to Henderson, indecision was certainly not one of them; in the autumn after the formation of the company, he and Nathaniel Hart personally visited the Cherokees and began the negotiations for the land. Henderson made the Indians promises, not of gold for their lands, but of many "white man's goods." The Cherokees listened to these propositions with pleasure, and with commendable prudence proposed that the Cherokee representatives should go to inspect the stores. To this Henderson assented, and after a discussion of a proposed meeting next spring the two men, accompanied by two Indian warriors and a woman, returned home.

Meanwhile, while the envoys of the Louisa Company and their dusky companions were crossing into eastern Carolina for the coveted stores, the Louisa Company itself was being reorganized. Leonard Bullock, James Hogg and David Hart increased the number of stockholders from six to nine. Each stockholder was to receive one-eighth part, since Bullock and David Hart ventured only one-sixteenth each. The

---

[7] Draper, MSS. *Life of Boone,* Vol. III, Chap. XI.

name of the company was changed from Louisa to Transylvania. The latter name suggested at once the character of the Kentucky lands and the impediments on the way into it.

In the spring of 1775, the wagons laden with goods [8] designed for the Cherokees by the Transylvania Company made their slow way across the Carolina mountains toward the appointed rendezvous on the Wataga River. The heavily laden wagons with their extraordinary cargo and their guard of two impassive warriors created much comment as they passed through the scattered settlements. The report got abroad and spread like wildfire that a new attempt was to be made to cross the Cumberlands and settle Kentucky. It was welcome news to a people whose eyes had long been turned thither. The Kentucky fever broke out anew and with greater violence than ever before. It pervaded all classes, and for a time seemed likely to depopulate the colony. Henderson's name became associated with the project and kindled additional enthusiasm. And when finally the insistent rumors were corroborated by the lips of Boone, the eagerness of the people could not longer be restrained. Boone had been employed and commissioned by the Transylvania Company to aid in the negotiation with the Cherokees, and at its completion to mark a road and lead the first settlers to the banks of the Kentucky. He selected from the ready frontiersmen thirty picked men and rendezvoused them at Long Island in the Holstein River, near the place selected for the treaty with the Cherokees.[9]

Boone, Henderson, Luttrell and Nathaniel Hart were to be the representatives of the Transylvania Company in

---

[8] The goods were bought at Fayetteville.
[9] Filson, *Autobiography of Boone*, p. 57.

the dealings with the Indians.[10] The four chiefs, Oconistoto, Attacullacula, Savanooko and Dragging Canoe were deputed by the Cherokees to represent them in the deliberations. The place of meeting was at Sycamore Shoals on the Wataga River. Here, then, in February, 1775, assembled the aforementioned chiefs of the Cherokees and about twelve hundred of the people.[11] At least one-half of these were warriors. Another chieftain, known as "Judge's Friend," had been kept at home for some reason but sent his proxy. Both sides were fully alive to the importance of the business to be transacted. The Cherokees were on the point of parting with their most valued possession. Kentucky was to them a paradise and a shrine. They loved the land because of the game in its level valleys. It was the land above all others where they delighted to hunt. To their minds Kentucky was the ideal country. Moreover, the Cherokees more than any other Indians, held the Kentucky land in veneration. The bones of their ancestors, so their tribal legend ran, lay thick beneath its surface. Under their savage exteriors they hid hearts by no means insensible to the pathos of their vanished forefathers. Truly, it was no trivial thing to give up the land that was called Kentucky. Such thoughts as these tempered their desire for gain and gave to their deliberations a dignity and a gravity not surpassed by the white men themselves. For Henderson and his associates also had much at stake. They were bargaining for an extensive country and money was not easy to find. And when the payment was made could they be sure of their purchase? Even if the Cherokees respected the treaty, would the northern Indians observe it? Supposing that Virginia

---

[10] Draper, MSS. *Life of Boone,* Vol. III, p. 169.
[11] Depositions of Chas. Robertson, *Cal. Va. St. Papers,* Vol. I, p. 291.

should again extend unscrupulous hands, as at Fort Pitt, what might not the future hold? Premonitions of such things caused Henderson to take the utmost precautions that the treaty should be fair and just, and that the Indians should fully understand the nature of it all. All halfbreeds among the Indians were required to attend and assist in interpreting.[12] Moreover, the best linguists among the Indian traders, including Ellis Harlan, Isaac Rogers, Thomas, Benjamin and Richard Paris, and Thomas Price were present and rendered active aid. Several men of note in the "settlements" were there; among which number was Isaac Shelby, later to become first governor of Kentucky. He was making plans for moving to Kentucky and more than suspected that Henderson was after the same lands as himself.[13]

From the time the contracting parties met until their departure, twenty days were consumed, but not all these were spent in business. The actual treaty-making seems to have taken up about five days while the remaining time was passed in feasting and revelry. On the first day,[14] Henderson and his companions called upon the Indians to show their title to the Kentucky lands. This the chiefs did, and Henderson satisfied himself by a most careful investigation that the Cherokees alone of all the people of that time were the rightful owners of the land. On the second day there came up the question of what lands Henderson wished to buy from the Indians. The Cherokees showed themselves unwilling to part with any lands except those lying to the north and east of the Kentucky River.

---

[12] Deposition of Samuel Wilson, *Cal. Va. St. Papers,* Vol. I, p. 282.
[13] Deposition of Isaac Shelby, *Cal. Va. St. Papers,* Vol. I, p. 296.
[14] Deposition of Jas. Robertson, *Cal. Va. St. Papers,* Vol. I, p. 285.

This region Henderson promptly refused to buy for the quite sufficient reason that Virginia had already bought it and was at that moment in possession. The Indians, unable to comprehend the ethical principle which prevented them from selling the same property as often as they pleased, were much incensed at Henderson's attitude, and, led by Dragging Canoe, they withdrew and broke up the conference. However, the lure of the "white man's goods" was too much for the Indian character and the following day found the Indians prepared to renew the conference. Henderson renewed his demands and the Indians finally agreed to them, though not without many complaints of the fewness of the goods to be given in exchange. It was at this juncture that Dragging Canoe in an impassioned address warned the white men that they had secured a "dark and bloody ground," a phrase that was to become widely famous. The region demanded by Henderson and yielded by the Indians lay between the Kentucky and the Cumberland rivers. On the fourth day nine deeds, one for each of the proprietors, were prepared and laid before the Indians for signing. The interpreters were present and read the documents to the chiefs, word for word, until they declared they thoroughly understood them. Then the chiefs signed. One of the interpreters, Vann,[15] as a result of a slight altercation with Henderson, at the last moment counseled the Indians to reject the treaty, but his advice fell on unheeding ears.

The boundary line of the land purchased by Henderson took its beginning from the Ohio River at the mouth of the Kentucky and ran up that stream to the head springs of its northernmost branch; thence the line ran overland

---

[15] Deposition of John Lowry, *Cal. Va. St. Papers,* Vol. I, p. 283.

to the top of Powell's Mountain in North Carolina, now Tennessee; thence it took its vague way along the ridge of the mountain until it reached a point where a northwest course struck the head springs of the southernmost branch of the Cumberland to the Ohio, and up that stream to the starting point. For this tract, goods amounting to ten thousand pounds sterling were given by Henderson to the Indians. In their eyes this seemed a huge amount, but they found when twelve hundred warriors shared in the division the *per capita* was surprisingly small. One warrior afterwards declared that his portion was represented by a single shirt.

After the chiefs had affixed their signatures to this deed, Henderson called their attention to the fact that the land he had bought of them was far off and that he had no entrance to it except through their territories or Virginia's. He proposed that they sell him for a further consideration a path [16] to Kentucky. This was to include Powell's Valley, in what is now Tennessee, and was to extend thence in a narrow path south of the Virginia line and into Kentucky. The actual limits of this path is today a matter of controversy and seems not to have been clearly understood then, unless by the contracting parties. It is certain that it included the land through which Boone a few days later blazed his way into Kentucky. It may be stated that for this "path" grant no money or goods passed into the hands of the Cherokees; the tribe was considerably in debt to the Indian trader, Carter,[17] and Henderson assumed the debt as a payment for the land. The nascent

---

[16] Deposition of Nathaniel Henderson, *Cal. Va. St. Papers*, Vol. I, p. 305.
[17] Deposition of Jas. Robertson, *Cal. Va. St. Papers*, Vol. I, p. 285.

Wataga settlement had a representative present at all the deliberations in the person of Charles Robertson.

The expense of the twenty days of treaty making was by no means small and was met by the Transylvania Company. They furnished beeves, flour, corn and other provisions for the entire assembly. To the credit of the company no liquor was given the Indians until the negotiations were completed. Hardly was the treaty signed, however, before the chiefs got gloriously intoxicated. The action of Henderson throughout is not open to criticism. There will not be found in history a treaty more fairly negotiated or more religiously observed.

For one hundred and thirty-five years the point has been debated whether the transfer was a legal one or not. Virginia took up the question almost before the ink was dry on the treaty and, of course, decided it in the negative. The royal Governor of North Carolina took similar action, and from that day to this the Transylvania Company and Henderson in particular has suffered condemnation at every hand. Were it not for the fact that historians, like animals of a more woolly appearance, are inclined to follow an accepted leader and that the action of the first judge, Virginia, was patently for self-aggrandizement, the verdict of the years might be accepted as final. Yet it might well seem strange to any truth-seeker that Henderson, one of the most eminent of colonial jurists, should be taken like a boy in a legal tangle, and that Boone, whose name was a synonym for honesty all along the frontier, should lend himself so completely to unlawful schemes. It may not, then, be entirely amiss that at least one more effort should be made to ascertain and make known the facts.

In a consideration of the title to Kentucky five different claimants must be noticed. These five are the Virginians, the English, the Shawnese—who may represent all the Indians immediately north of the Ohio—the Iroquois and the Cherokees. If there was any power to give a rightful title to Kentucky it was necessarily one of these.

The claim of Virginia to the western territory was based upon the charter [18] given them from the foundation of the colony. Therein it was specified that the domain of Virginia should extend from sea to sea and was interpreted by patriotic Virginians to mean that their colony grew wider as it grew further from the coast. Hence their seizure of Fort Pitt and the claiming of the Ohio as well as the Kentucky country. But the charter granting this extensive domain had been abrogated in 1624. Virginia's borders thereafter were become matters to be settled according to the kingly will. Virginia had become a royal province; her charter had been taken away from her and not another given. And in fact her boundaries had been fixed from time to time, not only to north and south, but to the west as well. Then, inasmuch as Virginia could not base her claim to Kentucky upon provisions of an annulled charter, unless the land were ceded her by one of the other four claimants, she could not possibly have any legal right to the country at all. A consideration of the other claimants will reveal whether or not any such cession ever was made.

The Shawnese, and the loosely allied tribes of the Ohio country, claimed Kentucky because of ancient possession and present desire. The Shawnese at one time, prior to

---

[18] McDonald, *Select Charters*, p. 17.

their removal to Ohio, had indubitably occupied Kentucky. They had lived along the Cumberland River and had given their own name to the stream. But neither Shawnese or others had occupied Kentucky, save by stealth, for nearly a century. They had been beaten by the Cherokees and conquered by the Iroquois. They were a vassal nation and had long acknowledged their dependence. Their claim, then, such as it was, had been taken over by the Six Nations who had conquered them and their country as completely as one tribe ever conquered another. The Ohio Indians admitted the Iroquois right to Kentucky and the Cherokees themselves acquiesced.[19] And, assuredly, neither Shawnee, nor Wyandot, nor Delaware, ever presumed to cede to Virginia the land that they had long since lost.

The Iroquois, then, had acquired as sound a title to Kentucky as an Indian ever had to property of any kind. By afterwards buying it from them the English acknowledged the claim, and Shawnese and Cherokees by acquiescing in the sale admitted its legality.[20] Thus the Iroquois title to Kentucky was unquestioned. But in a solemn treaty at Fort Stanwix, New York, on the fifth day of November, 1768, the Iroquois in the presence of the King's Commissioner, the Governor of New York, and representatives from Virginia and Pennsylvania, ceded to the English all the country east of the Ohio and Tennessee.[21] Three things are to be remembered in connection with this celebrated treaty of Fort Stanwix. The Shawnese and the Cherokees acquiesced in it; the Iroquois gave up all their

---

[19] Deposition of George Craig, *Cal. Va. State Papers*, Vol. IV, p. 140.
[20] Haywood, *History of Tennessee*, p. 80.
[21] *Documentary History of New York*, Vol. I, p. 587.

rights to the land; the title to Kentucky was ceded to the *English and not to Virginia*. Virginia had no more right to the country than before. England had acquired the right of eminent domain.

It is now necessary to consider the relations of the English and the Cherokees in order to understand why Henderson, knowing fully the provisions of the Fort Stanwix treaty, yet chose to buy his land from the Cherokees rather than to apply to the English government for a grant. While the provisions of the treaty were being arranged by Johnson and the reluctant ministers of the King could clearly foresee the result, they had begun straightway to make plans for alienating the territory they had unwillingly gained. At Hard Labor, South Carolina, a treaty was made with the Cherokees fixing the western boundary of Virginia by a line extending from a point on the North Carolina boundary, about thirty-six miles east of Long Island, to the Kanawha and down that stream to the Ohio. This boundary was somewhat west of the prior accepted boundary of Virginia, and for their agreement to this the Cherokees were expressly confirmed by the treaty in the possession of the lands west of the line. But the restless Virginians could not long be restrained within this boundary. October 18, 1770, at Lochaber,[22] in South Carolina, another treaty was made with the Cherokees by which the boundary was moved a little further west and the Cherokees again *confirmed in the possession of the remainder*. This time the line was to begin six miles east of Long Island and run to the Ohio. At this treaty the King's Indian commissioner was present, Major Lacey was there from Virginia, and James Sampson represented

---

[22] Summers, *History of Southwest Virginia*, pp. 90 and 111.

South Carolina. So on two occasions and by solemn treaties the English had confirmed the Cherokee title to the Kentucky country. Kentucky, having passed from Cherokee and Shawnese to Iroquois, and from Iroquois to English, had by English cession been restored to Cherokee. But not all of it was destined to come back into their hands. A certain Colonel Donelson was appointed to run the new boundary line, but instead of following the provisions of the treaty he passed from Long Island to the headwaters of the Kentucky River and down it to the Ohio. An enormous territory was thus gained for Virginia.[23]

Henderson in his negotiations with the Cherokees at Wataga had in his possession a copy of the Lochaber treaty. He knew, then, that the title of Kentucky rested with the Cherokees, and he knew, also, of Donelson's action in seizing for Virginia all the lands east and north of the Kentucky River, hence his refusal to buy such lands notwithstanding the eagerness of the Indian to sell. He was careful to buy only to the west and south of the Kentucky, and therefore secured lands outside the jurisdiction of Virginia.

The necessary conclusions from the facts as presented are, that since Shawnee had yielded to Iroquois, and Iroquois to English, and English had confirmed to Cherokee, the Kentucky lands were Cherokee possessions with the English government holding the right of eminent domain. The treaties of Lochaber and Hard Labor had fixed the western limits of Virginia, a boundary which Donelson unfairly extended to the Kentucky. Assuredly, then, the lands beyond the Kentucky did not belong to Virginia,

---

[23] **Draper, MSS.** *Life of Boone.* Donelson justified his act by saying that an Indian chief suggested the change on the ground that the Indians preferred natural boundaries.

they had never even been claimed by her. The treaties of Hard Labor and Lochaber had effectually checked her western expansion and must not be overlooked in any consideration of her later claims.

Henderson made no pretense of acquiring eminent domain. He recognized the sovereignty of England. The right of individuals to buy land of the Indians was one that on many occasions had been upheld by the Crown. Henderson, then, did not err in this. The right of a people to organize for local self-government was as old as the English race and colonial history afforded many examples of it, notably at Wataga. Henderson, therefore, did no unlawful thing in establishing the Transylvania government. There can be little doubt that if the Revolution had not intervened, Transylvania would have been recognized by the Crown as a separate colony. The confusion of Revolutionary times gave Virginia her opportunity to exploit her claims. As to the King's proclamation forbidding settlement in Kentucky, it was never construed as binding. No officer of the Crown observed it. The colonists shrewdly guessed at the truth, that it was intended only as a balm to Indian feelings. Henderson violated no law in settling Kentucky.

After the treaty was completed Henderson announced the terms on which he would sell land to settlers in the proposed Transylvania colony.[24] To those whose daring and energy induced them to accompany Boone or himself as the initial settlers, he announced that he would grant six hundred and forty acres at twenty shillings per hundred acres. Three hundred and twenty acres additional could be secured by bringing in a taxable settler. Hen-

---

[24] Collins, Vol. II, p. 512.

derson was careful to explain that this price would be given only to the first settlers and that there would be an increase after the first settlement was made.[25] With this clear understanding the journey was begun to Kentucky.

Boone and his companions of thirty picked and mounted men had the task of preceding the others and marking out a trace to the new settlement. The party included Squire Boone, Richard Calloway and Felix Walker. Captain William Twetty, with eight men under his command, was also among the number. The objective point was the mouth of Otter Creek on the south bank of the Kentucky River. This was a place frequently visited by Boone on his previous trips to Kentucky and one in which he took much delight. To the mind of the simple-hearted hunter it seemed an ideal location for a town and he had not been sparing in its praises to Henderson. The task of Boone was not to make a road but to mark a trace. Those that were to come after were either on foot or at most only accompanied by pack horses. The trace was to be principally for their guidance.

Boone began his journey even before the Wataga treaty was completed. Crossing into Kentucky by Cumberland Gap, he entered the well-beaten war road of the Shawnese and Cherokees and followed it northward for fifty miles.[26] Then leaving the war road, he traveled over a buffalo road to the "Hazel Patch," and thence across a trackless wilderness until he reached Rockcastle River. Up to this point the task had been an easy one; the road-making had consisted in blazing with their hatchets the trees along the

---

[25] Deposition of John Floyd, *Cal. Va. St. Papers,* Vol. I, p. 309.
[26] Speed, *Wilderness Road,* p. 26.

road. But now a more serious labor confronted them; the forests were full of fallen timber and dead brush. For twenty miles the company had literally to hew their way. No sooner had they successfully passed through this wearisome region than they encountered one of the wild cane fields that abounded in Kentucky.[27] Their path through this was as difficult as through the brush. But after thirty miles they reached the end of the cane and "began to discover the pleasing and rapturous appearance of the plains." Upon this plain the pathfinders entered, and guided by Boone made their way rapidly to the Kentucky River. No indications of Indians had been observed on the way and they had almost completed their journey without an interruption. But on the twenty-fifth of March, when they had come within fifteen miles of their destination, the unexpected blow from the Indians came. The party, while sleeping in fancied security, was fired upon at daybreak. A colored servant was killed by the volley and Walker and Twetty were badly wounded.[28] An Indian sprang forward to scalp Twetty but a faithful bulldog bore him to the ground. His red companions tomahawked the dog and then being but a feeble band all quickly withdrew. Boone had calmly rallied his men after the first surprise and saved the property. The ardor of some of the party was much chilled by this incident and they immediately set out for home. Both Twetty and Walker were in great suffering from their wounds, and as they were unable to be moved, Boone hastily constructed a rude fort for their protection while waiting. Here Twetty

---

[27] Narrative of Felix Walker. This is given in Collins, Vol. II, p. 497.
[28] Bradford, *Notes on Kentucky*, p. 22.

died the next day and the fort was christened in his memory Fort Twetty.[29]

Boone remained encamped at this point until the first of April. While inactive he wrote and dispatched to Henderson a letter [30] relating the story of the Indian attack, but urging Henderson to come on to Kentucky as quickly as possible. He stated in his letter that he was going to start that very day for the mouth of Otter Creek and promised to send ten men to meet him if he so desired.

Meanwhile Henderson, having finished the treaty at Wataga, had started for "Louisa" on the twentieth of March.[31] When Boone's letter reached him April 7th, he had almost arrived at Cumberland Gap. Hardly had he received the news, when the settlers fleeing from Kentucky began to come into camp. In one day he met forty fugitives and could prevail on but one of them to go back with him. Moreover, some members of his own party, being Virginians, and probably having no great affection for their Carolinian leader, left and went home.[32] On the tenth he determined to send a messenger at once to Boone and inform him that he was on his way. Volunteers were not abundant for the perilous task; by the promise of ten thousand acres of land [33] and by many solicitations, he finally prevailed upon Captain William Cocke to make the trip. He, himself, with the remainder of his company, pushed on over the "trace" as swiftly as possible. On

---

[29] Unknown to Boone, there was encamped only six miles away another party of white hunters from Virginia. These were attacked by the Indians two nights later and lost two men killed and three wounded.
[30] Boone to Henderson, Collins, Vol. II, p. 498.
[31] Henderson's "Journal," *Draper Manuscripts.*
[32] Even Captain Hart retreated and decided, as Henderson ironically states, to raise corn at home for the Kentucky people.
[33] Cocke *vs.* Henderson, *Cal. Va. St. Papers.*

the eighteenth he was met by Stoner with pack horses and an escort promised by Boone in his letter. Two days later he reached the Kentucky River and found that Boone had already arrived and constructed a rough fort.

A candid admirer of Boone might well be at a loss to say whether instinct or reason had induced him to select such an unsuitable place for a settlement. He designed to build the town in the narrow valley that lay along the banks of the Kentucky. On the north side ran the narrow current of the stream, on whose northern banks arose high and precipitous cliffs. From their summits a rifleman could command any point in the valley across the river. Both banks of the river were thickly screened by the trees; these were never felled and afforded an easy approach to the fort. On the south side, lofty hills arose at no great distance from the fort. They, like the cliffs on the other side of the river, commanded the fort. On all sides the fort lay exposed to any enemy of determination and skill.

In Boone's party when he had arrived at the Kentucky were about twenty-five men; Henderson had brought in forty more.[34] Accommodations had to be provided for this additional number. Boone had built his cabin on the west bank of a little stream that flows into the Kentucky about one-half mile below Otter Creek. Henderson found it impracticable to build cabins for his men at the same place and after reflection he decided to build a fort on the east, some three hundred yards away. By the twenty-second of April the fort was under way and lots had been laid off for the men. The men were to draw for the lots, and here it was that Henderson encountered his first

---

[34] Henderson's "Journal."

opposition. Robert McAfee [35] refused to take part in the lottery, saying he wished to go some fifty miles down the river and make a settlement. Nevertheless, the drawing was made, houses were built, a magazine erected and seed planted. A few days later Captain Harrod and Colonel Slaughter came into the fort from their settlement on Salt River. Captain John Floyd also put in his appearance, and because he was deputy-surveyor of Fincastle County, gave Henderson considerable anxiety.

There is no reason to believe that Henderson had ever intended to claim or assert any right of government over the territory he had purchased.[36] The right of eminent domain and of government, as he very well knew, belonged to England. But a quarrel broke out between Slaughter and Harrod in regard to their land on Salt River, and Henderson, much embarrassed, proposed that the different settlements in Kentucky should send delegates to Boonesborough and form a representative government.

For Boonesborough was not the only settlement in Kentucky at this time.[37] There were three others that deserved the name; these were Harrodstown, Boiling Springs and Saint Asaph. The story of their settling must be briefly told.

It has already been related how Harrod and a company of Virginians had laid out Harrodstown in the spring of 1774, but after being warned of impending war by Boone

---

[35] The McAfees had returned to Kentucky in March, and after planting a crop had set out for Virginia. They met Henderson, and all but James returned with him.

[36] Deposition of John Floyd, *Cal. Va. St. Papers*, Vol. I, p. 309.

[37] There were several bands of white men in Kentucky. Kenton had returned in the early spring, had found the "cane land" and was living in a cabin where Washington now stands. The Hinkston company of fifteen men were encamped on the creek of that name. Floyd's company of thirty men were encamped on Dick's River.

and Stoner had abandoned their "improvements." In March, 1775, accompanied by fifty men he had returned to his abandoned settlement. The news of Boone's misfortune at the hands of the Indians had caused many of his men to return home, but at the time Henderson called the convention Harrodstown was generally considered a strong settlement. It is worthy of note that it enjoys the distinction of being the first settlement in Kentucky. Boiling Springs had also been settled by Harrod and his companions, but was not a fortified place nor as large as Harrodstown.

Saint Asaph had been founded by Benjamin Logan and was quite generally known as Logan's Fort.[38] Logan was a Virginian, and starting to Kentucky had fallen in with Henderson and made the trip with him. Becoming displeased with Henderson's plans, he separated from him at Rockcastle River, and cutting a road [39] of his own westwardly he established a settlement near the present site of Stanford. The character and reputation of Logan was such that in a few weeks numerous settlers were attracted thither and Saint Asaph shortly grew to be an important place.

From the four settlements in Kentucky, Henderson called for delegates to be elected and meet at Boonesborough.[40] The delegates arrived and on May 23d held their first meeting under a great elm tree near the "lick." This was between the fort and Boone's stockade. Slaughter was selected as chairman of the convention much to the chagrin, doubtless, of Captain Harrod. Henderson opened

---
[38] Speed, *Wilderness Road*, p. 27.
[39] This road was extended to Danville and Louisville and soon superseded Boone's as the main highway to Virginia.
[40] Henderson's "Journal."

their deliberations with an address in which he pointed out several matters for their consideration and denounced the preclamation recently issued against him by Governor Dunmore.[41] To this speech the convention replied in an address wherein they asserted their right to frame local laws without giving umbrage to Great Britain or any of the colonies.

The convention remained in session until the twenty-seventh, and during that time passed nine laws. These laws concerned themselves with a variety of topics; establishing courts, regulating the militia, punishing criminals, preventing profanity and Sabbath breaking, writs of attachment, clerk's and sheriff's fees, preserving the range, improving the breed of horses, and, finally, preserving the game. This last law was made necessary by the fact that the abundant game of the region was already fast disappearing, owing to reckless hunting by the settlers. The law for improving their horses shows that even at this date the Kentucky people were interested in the subject that later, according to popular report, enjoyed their exclusive attention.

At intervals throughout their lawmaking the legislators concerned themselves with other things. A committee was appointed to confer with Henderson concerning a suitable name for the colony, Henderson suggested "Transylvania" and the name was adopted. Later another committee, consisting of Boone, Harrod and Cocke, was appointed to urge the company to grant no land to newcomers save on the original conditions—higher prices than to the first settlers. Harrod's presence on this committee was significant, as he was later to change his attitude entirely. Be-

---

[41] Journal of the Convention, *American Archives*, Vol. IV, p. 546.

fore the convention adjourned, Henderson, inviting open investigation, appeared before them and displayed the deed the Indians had given him at Wataga. Finally on the last day of the session he entered into a solemn and written covenant with the people. By the provisions of this contract, which merits the name of a constitution, delegates were to be elected and meet annually, judges were to be appointed by the proprietors but answerable to the people; all civil and military officers were to be appointed by the proprietors, there should be a surveyor-general who should not be a partner in the purchase, and the legislative authority thereafter should consist of the delegates, a council of twelve men and the proprietors. The agreement was signed by Henderson, Nathaniel Hart, Luttrell and Slaughter. It is significant that no mention was made of executive authority.

The convention adjourned on the twenty-seventh to meet again in September. The best men of the settlements had taken part in it and they were, as Henderson testified, a fine body of men. Their work had been done well and with dignity. They went to their homes well pleased with the Transylvania Company and its treatment of themselves.

TRANSYLVANIA AND VIRGINIA.

AFTER the departure of the delegates, Boonesborough settled down to the by no means humdrum life of a provincial capital. The center and the nucleus of the town was the fort; it was built in the form of a parallelogram and measured, probably, some two hundred and sixty feet in length by one hundred and eighty in breadth.[1] The walls of the fortification were composed of the walls of the settlers' cabins and interstices filled with palisades. At each of the four corners was a cabin of two stories which served as a watchtower and a redoubt in case of war. All the cabins had their roofs sloping inward so that they might be less readily set on fire by the enemy. On the opposite side of the fort were gates. But not all the settlers were located in the fort; Boone had erected two cabins on the other side of the "lick." Mr. Hart, also, one of the proprietors, to show his independence of Henderson, built his cabin outside the fort. Not a few others followed his example, and it was only in case of danger that all the settlers lived within the fortification. In fact, in times of peace not all the cabins within the fort were occupied by any means.[2]

There were at the beginning of June about sixty men, and no women, within Boonesborough.[3] As a means of subsistence all were engaged in hunting or in raising Indian corn. The former was much the more popular, and strong persuasion had sometimes to be used in order that corn-

---
[1] Rancke, *Boonesborough*, p. 35.
[2] There were twenty-six cabins and four blockhouses in the fort.
[3] Henderson's Letter to Colleagues, June 12, 1775, in Rancke's *Boonesborough*.

raising might not be altogether neglected. In one of the block houses Henderson made his home and opened a store. Goods of various kinds were sold here and on credit. Greater reliance was put on the store for provision than even at first. For reckless hunting, as the Convention had noted, had already resulted in the destruction of much of the game and the gradual driving out of the remainder. Hunters had now to go fifteen and often thirty miles before finding any game at all.[4] Yet the men still preferred the life of a hunter to any other. Only reluctantly did they engage in other occupations. When by chance any one wished to employ laborers he was compelled to pay three times the wages that prevailed in Virginia or on the Yadkin. The truth was, as Henderson wrote home to one of his colleagues, that many of the settlers were idle and worthless, having come to Kentucky merely that they might go back home and boast of their journey. The people when they did work were scattered over the little farms which extended two miles along the river and Otter Creek. They went to the fields without their guns and, apparently, had forgotten all about their former disaster. Boone had finished his little stockade to the west of the "lick" soon after arriving, but so great was the seeming sense of security that no amount of solicitation was able to induce the men to complete the main fort.

In all Kentucky there were in the summer of 1775 some three hundred men.[5] Most of these, outside of Boonesborough, were at Harrodstown, Logan's and Boiling Springs, but there were several minor parties in different sections of the country. Kenton was occupying a cabin where Washington now stands; Hinkston with fifteen men

---
[4] Henderson's "Journal."
[5] Butler, *Kentucky*, p. 80.

was encamped on the stream that now bears his name; Miller with fourteen men was giving his name to a well-known creek; McConnell with a small band was loitering near Kenton; Lindsday and others were encamped around the spring that was later to be enclosed in the town of Lexington. In all, the various parties had about two hundred acres of land under cultivation.

Kentucky was fast becoming a white man's land. Henderson had opened a land office at Boonesborough [6] and was rapidly granting land to actual settlers. He had also made out commissions for local officers at Logan's, Boiling Springs and Harrodstown. He had taken occasion to personally visit the three forts and found with a degree of pleasure that, though provisions, and especially salt, were scarce, the people seemed prosperous and well pleased with Kentucky and the Company.

But, as Henderson very well knew, there was no such tranquil life before him and his colleagues. Virginia and North Carolina had both, through their governors, denounced him and his treaty in no measured terms. According to the Governor of Virginia, the infant colony of Transylvania was an asylum for rogues and debtors; Henderson, moreover, was a disorderly person of whom the loving subjects of His Majesty should beware;[7] His Majesty had reserved Kentucky for other uses and all his civil and military officers should unite in throwing out the said Henderson. Henderson had, in opening the convention, adverted to the admirable solicitude of Virginia's royal Governor and then gone calmly on with his undertaking. But on some of the settlers the proclamation was

---

[6] Henderson's "Journal."
[7] Dunmore's Proclamation in the *American Archives*, Vol. II, p. 174.

having a different effect. Over at Harrodstown and Boiling Springs, where Captain Harrod's influence was paramount, disaffection began to appear. Hite was apparently the leader in the movement, but the guiding hand was that of Harrod. That the revolt should come to light at Harrodstown was very natural. It had been settled long before Boonesborough and was not pleased to be thrust in the background while a later settlement secured and enjoyed the honor of being the capital.[8] The settlers of the town had located their claim under Virginia government and on reflection did not enjoy the prospect of exchanging the ineffective rule of that province for the specific regulations of the Transylvania Company. Land was cheaper under Virginia land laws than under Transylvania. Over at Logan's Fort, Logan himself had, from his quarrel with Henderson, held sullenly aloof from things Transylvanian; he was a powerful influence in the new country and his attitude helped spread the disaffection. Finally, George Rogers Clarke found his way to Harrodstown in the spring of 1775, and at once cast himself into the fight against Henderson. This ambitious, unscrupulous and intemperate man was a native of Albermarle County, Virginia, had been a neighbor of Jefferson and a schoolmate of Madison's, and had for several years before his appearance in Kentucky lived a roving and somewhat malodorous life as a frontier surveyor.[9] He had been an associate of Cresap and Connolly in the preliminaries of Dunmore's War, and later became their staunch defender. He had served in the

---

[8] This ill-feeling between the two towns was accentuated by the fact that the Boonesborough people were Carolinians; Harrodstown, Virginians.

[9] English, *Life of Clarke*, Chap. II.

war and had made the acquaintance of Harrod, Kenton, Hite and other pioneers of Kentucky. He was a deputy-surveyor under Hancock Lee.[10] Clarke was perhaps the only man in Kentucky at that time the equal of Henderson. To his fiery and ambitious spirit the claims of the Transylvania Company were like a challenge to battle. He worked during the summer secretly against Henderson and returned in the fall to Virginia.

It so happened that within the course of this critical summer both Boone and Henderson felt constrained to leave their newly planted colony. Boone started home June 13th, for the purpose of leading out his family and neighbors to Boonesborough.[11] Henderson, T. Hart and Luttrell set out in August for the North Carolina settlements in order to attend a meeting of Proprietors.[12] Nathaniel Henderson remained at Boonesborough as justice of the peace. So Transylvania was left without a guide. David and Nathaniel Hart, it is true, remained, but they had by this time become thoroughly at variance with Henderson and were rather disturbing agents than leaders.

The proprietors assembled at Oxford, N. C., the twenty-eighth of September. Their meeting was a busy one and many things of importance were done. One of their own number, John Williams, was designated to be a permanent land agent at Boonesborough and his salary was fixed at one hundred and fifty pounds.[13] A vote of thanks was given Calloway and Boone for their efforts in behalf of the colony, and the latter was voted two thousand acres

---

[10] Clarke settled at Leestown.
[11] Filson, *Autobiography of Boone*, p. 57.
[12] Rancke, *Boonesborough*, p. 38.
[13] *American Archives*, Vol. IV, p. 554.

of land, while the former's son was given six hundred and forty acres. James Hogg was chosen to represent the colony in the Continental Congress then sitting at Philadelphia, and a memorial was given him to present to that body. The price of land was raised from twenty to fifty shillings per hundred acres. It will be remembered that Henderson, before starting from Boonesborough, had told the prospective settlers that this would be the case. Then, after preparing some elaborate advertisements to be sent through the colonies, the meeting adjourned.

Williams speedily set out for Boonesborough and reached the fort in the last days of December.[14] He found that Boone had returned the first of September and had brought his wife and children with him. Several others, including Calloway, had brought out their families and Boonesborough began to acquire a more domestic appearance. Boone, in fact, had started back with a party of thirty, but some of them under the leadership of the hotheaded Hugh McGary had gone to Harrodstown. Michael Stoner, a quiet, indefatigable "Dutchman" and the official hunter of Boonesborough, had one day fallen in with Kenton[15] at the Lower Blue Licks and had surprised that worthy very much with the information that there were other occupants of Kentucky than himself. Kenton had straightway returned with Stoner and was now at Hinkston. Floyd had been left by Henderson in charge of the land office and had done a flourishing business. There had been little evidence of Indian hostility except that Kenton had lost a companion near Lower Blue Licks.

The first act of Colonel Williams was to select a man for the very important office of surveyor-general. That

---

[14] Draper, MSS. *Life of Boone*, Vol. IV, p. 52.
[15] Hartley, *Life of Kenton*, Chap. II.

he might make no mistake in this, he resolved to call together the Assembly.[16] But it was the dead of winter and few were able to come; those that did come unanimously recommended Floyd for the place. Nathaniel Henderson was put in charge of the entering office. Under the direction of these two men the locating of land went on rapidly; by the first of January there were nearly nine hundred claims recorded and many thousand acres surveyed. The people, as a rule, seemed well affected towards the company, save those at Harrodstown. Here the men were binding themselves into a league to hold no land save on the original terms, and four of them, Hite, Bowman, Wharton and McAfee, presented to Williams a remonstrance against the increase in prices.[17] Williams answered with a spirited defense of the Company. He made preparations, however, to go to Harrodstown himself and open a land office to see if he were able to allay the growing excitement. Of all the Kentucky country, the most valued part was that around the Falls of the Ohio. Great estates had been secured there by a few enterprising settlers and of this the Harrodstown people bitterly complained. Williams at once proclaimed that no more lands should be surveyed there except in tracts of a thousand acres or less; these, moreover, to be forfeited unless settled at once. Williams also announced his intention of laying off a town there in the early spring. But when spring came he could not find the requisite number of men for the undertaking, for there had been an Indian attack at Boonesborough and many people, consequently, had found it imperative to look after their affairs in Virginia or Carolina. Colonel

---

[16] Williams' Letter to the Proprietors, *American Archives*, Vol. IV, p. 559.
[17] *Cal. Va. St. Papers*, Vol. I.

Campbell,[18] accompanied by two boys, had crossed the river at Boonesborough for a hunt. Almost immediately the Shawnese had set upon them and scalped the boys, but Campbell escaped. Boone started in pursuit, found one of the boys scalped, tracked the Indians to the Ohio, but made no discovery of the fate of the other boy.

Meanwhile Hogg had proceeded to Philadelphia on his mission of securing from the Continental Congress a recognition of the Transylvania colony.[19] He had sanguine expectations of success. The plans of the Transylvania Company had been under consideration in the Virginia Convention and had received warm support from both Jefferson and Henry. Henry, in pre-revolutionary times, had himself negotiated for a share in the Transylvania Company. Henderson had written personal letters of thanks to both Jefferson and Henry and thought he could count on their support.[20] But times had changed. Henry now saw a way of expanding Virginia at the expense of Transylvania, whereas before the suppressing of Transylvania would have helped only England. So the Virginia delegates in the Congress opposed the recognition, and Jefferson "gently hinted" that the Kentucky country really belonged to Virginia. Other members of the Congress, notably the two Adamses and Silas Deane, were favorably inclined to the colony, and, in general, acknowledged the validity of the charter. But against the opposition of Virginia nothing could be done.

In the spring of 1776, George Rogers Clarke reappeared at Harrodstown and the bad feeling there came

---

[18] Williams' Letter to Proprietors, Perrin's *History of Kentucky*, p. 136.
[19] Proprietors to Henry and Jefferson, in Rancke's *Boonesborough* (Appendix).
[20] *American Archives*, Vol. IV, p. 543.

rapidly to a head.[21] At his suggestion a convention was called at Harrodstown, June 6th, which decided to appoint Clarke and Gabriel Jones as delegates to the Virginia Convention. The two were instructed to appeal to Virginia to overthrow Transylvania and incorporate the country under her own government. At the same time Slaughter and Harrod were appointed to visit the northern Indians and find out their intentions in the war that was just begun between the colonies and England.[22] For at that critical time the attitude of the Indians was of great importance to all Kentucky. Every one knew the provisions of the treaty that had closed Dunmore's war; they also knew the extreme improbability of their being kept. In fact, the Indians were already violating it; they had killed two boys at Boonesborough, murdered Lee at Leestown, and were constantly prowling in predatory bands throughout the land.

The action of the Harrodstown people was not at all to Clarke's liking; he preferred independence first and negotiation with Virginia later. He knew, also, enough about the Tidewater brand of statesmanship to realize that for himself and Jones a seat in the Virginia Assembly was about as attainable as a habitation in the Elysian fields. Nevertheless, they undertook the journey and set out for Williamsburg.[23] They carried with them a petition to the Virginia Assembly to reassert her claim to Kentucky and relieve the land from the tyranny and exactions of Henderson. The petitioners stated that they were convinced the land belonged to Virginia and that the reason for the lateness of their action was because they had only recently

---

[21] English, *Life of Clarke*, p. 68.
[22] Draper, MSS. *Life of Boone*, Vol. IV, p. 74.
[23] *American Archives*, Vol. VI, p. 1529.

heard of the treaty of Fort Stanwix. This statement would indicate either a very slow rate of speed for colonial news or else an extraordinary deafness on the part of the citizenship of Harrodstown.

When the two envoys had come into the neighborhood of Charlottesville, they found that the elusive Assembly had already adjourned, not to meet again until October.[24] Jones, thereupon, made his way to the Holstein Valley for a visit, but Clarke pushed on to Hanover County to see the Governor. The Governor of Virginia was Patrick Henry, who was finding in patriotism and office holding a quick forgetfulness of his early negotiations with the Transylvania Company. By him Clarke was received in a most cordial and noncommittal manner. Clarke was given a letter to Virginia's executive council and immediately demanded of it an assumption of jurisdiction over Kentucky. The form of the jurisdiction, Clarke urged, should be the sending of five hundred pounds of powder across the mountains, so that Harrodstown might defend itself against the Indians. The council after much hesitation declared it could not assert jurisdiction, but was willing to lend Clarke the powder. Clarke lost no time in rejecting this offer and declared that Kentucky would assert her independence. Thereupon the council, perhaps not to his joy, granted his request and gave him an order for the powder.

This action foreshadowed the permanent policy of Virginia. When her Assembly met in the autumn Jones and Clarke were present and handed in the Harrodstown petition.[25] It was signed by eighty-four men, eighty-three of whom sank, or remained, in merited oblivion. Harrod,

---

[24] The assembly had met at Williamsburg.
[25] *American Archives*, Vol. VI, p. 1573.

alone, was a man of worth. He had been a member of the Boonesborough Convention and was much trusted by Henderson. A satisfactory reason for his change of heart has not appeared after a century of searching. Henderson was there, also, and Campbell, to present the claims of Transylvania. But Virginia's thirst had not been satiated by the confiscation of Indiana or the theft of Fort Pitt. It was in vain that Henderson called to their memory the legal opinions of the Imperial counsellor, or recounted his hardships in settling the land. The Assembly passed an act incorporating all Kentucky as far as the Tennessee River and naming it Kentucky County.[26]

Transylvania ended, as it began, in bloodshed. As the Colony grew unconsciously to a close, Indian activities were reported in many places. Two of these deserve, perhaps, a place in history. At Boonesborough, Jemima Boone, suffering from a cane stab in her foot, persuaded her two friends Frances and Elizabeth Calloway to join her in a canoe ride that she might bathe the injured foot in the cool water.[27] While the attention of the three was given to other things, the canoe gradually drifted down stream and went aground on a sandbar near the northern shore. Immediately five Indians sprang into the water from their place of concealment and seized the canoe. Notwithstanding Elizabeth Calloway's use of the paddle, the girls were quickly overpowered, hurried on shore and marched rapidly northward. The men at the fort were apprised of the capture by the shrieks of the girls and at once hurried in pursuit; Boone, with seven men, followed on foot while others followed on horseback. The capture was made on Sunday afternoon and the following

---

[26] Hening's *Statutes*, Vol. IV, p. 257.
[27] Draper, MSS. *Life of Boone*, Vol. IV, p. 78.

HISTORY OF PIONEER KENTUCKY

Tuesday morning the pursuers came up with the Indians as they were preparing their breakfast near the Lower Blue Licks. A swift rescue was effected with but one Indian escaping. The affair had its romantic side in the fact that three of Boone's men—Holder, Henderson and Calloway—were the lovers and later the husbands of Frances Calloway, Elizabeth Calloway and Jemima Boone.

The second occasion of Indian activity was less romantic and more perilous. In December, Jones and Clarke, returning from Williamsburg, came by way of Fort Pitt in order to get the powder collected for them there by Virginia.[28] A small boat and seven boatmen were secured and the party started down the Ohio for Kentucky. But the Indians had news of the cargo and lost no time in pursuing. Clarke, however, reached Three Islands near the present Maysville, and disembarking secreted the powder along the banks of Limestone Creek and set the boat adrift as a decoy. Then the whole party set out overland for central Kentucky to secure help in bringing in the ammunition. On the west fork of Licking they came upon the deserted cabin of Hinkston and found several surveyors in the vicinity. These told them Captain Todd was near with enough men to bring in the powder. Todd not appearing, Clarke with two companions, and guided by Kenton, pushed on to Harrodstown. Hardly had he left when Todd appeared; though he had but six men he yet resolved on hearing of the powder, to go and bring it in. His rashness received a speedy reward. At the Lower Blue Licks he was ambushed by the Indians who had found Clarke's trail and were following him. Two men were killed, of whom Jones was one, and two captured; Todd

---

[28] Bradford, *Notes on Kentucky*, p. 25.

and the others escaped to McClellan's Fort. Clarke returning from Harrodstown found them here and the whole party were soon attacked by the victorious Indians. The red men, however, were beaten and their leader killed. Clarke then safely carried in the powder.

In this connection it may not be inappropriate to sketch the future fortunes of the Transylvania proprietors. The act creating Kentucky County and nullifying Transylvania was passed in the autumn of 1776. A committee had been appointed by the Virginia Convention the preceding July to investigate the Henderson purchase and report. William Russell, Arthur Campbell, Thomas Madison, Edmund Winston, John Bowyer, John May, Samuel McDowell, J. Harvey, Abram Hite, Charles Sims, James Woods, Hugh Innes, Paul Carrington, Bennet Goode and Joseph Speed composed the committee and gave in their report in the winter of 1778. Virginia by establishing Kentucky County had prejudged the case. The committee in the course of a period of investigation extending over two years, heard the evidence of practically every person of importance connected with the affair. The depositions are preserved in the Calendar of Virginia State Papers and are almost without exception favorable to Henderson. But when the committee made its report affairs were too far gone to ever be turned back. Henderson had kept up a continual agitation before the Virginia Assembly and that body in the fall of 1778, in tardy and partial compensation, gave him two hundred thousand acres of land at the mouth of Green River, Kentucky.

North Carolina took a similar action, allowing him two hundred thousand acres around the present Nashville. It will be remembered that Henderson's purchase extended far down into Tennessee, and the territory now granted him was a part of the original tract. Henderson removed to his North Carolina property and enjoyed many honors at the hands of his fellow citizens until his death. He was once to revisit Kentucky in 1780, when he made a short stay at his old capital Boonesborough while he collected supplies for his new post on the Cumberland. North Carolina appointed him one of her commissioners to run the boundary line between that State and Virginia, and he later served as a member of the North Carolina Legislature. There are few cases in history where a man after being denounced by a government as a traitor, enjoyed such high honors at its hands. Henderson's later career speaks well for the uprightness and rectitude of his life.

KENTUCKY COUNTY.

WHILE Virginia and Transylvania had been wrangling about Kentucky, the ill-feeling between England and her colonies had reached a climax. On the fourth of July, 1776, after a year of hostilities, the colonies had asserted their independence and thenceforth the revolt widened into a revolution. The struggle was characterized on both sides by weird inefficiency and brutality. It was a contest in which the one country was not able unaided to attack nor the other powerful unaided to defend. England was hindered by intervening oceans, hampered by inefficient or half-hearted commanders, and harassed by a network of enemies; the colonies were doomed to divided action and untried counsels. Neither could utilize its full strength and both speedily began a search for allies. The colonies obtained help from abroad and contended against England to secure the aid of the Indians at home. But in the rivalry for Indian assistance the colonists were from the beginning at a hopeless disadvantage. Of the Indians, some tribes, as the Six Nations, preferred the English to colonist because of long alliance; others, and they were the most numerous, took the side of the English because of the fact that they hated the colonists, a hatred sufficiently justified by their past experience. So, not without great outlay of gifts and persuasion, the Indians of all sections took up arms for the English. Nor was the course of England one of unusual turpitude; the colonists did the same. The American condemnation of English policy in this instance is apparently due to the fact that England obtained the alliance which the colonists could only desire.

There can be no real understanding of Kentucky history without a clear conception of conditions existing in the region north of the Ohio River. The history of Kentucky is inextricably mingled with that of the northern Indians and of early Canada. At the beginning of the Revolution Sir Guy Carleton was sent out from England to be Governor of Canada. His capital was at Quebec and he had jurisdiction over all the British possessions not within the limits of the thirteen original colonies. Acting under Carleton were several lieutenant-governors located at the exposed forts on the Canadian frontier. The office of Superintendents of Indian Affairs was filled by these lieutenant-governors and their chief duty was to keep the Indian tribes well disposed to England and hostile to her enemies. To Henry Hamilton, residing at Detroit and managing the Indians from that place, fell the duty of arranging the Indian forays into Kentucky. He arrived at Detroit in November, 1775, and performed most admirably the duties of his trying situation until he was captured by Clarke in 1778. Before his appointment he had seen service in the English army as a lieutenant and possessed respectable military ability. He was personally a kind-hearted, genial man who constantly did all in his power to mitigate the horrors of savage warfare. To the north and west of Detroit was the fort of Michilimacinack where De Peyster held command of two companies of soldiers and acted as Superintendent of Indian Affairs in the absence of the Lieutenant-Governor, Patrick Sinclair. For the various towns in the Illinois, David Abbot was the lieutenant-governor and had his headquarters at Vincennes.[1]

---

[1] Matthew Johnson had been appointed Lieutenant-Governor of the Illinois country, but never reached his post—a fact which did not at all prevent him from drawing the salary pertaining to it.

England possessed on the Great Lakes a small but very efficient navy, built for the most part at Detroit. There were four schooners and four sloops on Lake Erie, one sloop on Lake Huron and one on Lake Michigan. In addition to this naval force Hamilton held about five hundred men under the command of Captain Lernoult. Among these were two companies of Rangers which it was the custom to intermix with the Indians on their expeditions. On such occasions both Indians and Rangers were put under the special command of "Indian officers," who were men that had by long service become thoroughly familiar with Indian manners and customs. These officers were never Indians.

Such were the military arrangements of the English in the northwest. On the colonial side, Fort Pitt, at the present site of Pittsburg, occupied the same position that Detroit held among the English. There, early in 1776, the Continental Congress had placed George Morgan as Indian agent for the tribes north of the Ohio, with wide instructions for dealing with the Indians. At the same place they had located General Edward Hand of the Continental army to have charge of the military operations that might be necessary in the west. Fort Pitt was at this time in the possession of the Virginians; they had built several other forts along the lower course of the Ohio, as a step toward retaining their hold on the western regions. Of these, Fort Henry, where Wheeling, West Virginia, now stands, and Fort Randolph, at the mouth of the Great Kanawha, were the most important.

There was a continued rivalry between Hamilton at Detroit and Morgan at Fort Pitt to secure the active or passive assistance of the Indians. In the summer of 1775, Carleton sent emissaries to the various tribes, inciting them to take up arms for the King. In the spring of 1776 a grand treaty was held at Detroit where, after five days consumed in speeches, the Indians definitely declared for England. Morgan, however, soon heard of this, and by a personal visit to the Delawares and Shawnese, did much to nullify Hamilton's work. He induced many of the tribes to attend a meeting at Fort Pitt and make a treaty of peace. He went even further and planned an expedition to capture the British posts in the Illinois, but his plans miscarried. In the spring of 1777, Hamilton had another meeting with the Indians at Detroit, delivered the war hatchet and many presents to them and sent them out on the warpath toward the forts south of the Ohio. Before the year was out more than a thousand warriors, officered by Englishmen, were hovering around the little forts at Fort Pitt, Henry, Randolph and the Kentucky stockades.

Of the frontier posts against which this force was directed, none were more exposed than those in Kentucky. It lay like a shield across the western region of Virginia and penetrated the Indian country for two hundred miles. The feeblest vision could foresee that there were troublous times in store for Kentucky if the Indians should again take the warpath. Moreover, at this time of greatest need the Kentucky settlements were at their weakest stage. Indian depredations and the rumors of war had, at the opening of 1777, well-nigh depopulated the country. Three hundred people [2] had left the country and seven stations had been abandoned.[3] Boonesborough, Harrodstown and McClelland's alone survived, and the last named was abandoned in the early days of 1777. There were,

---
[2] Draper, MSS. *Life of Boone*, Vol. IV, p. 104.
[3] Huston's, Hinkston's, Bryant's, Whitley's, Logan's, Harrod's and Leestown.

then, in the beginning of 1777, but two settlements and a possible one hundred and fifty men in Kentucky. Many of the people from the abandoned forts had found refuge at Boonesborough or Harrodstown, the latter gaining many accessions, particularly from Logan's [4] and McClelland's. The enmity between Boonesborough and Harrodstown had not abated. Rather had it increased because of Virginia's action in making Harrodstown the capital of the new county.

The year opened with two months of deceptive calm. The Indians committed no depredations and seemed to have abandoned, or at least to have deferred, their wrath against Kentucky. In February Logan moved his family back to Saint Asaph and reoccupied his fort. The settlers began to recover their spirits and venture away from the support and protection of the stockades. Such peaceful times were destined, however, to be by no means lasting. Already the British Governor of Canada was directing his Indian allies toward Kentucky with comprehensive instructions to destroy the settlements there. The blow was not long in falling. But even the short delay of a few weeks had sufficed for completing the military organization of the people. Colonel Bowman [5] was to lead a regiment of troops from Virginia; Clarke, who had been commissioned Major, personally commanded at Harrodstown; Captain Calloway and Captain Boone had charge at Boonesborough, and Captain Logan was supreme at Saint Asaph. Clarke was in charge of the entire militia of the county until Bowman arrived in September.[6]

---
[4] Logan himself with his slaves remained at the fort to continue his improvements.
[5] Morehead, *Settlement of Kentucky*, p. 59.
[6] Bradford, *Notes on Kentucky*, p. 26.

The Indians, in their attempt to destroy the Kentucky settlements, struck first at Harrodstown. Their forces were under the command of the great chieftain, Blackfish, and their coming was as silent as Indian caution could make it. Accident alone saved the fort from murderous surprise. It so happened that the two Ray brothers,[7] accompanied by William Coomes and Thomas Shores, had gone a little distance from the fort in order to clear some land. Three of them in the course of the day started off to visit a neighboring sugar camp, leaving Coomes at work in the clearing. The three fell in with Blackfish's Indians and two were killed at the first volley.[8] But James Ray, who possessed what were possibly the longest legs on the western continent, took to his heels and made his escape while the Indians stood dumfounded at his speed. Reaching the fort, he gave the alarm, and McGary, with thirty men, set out for the sugar camp.[9] They found the lifeless body of William Ray and soon came upon Coomes who had discovered the Indians, but had concealed himself so thoroughly that he escaped detection.

This incident occurred on the sixth of March, and the Indians, chagrined at their failure to surprise the fort, abandoned the attack for two days, hoping to lull the white men into a sense of security. At the expiration of this time they set fire to an isolated cabin outside the fort in order to lure the settlers to come out. The white men, apparently untaught by the death of Ray, rushed out to extinguish the flames, only to find themselves face to face with an overwhelming number of savages. Aided,

---

[7] Spalding, *Sketches of Early Catholic Missions in Kentucky*, p. 35.
[8] Clarke in his "Diary" says both men were killed.
[9] On hearing the news the anguished McGary upbraided Harrod for neglecting the defense of the fort. A conflict between the two was prevented only by the earnest efforts of McGary's wife.

however, by the forests, the settlers succeeded in reaching the fort. Four white men were wounded and one Indian killed. After killing all the cattle they could find, the Indians withdrew, but roving bands continued to molest the fort throughout the year. Probably a score of men were lost by the three forts through isolated murders and many more in the concerted attacks. Truly, as Draper has said, "The year 1777 was one of constant watchfulness and anxiety in Kentucky."

It is a striking revelation of the pioneer character, that in the midst of such suffering and anxiety, they seemed to have no thought of leaving their exposed position. Notwithstanding the Indian massacres, they proceeded with the organization of their government for all the world as if Kentucky was a land of peace and destined to lasting quiet. On April 19th, an election—the second in Kentucky—was held, and Calloway and John Todd chosen to represent the county in the Virginia Legislature. Clarke worked without ceasing to improve the military condition of the county. In April he called upon the commanders of the different forts to appoint two patrols, each to range along the Ohio and give notice of Indian approach. From Boonesborough, Boone appointed Kenton and Thomas Brooks; Harrod named Moore and Collier; and Logan, Conrad and Martin. These were to range by turns in pairs along the Ohio, changing each week. They did excellent service, but were more than once eluded by their crafty foes. At the same time Clarke dispatched two men [10] to the Illinois country to gather information for a scheme he had in mind.

---

[10] Linn and Moore. Bradford, *Notes on Kentucky*, p. 27.

The most northern, and consequently the most exposed of the three settlements, was Boonesborough; against it the Indians directed their attacks with even greater fury than against Harrodstown. The first attempt was made on April 15th by the same Indians who had shortly before retired from Harrodstown.[11] There were only twenty-two "guns" in the fort as compared to the hundred under the command of Blackfish, yet after two days of fighting, the Indians withdrew in complete discomfiture. They continued, however, to infest the forest and to cut off all stragglers, keeping the settlers confined to the fort. On April 24th, about forty or fifty of the original band made another concerted attack on the fort. Attacking and tomahawking a laboring man near the gate, they drew Boone outside by feigning a retreat. Boone, pursuing with ten men, suddenly found himself cut off from the fort. He only regained it after desperate efforts.[12] Seven men, including Boone, were wounded and the fort was besieged for three days. On May 23d a third attempt was made, and the fighting lasted two days, resulting in no loss to the whites except three men slightly wounded.[13]

Now the wrath of the Indians was turned against Logan's. Leaving prowling bands to prevent the sending of aid from Boonesborough or Harrodstown, the Indians in large numbers [14] marched secretly on Logan's. On the morning of the twentieth of May they appeared before the fort and surprised the women milking the cows while a few men were standing on guard with ready rifles. Of the

---

[11] Filson, *Autobiography of Boone*, p. 58.
[12] It was in the desperate attempt to regain the fort that Kenton twice saved the life of Boone, the second time carrying him bodily into the fort after he was wounded.
[13] Clarke's "Diary."
[14] Smith estimates the number at 100.

white men one was killed by the first volley and two were wounded;[15] the women and the other men reached the fort unharmed.

From this time until the close of the year, there was as little rest for Logan's as for Boonesborough or Harrodstown. Yet it would be the reverse of the truth to refer, as many have done, to the *siege* of the fort. Kentucky in 1777 was continually infested by Hamilton's savages, but for the most part they confined themselves to prowling through the forests, lurking around the forts and along the trails in small bodies, in the hope of killing from ambush whatever white men might come in their way. They were particularly successful in preventing communication between the forts. Yet there is every evidence that the settlers did not consider themselves in particular danger within their stockades. They continued, in fact, all their usual occupations, planting their crops and going on hunting trips whenever opportunity presented itself. Several times in the summer the savages appeared in force before the different forts, as in the attacks previously mentioned, but these attacks were of short duration and resulted invariably in favor of the white men. The greatest danger to which the settlers were exposed came from concealed Indians when they were out hunting or tending their crops. There was also the anxiety caused by the gradual

---

[15] Of the wounded men one named Harrison staggered and fell some distance from the fort, whence the little garrison could plainly see him bleeding and pathetically trying to rise. Logan and a friend named Martin resolved to attempt a rescue, but Martin's courage failed him when the gate was opened, and Logan was left to face the Indians alone. Running straight into the Indian fire, he reached the wounded man, swung him with easy strength to his shoulders and returned amid a hail of bullets, unharmed. Logan was a giant physically, and the early history of Kentucky abounds in stories of his exploits. It may be said in passing that his mental and moral equipments surpassed even his physical. He was probably the most heroic figure that ever trod Kentucky soil.

diminishing of their ammunition and the small prospect of getting more. Logan's Fort suffered more from this cause than did either of the others, and it was this fact that caused Logan to make his celebrated trip to the Holstein in the midst of the trouble that was come on Kentucky. He managed to elude the Indians, and, after many privations, reached the Holstein settlements two hundred miles to the east. Within two days he returned to his fort, while his companions followed him a little later, bringing four kegs of powder and four horseloads of lead.[16] The feat was heroic, but it is absurd to represent him stealing out of a besieged fort and running the gauntlet of Indians that beset his path.

On the first of August Colonel Bowman arrived at Boonesborough from Virginia with a much-needed enforcement of one hundred militia.[17] This was the end of the Indian troubles for that year. But even at the last moment the savages contrived to strike a blow. Learning of the coming of Bowman's men, they had carefully prepared an ambuscade into which the advance guard of the white men unsuspectingly fell. Several were killed before the main body came up and drove off the Indians. Upon the dead the Indians placed a proclamation signed by Hamilton, which proclaimed pardon and forgiveness to all the Kentuckians who would return to the allegiance of their Lord George III, and denouncing all who should neglect to so conduct themselves. What course the Kentuckians would, in the face of this magnanimous offer, have taken can only be conjectured, inasmuch as the papers fell into the hands of Logan, who, with lamentable lack

---

[16] Draper, MSS. *Life of Boone,* Vol. IV, p. 131.
[17] He first came to Boonesborough where he was informed of Logan's distress.

of respect for royal communications, promptly destroyed them. Notwithstanding the multiple guesses of succeeding historians in regard to the reason for Logan's action, it would not seem to require elaborate explanation. It was the most natural action for a man who in all his simple, heroic life never dallied with dishonor.

With the coming of Bowman and his men, the long harassed pioneers took heart anew. Already a company of North Carolinians, numbering forty-five, had entered Kentucky and joined, as was natural, their friends at Boonesborough.[18] These additions made it possible for the little garrison to take the offensive. Even in June Major Smith, with seventeen other Boonesborough men, had ventured as far northward as the Ohio in pursuit of an Indian band, one of whom they killed. Returning, they surprised and scattered an Indian force of thirty and arrived safely at home with but one man wounded. A little later the Indians, in revenge, besieged the fort for the fourth time in the course of the year. Numbering two hundred, they kept up the siege for two days and nights with much clamor and no success. They then withdrew and Boonesborough enjoyed a respite after five months of constant anxiety. Harrodstown enjoyed the honor of bringing the year's hostilities to a fortunate close. Here Clarke, forewarned of the Indians by the uneasiness of the cattle, flanked their ambuscade, killed four and scattered the remainder in all directions. No further Indian conflicts worthy of the name occurred in the Kentucky country till 1778.

From a record of Indian contests, it is pleasant to return to a story of more peaceful happenings. Virginia, in supporting the cause of liberty against England, had been

---

[18] July 25th, Captain Watkins was in command.

slow to organize the county she had with such dubious morality acquired. True, the militia had been put in shape by Clarke in the early spring, but of civil government or regulation there was none. In the tumults of Indian warfare the pioneers had not needed or desired other than military law; now that the land was enjoying, or at least experiencing, a period of quiet, there came an opportunity and a desire for civil justice. By the act erecting Kentucky out of Fincastle County, Harrodstown was fixed upon as the seat of government.[19] The reason for this action is more evident than its justice. Here, on the second day of September, 1777, assembled the first [20] court ever held in Kentucky. It was styled the Court of Quarter Sessions and was composed of five judges. These were John Todd, John Floyd, Benjamin Logan, John Bowman and Richard Calloway. None of these men were jurists, but they were all men that honored the law and loved justice. Perhaps no other five men could be named who deserved more of Kentucky or suffered more for her sake. A record of their lives would almost be a history of their country. Todd became one of the most eminent of Kentuckians and was honored abundantly even before his death. It may be sufficient to say of Floyd that he was the best beloved man in Kentucky. The deeds of Logan were such as to require no comment. Bowmen and Calloway were both heroic figures and strove with all their might in behalf of their land and their people. Of the Court of Quarter Sessions Levi Todd was clerk. The entire military and civil provisions of the act creating Kentucky

---

[19] Hening, *Statutes,* Vol. IX, pp. 257, 258.
[20] Trabue, in his *Autobiography,* mentions a court held at Logan's in July. Bowman, Riddle, Calloway and Logan were judges and Levi Todd, clerk.

were now put into effect and Kentuckians soon found themselves living under a well-organized form of government. In the military organization to which allusion has already been made, John Bowman was county-lieutenant, Anthony Bledsoe, lieutenant-colonel, George Rogers Clarke, major, and Boone, Harrod, Todd and Logan, captains. Logan also served as the first sheriff of the new county, while John May was the official surveyor. Ten justices of peace in the different stations lent their influence in preserving order among the sometimes unruly backwoodsmen.[21]

While this Court was in session at Harrodstown a census was taken of the town.[22] It was found to have a population of 198, of whom 24 were women. There were 81 arms-bearing men and 4 who were unfit for service. White children under the age of ten numbered 58; over ten, 12. There were 19 slaves, 7 of whom were less than ten years old. A census was most probably taken at other forts at the same time as at Harrodstown, but unfortunately it has not been preserved. The combined population of Boonesborough and Logan's probably did not equal that of Harrodstown. The population was, in fact, during the year rarely the same for any two weeks. Individuals and companies were constantly arriving and departing. The arrival of Bowman and Watkins has already been mentioned. In October Clarke, with twenty-two men, started from Harrodstown for Virginia, and was joined by fifty-five men from Logan's. The next day Captain Montgomery came into Logan's with thirty-eight men. In September, W. B. Smith, who had gone to the Yadkin to secure aid, had succeeded in piloting into Boonesborough Captain Holder and forty-eight men. In this manner the popula-

---

[21] Cowan's "Journal."
[22] Draper, MSS. *Life of Boone,* Vol. IV, p. 134.

tion changed from day to day. With the closing of the year Kentucky had practically the same population as in its beginning.

What Clarke's reasons were for leaving Kentucky and returning to Virginia are unknown.[23] He had declared his intention to resign his commission as major and not again to hold a military command unless there was imperative need. There can be little doubt that the principal motive influencing him in returning to Virginia was the desire to lay before Governor Henry a plan he had formed for invading the Northwest and capturing the English posts in the Illinois.[24] He had, while in Virginia the previous year, learned of Morgan's proposed conquest of the Illinois, and it was doubtless this fact that caused him to send the two spies there to find out the condition of the country. These two men, after a roundabout journey by way of the Cumberland River, had visited Kaskaskia on the Mississippi, and on the twenty-second of June had returned with a vast store of information. They reported that the British were constantly sending out war parties from the Illinois posts; that the militia in these posts were well trained, but had little fear of an American invasion; that the French *habitants* were by no means ardent in their affection for the English; that the Spanish to the west were well disposed to the Americans, but that the English were closely watching the lower course of the Mississippi and the Ohio.[25] The first part of this report was untrue, but the remainder extremely accurate, and no doubt

---

[23] Clarke's ostensible mission was to have the militia accounts drafted.
[24] Clarke's action from the time of leaving Kentucky until the capture of Vincennes are most minutely and critically set forth in Consul Butterfield's *Conquest of the Illinois*.
[25] Clarke's "Memoir," Dillon's *Indiana*, p. 118.

as Clarke reflected on the situation, he became convinced that the capture of the British posts was both feasible and necessary.

In the summer [26] Clarke had sent Harrod and a companion to Fort Pitt, apparently for ammunition; they had brought back the report that there was no apparent prospects of peace. This fact and his knowledge of the weakness of the British determined Clarke. To his ambitious mind it seemed that a continued war and a weak enemy presented an opportunity not to be neglected. Accordingly, while the feeble settlement of Kentucky were engaged in a life and death struggle with the enemy at their gates, Clarke determined to carry the war into the enemy's country. That the enemy could enter Kentucky as well as he could enter Illinois was a thought that apparently never entered his mind. That he might fail to conquer Illinois if he attempted it, or even when it was captured the Indians might insist on continuing their war against Kentucky, were thoughts that he apparently failed to entertain. No benefit could come to Kentucky save by a cessation of Indian attacks. But the prospect of American neighbors in Illinois was well calculated to enrage the Indians without serving to overawe them. Kentucky had nothing to gain from the project. It was for the benefit of Virginia.

In December Clarke reached Williamsburg and laid his plan before Henry, the governor. Henry entered into the plans with the same enthusiasm he had displayed in confiscating Transylvania; it was another opportunity for acquiring a goodly amount of territory without the inconvenience of paying for it. But as the success of the expe-

---
[26] Clarke's "Diary," May 18th.

dition would depend on the secrecy with which it was conducted, Henry decided not to communicate the plan to the Legislature where, as he knew, there was wont to be an enormous output of the English language on very slight provocation. He called into his counsel Jefferson, Madison, Wythe and Mason, and discussed the plan of Clarke's until January. In making up their minds to aid Clarke, these worthy sons of Virginia were far from being actuated by any such abstract idea of safeguarding Kentucky. But the opportunity was come to put into effect Virginia's oft-repeated claim of sovereignty over all the northwest territory. It was not characteristic of Virginians to hesitate at such a time.

The plan which Clarke's fertile mind had originated and which the Virginia statesmen had discussed in such detail was not concerned primarily with Detroit, but aimed at the conquest of the whole country between the Ohio and the Great Lakes. In this region the British held a number of posts recently taken from the French and serving as bases for dealing with the Indians. Of these the chief were Kaskaskia on the Mississippi and Vincennes on the Wabash. Cahokia, not far from Kaskaskia, was also an important stronghold. Clarke aimed specifically at Kaskaskia; his other operations were to be determined by fortune. He wished, if possible, to get possession of Hamilton, whom he termed the "great hair buyer," and to capture Detroit if circumstances would allow.

On January 2, 1778, he received from Henry two sets of instructions [27] in regard to the expedition, and the next day a letter reached him from Jefferson, Wythe and Mason. Henry, in one set of instructions meant for public con-

---

[27] English, *Life of Clarke,* p. 95.

sumption, addressed Clarke as lieutenant-colonel and authorized him to enlist seven companies of fifty men each from any part of Virginia. Said men were to serve three months and were to follow Clarke to Kentucky, where they should obey such orders and directions as he might give them. The second set of instructions was private and authorized Colonel Clarke to enlist seven companies of men for the purpose of marching against Kaskaskia. The letter from Jefferson, Wythe and Mason promised in the name of Virginia three hundred acres of land for each volunteer if the expedition should prove successful.

Clarke's instructions called for three hundred and fifty men, and he set to work at once to raise the number. Captain W. B. Smith was sent to take charge of the enlistment of four companies in the Holstein settlement. Captain Leonard Helm was to raise a company in Fauquier County and Captain Joseph Bowman one in Frederick County. Clarke himself, aided by Captain William Harrod, took charge of the recruiting in the Monongahela country. As is evident from the location of these men, the army was to be made up of men from the west of the Alleghanies. For whatever reason Tidewater Virginia was not to be a party to the undertaking. Clarke had fixed upon Redstone [28] as the rendezvous for all the men save those recruited in the Holstein; they were to meet him at the Falls of the Ohio.[29] Redstone on the Monongahela was in the territory then claimed by Virginia but later confirmed to Pennsylvania. None of the officers engaged in the recruiting or the men whom they were to enlist knew the real object of the movement; they thought, as Clarke proclaimed, that the force was designed to protect Kentucky.

---

[28] Now Brownsville.
[29] Pirtle, *Clarke's Campaign in the Illinois*, p. 25.

In Clarke's private instructions he was ordered to apply to General Hand at Fort Pitt for powder and lead.[30] He was given twelve hundred pounds in Virginia currency and was authorized to draw on Oliver Pollock, Virginia's agent in New Orleans, for whatever additional money he might need. As far as paper plans were concerned the expedition was well contrived; unforeseen obstacles soon began to present themselves. In the first place the Monongahelians obstinately refused to enlist; Clarke's public instructions proved a source of embarrassment, inasmuch as the frontiersmen were not at all interested in Kentucky and would not enlist for the purpose of guarding her. The section was in a turmoil over the conflicting claims of Virginia and Pennsylvania, and this made recruiting difficult. Bowman and Helm each succeeded in raising a company, only to have most of them desert at the last moment.[31] In thorough disgust Clarke set out for Redstone on the twelfth of May with what men he could secure—one hundred and fifty—divided into three companies. They were commanded by Bowman, Helm and Harrod. Some twenty families of emigrants accompanied the army, designing to settle in Kentucky.[32]

General Hand at Fort Pitt did all in his power to help the expedition. He furnished ammunition and supplies from his stores at that place and at Wheeling. Taking on these supplies, Clarke moved down the Ohio in rowboats for the Falls, where Captain Smith had written he would meet him with two hundred men. At Fort Randolph on the Kanawha he was joined by a company of men under

---

[30] Henry, *Patrick Henry*, Vol. I, pp. 603-605.
[31] Dillon, *Indiana*, p. 121.
[32] *Southern Bivouac* of January, 1884.

Captain James O'Hara,[33] bound for the Spanish settlement Ozark at the mouth of the Arkansas. Resisting the importunities of the garrison to join in the pursuit of a body of Indians who had just closed an unsuccessful attack on the fort, Clarke kept on his way until he reached the mouth of the Kentucky, where he soon learned on inquiry that Captain Smith had not yet reached Kentucky. Only a few of his men under Captain Dillard had come, and Clarke, in order to secure others, wrote to John Bowman at Harrodstown to collect these men of Dillard's and with what others he was able to meet him at the Falls, where he intended to build a post.[34] On the twenty-seventh of May he reached the Falls and landed his men on Corn Island (opposite Louisville) in order that he might more easily restrain his force from deserting when he disclosed his real destination as he intended to do here.

Captain Bowman was not able to secure more than twenty Kentuckians to march to the Falls, and even this small number proved reluctant to accompany Clarke to Kaskaskia, when he finally made known to officers and men his real destination. The Holstein men went even further; the majority of Dillard's men, led by Lieutenant Hutchins, escaped the night before the day fixed upon for departure.[35] They were pursued by mounted men and overtaken twenty miles away on the road to Harrodstown. Seven were retaken, but the others escaped to Harrodstown, where, after some reluctance, they were received. There were left now on the island about one hundred and eighty men that were to compose the army. These were divided into four

---

[33] When Clarke stopped at the mouth of the Kentucky, O'Hara's company continued on down the river.

[34] Butler, *History of Kentucky*, p. 49.

[35] Monnette, *History of the Valley of the Mississippi*, Vol. I, p. 418 (note).

companies under Helm, Harrod, Bowman and Montgomery.[36] Having previously built a block house on the island, Clarke put in it a part of his supplies, left seven soldiers and ten families of the Redstone immigrants, and, with the little army, started down the Ohio, June 24th.[37]

On the twenty-eighth of June he landed his men on a small island in the mouth of the Tennessee River. From this point he intended to march overland to Kaskaskia. He had hardly landed before his soldiers fell in with a boat of hunters,[38] who proved to have left Kaskaskia eight days before. Clarke administered the oath of allegiance and questioned them. They were Americans and asked permission to go with him. Clarke gave it and engaged one of them to guide them to Kaskaskia. In the evening of this day the force rowed ten miles down the river and landed about a mile above old Fort Massac[39] on the Illinois side. Spending the night here and concealing their boats in a creek, they began on the morning of the twenty-ninth their journey of one hundred and forty miles to Kaskaskia.

The progress and success of this expedition is only indirectly a part of Kentucky history; its formation has deserved notice because of the popular fallacy that it was a Kentucky enterprise. Of the whole force of Clarke's men only twenty could be classed as Kentuckians. From

---

[36] Pirtle, *Clarke's Campaign in the Illinois;* Letter of G. R. Clarke, November 19, 1779.

[37] A total eclipse of the sun began as the boats entered the Rapids.

[38] These hunters were six in number and were under the leadership of John Duff. The man taken for a guide was John Sanders.

[39] Fort Massac was on the north side of the Ohio, ten miles below the mouth of the Tennessee. Its official name given it by the French when they built it and who then occupied the valley of the Ohio was l'Assomption. It was erected in 1756 (some writers claim it was only strengthened, and was built much earlier) to counteract the building by the English of Fort Loudon on the upper waters of the Tennessee. . . . It was of course unoccupied at the date of Clarke's visit.—Butterfield, *Clarke's Conquest of the Illinois,* p. 591.

Boonesborough only Kenton and Haggin joined the enterprise. Kentucky would have none of it. There was, in the first place, some little resentment felt against Clarke by those who felt that Henderson had been badly used. But perhaps the greater reason was that Kentucky and especially Boonesborough was expecting an Indian invasion. It seemed to them the height of folly to invade another country while leaving their own defenseless against attack. Nor does it speak very well for the military genius of Clarke that at the very time when Kentucky needed all her resources he was engaged in an effort to enroll her militia for an external war. Surely it would have been better tactics to defeat the enemy at the gates.

THE GREAT INVASION.

IT WAS from the north that Kentucky was expecting the Indian attack. The Shawnese were again, as in the preceding year, planning destruction for the settlements. A lack of allies, intervening distance, and even a sense of honor held the Cherokees in restraint; Kentucky was never to suffer an attack from the south. From Detroit and her other Canadian posts England let no opportunity pass for arousing the Indians. One hundred dollars was the price paid for a prisoner; one-half that sum for a scalp.[1] The British agents had been active and successful. They were busy sending out officers among the Indians to reduce them to some discipline of war. Their trading posts throughout the north were become depots of supplies which the Indians were encouraged to rally around in order to receive provisions and to secure gifts. As for the Indians, they were well pleased with their new friends; they were quick to pledge allegiance and to promise aid. England constantly kept the barbarian eye turned toward Kentucky and continually used her utmost arts to direct their anger thither. As an assistance for their raids there had been constructed on the Ohio River a regular ferryboat on which the Indians might pass from shore to shore.[2] The English honored the chiefs, armed the warriors and attentively cared for the interests of all. Yet, in the utilizing of the Indians against Kentucky, it must be conceded that England tried sincerely to mitigate the inhumanity of her

---
[1] Draper, MSS. *Life of Boone,* Vol. IV, p. 170.
[2] It was made of buffalo hides attached to a framework. When not in use it was hidden along the bank.

red allies. Stringent orders were given and resolute precaution were taken against the torturing of prisoners. The price of a prisoner was double that of a scalp. Nor did they fail in their humane efforts; Indian warfare was more civilized in 1778 than in any previous year. Prisoners were more kindly treated and agreements were more faithfully observed.

The British efforts towards arousing the Indians were powerfully seconded by colonial treachery. Of the two great Shawnese chieftains, Blackfish urged war and Cornstalk consistently favored peace. In the autumn of 1777 the latter, while on a friendly visit to Captain Arbuckle at Point Pleasant, was foully and treacherously murdered. The outraged Indians hastened to arms. They turned their rage first against Wheeling and only withdrew after losing one-fourth of their number. Enraged by their defeat, they prepared a new expedition, and this in the first days of 1778 directed its march to Kentucky. There were one hundred and two men in the party, of whom two were Canadians, eighty Shawnese and the remainder Miamis.

In the three settlements of Kentucky the pioneers were experiencing a scarcity of salt. It was their custom to make this from the various licks from time to time as a public enterprise; but because of continuous Indian attacks in 1777, the supply was now running short.[3] Accordingly, a company of men was enrolled from the different posts for the purpose of visiting Lower Blue Licks and making salt there for the various garrisons. Boone was the hunter and guide for the company. They set out on New Year's Day and worked in peace until the seventh of February. On that day Boone, while out hunting some distance away,

---

[3] Filson, *Autobiography of Boone,* p. 60.

fell in with the previously mentioned band of Shawnese and Miamis on their way to Boonesborough.[4] He was numbed by the cold and in no condition to fight, even had there been no disparity of numbers. He tried to escape by flight, but was soon captured. The Shawnese were more than pleased when they recognized their prisoner. They had known Boone ever since they had taken him and Stewart in central Kentucky. He was known to them personally and by reputation. But they were far from feeling toward him the animosity usually displayed to their white foes. Rather their feeling was one of admiration and even of affection. Boone held much the same place in their hearts as in the hearts of the schoolchildren of today; he was their hero. History, in fact, has no stranger anomaly than the relations of Boone and the Shawnese. Year after year they fought as foes, but countless incidents show the good feeling existing between them; for Boone had much the same feeling for the Shawnese as they had for himself. He felt entirely at home when chance threw him among them. He had a strong appreciation of their mode of life and differed from them only in color and disposition. So the Shawnese were in great glee at taking Boone, and Boone, knowing well their feeling toward himself, felt no fear of suffering any injury at their hands.

The Indians, even before taking Boone, had discovered his companions at the lick, but had not molested them. They let themselves be cajoled by Boone into a promise of kind treatment if the men should surrender. This surrender Boone undertook to bring about. He led the Indians

---

[4] Charles Beaubien and Pierre Lorimer were the Canadian leaders. They had raised the Miamis from their town on the Maumee and the Shawnese from Piqua and Chillicothe. Beaubien and Lorimer were "Indian officers" in the British service.

to the lick, and, after some argument, induced the men to give up their arms on his personal assurance that they should not be harmed. The influence of Boone and the ameliorating effect of English orders is well shown by the fact that the Indians faithfully observed their promise. The red chieftains informed Boone that they were on their way to Boonesborough and would greatly appreciate any information he might give them relative to its strength. Boone, well knowing the defenseless condition at Boonesborough, solemnly asserted that the fort was impregnable to attack and a large garrison was constantly on guard and looking for these same invaders; that because of his deep affection for his red brothers he would advise that the attack be postponed until another day. His red brothers, having some knowledge of their own, through their spies, in regard to the actual condition of things at Boonesborough, probably took Boone's statement with several grains of salt. They knew that the fort was unfinished and manned by a feeble garrison. But so pleased were they with Boone, whose imaginative faculty endeared him to his captors no less than did his prowess, that they determined to abandon the expedition and retrace their steps.[5] Moreover, they saw in the ransom of the prisoners a rich opportunity for securing much "firewater," the deep affection for which among the Shawnese is a strong indication of their having once been Kentuckians.

Not all the men, however, had been made prisoners. Three of them had fortunately been dispatched to Boonesborough to carry in the salt they had made.[6] After performing their task they returned to the Licks to assist in

---

[5] Beaubien and Lorimer both wanted to go on against Boonesborough. The former was so incensed at the action of the Indians that he shortly afterwards abandoned them and went to Detroit.

[6] Filson, *Autobiography of Boone*, p. 60.

the salt-making. They were not long in perceiving that misfortune had befallen the others, though whether imprisonment or death they were, of course, unable to judge. Hurrying back, they reported the news to the panic-stricken fort. Such a blow had never before been struck against Kentucky; after the hostile encounters of the preceding year the pioneers had no hope that mercy would be shown to any one that fell into the hands of the Indians. The captives were given up for lost and their families mourned them as dead. An exodus began to Carolina and Virginia, and Boone's wife was in the departing number. The forts, and particularly Boonesborough, stood on guard continually. Everyone waited in vain for the attack they knew to be inevitable.

Meanwhile Boone and his companions were being conducted to Old Chillicothe. It was a three days' journey thither and the weather was severe. Much suffering resulted both to captives and captors, but it is to the credit of the Indians that they did what they could to alleviate the pain of their prisoners. They shared with them their food and blankets. Indeed, they kept with scrupulous exactness their promise given to Boone that all should be treated well. This unusual conduct was probably caused as much by expectation of bounties as by any altruistic conception of honor. They remained at Old Chillicothe only for a short time. On the tenth of March Boone and ten others were sent on under the guard of forty Indians to Detroit. Here the ten were exchanged for the promised reward, but the Indians were firm in their refusal to part with Boone. It was in vain that Hamilton offered five times the usual ransom; the Indians would not let him go on any terms. Nor did Boone himself display any great desire to be ransomed. He refused to countenance any of the numerous plans suggested by the English for his detention, and even refused the gifts of some articles of comfort pressed upon him. In fact, Boone was in no hurry to give up his Indian life; as long as peace obtained between them and his friends in Kentucky he was quite content to remain with them on equal terms. At Detroit the English seemed to place great confidence in him. Boone, on his part, conversed freely with the English in regard to Kentucky, telling them how the crops had been destroyed the previous year and that the settlements were in a bad way, with no hope of getting help from Congress.[7] It is possible that he even promised to aid them in their plans against Kentucky. There is no reason to believe that Boone was doing more than exercising that talent of which he was very proud—the talent of "fooling" his enemies. But the British and even the Indians listened to his words as to Holy Writ.

At length, heavy laden with "firewater" and other tangible proofs of British affection, the Indians set out on their return to Old Chillicothe. Boone, of course, accompanied them. Arriving, the Indians, as a special mark of their affection, decided to admit Boone to membership in their tribe;[8] he was to become the son of a chief.[9] As a preliminary to entering into a relation so desirable it was necessary for Boone to take part in several ceremonies. He had to submit to having his hair plucked out by root; only a small scalp lock on top was allowed to remain. The pain of this process was probably not lessened by the fact that it was done by women. He was then led into the

---

[7] *Haldimand Papers,* Hamilton to Carleton, April 25, 1778. (Michigan Pioneer and Historical Collections, Vol. IX, p. 435.)
[8] The sixteen companies of Boone were also adopted.
[9] Blackfish.

river and rubbed thoroughly to take out his white blood; in all probability some of his blood was taken out in reality before the ceremony was finished. Then, dressed in Indian fashion with gay feathers in his scalp lock, he was taken into the council house and listened while the old men, as is the custom of old men, spoke eloquently of the golden opportunities before him. He was then given a coat of paint of many colors and given a huge banquet which, being somewhat unaccustomed to dog meat and similar delicacies, he probably found the most trying part of his initiation. The Indians, with a grave sense of humor, named him the Big Turtle, a name probably called forth by the small height and comfortable girth of the new member. He was also presented with a dog and a squaw.

Boone did not pretend, and there is no reason to believe, that he disliked the life that followed. He was treated by the Indians as one of themselves and took part in all their activities. He was taken along on all hunting trips and quite won the heart of his father by keeping him supplied with meat. When he took part in their shooting matches a delicate situation arose, inasmuch as he was obliged to shoot worse than his opponents in order not to arouse their jealousy. This was a difficult task, as the Shawnese were notoriously poor marksmen and could rarely be trusted to hit anything smaller than the solar system. However, Boone so managed that he every day grew in favor with the Indians. The nominal guard that was at first kept over him was gradually relaxed until finally he was allowed to come and go as he pleased. Boone made no efforts to escape; he was unfeignedly enjoying himself. Moreover, he was probably somewhat diffident about exposing his scalp lock and other Indian acquisitions to the jests and jibes of his rough neighbors at home. The wandering Indians drifted in June toward the Scioto Salt Lick to lay in a supply of salt. Boone went along, and when he returned to Chillicothe was startled to find a large force of Indians painted and ready to march on Kentucky.

Clearly this put a new light on things. Content to live and hunt with the Indians on friendly terms while Kentucky was at peace, the sturdy old pioneer could not remain passive and see his old companions endangered. On the sixteenth of June he set out for his usual hunt and did not return. He made straight for Boonesborough, one hundred and sixty miles away. Fearing pursuit, he did not dare to stop to kill anything, and during the entire five days he was on the road he ate but one meal.[10] He came to Boonesborough on the twentieth and was received as one from the dead. The pioneers had long since given him up as lost and were overjoyed to find him alive.[11]

Boone's stay with the Shawnese was a powerful factor in preserving for so any months a peace between red men and white. The Indians could but know that a move on Kentucky would cause Boone to bring his Indian life to a speedy close; and their hearts were set on keeping Boone. The latter, for his part, understood that the Indians would not seriously molest Kentucky while he was among them. This knowledge must have strongly inclined him to defer his escape and appear content with Indian ways. But Hamilton, in a great conference held with the Indians at Detroit in June, had, by dint of extraordinary efforts, induced the Indians to take the warpath. Evidently there were to be few moments of peace for Kentucky in the near future.

---

[10] He had brought this with him.
[11] Bradford, *Notes on Kentucky*, p. 31.

When Boone reached the fort he found it garrisoned by some sixty men, one-third of whom were unfit for fighting.[12] The fort, despite a multitude of dangers, had never been finished. When Boone told his story the men began to apply themselves to bettering its condition and soon had it in good shape. Meanwhile the days wore on and no attack came. Several days after Boone there arrived at the fort a certain Stephen Hancock,[13] who had been surrendered at the Lower Blue Licks and had been living in captivity since. He reported that on account of Boone's escape the Shawnese had postponed the expedition against Kentucky for three weeks. This was agreeable news to the Boonesborough men, but the remainder of his story was not so pleasant. He related how Boone while at Detroit had been on friendly terms with Governor Hamilton and had promised to deliver Boonesborough and its garrison into the hands of the British and Indians if opportunity should arise.[14] This story, undoubtedly true and not denied by Boone, was not long in causing a complete revulsion of feeling. Boone became no longer a popular hero, but a despised renegade. His old friend Calloway, now a colonel of militia, openly advocated that he be courtmartialed and punished. The ambitious W. B. Smith came forward with the claim that he himself had been substituted for both Calloway and Boone[15] in the command of the fort. Some of the garrison still clung to Boone, and were willing to believe his story that he had not intended to keep his promises to the British and Shawnese,

---

[12] Draper, MSS. *Life of Boone*, Vol. IV, p. 217.
[13] Draper and Rancke agree that Hancock came after Boone. Trabue, a contemporary, says that Hancock came before Boone. It seems certain that the former view is the correct one.
[14] *Autobiography of Daniel Trabue*.
[15] Rancke, *Boonesborough*, p. 98.

but was deliberately deceiving them. Affairs were in a most chaotic condition, but as time wore on Boone gradually regained his old place in the esteem of the people.

The three weeks mentioned by Hancock were passed and still no sight of the enemy. Boone urged that a counter expedition be sent against the Shawnese town of Paint Lick near the Scioto. The wary old hunter had ascertained that Indian spies were lurking around the settlements, and he well knew the trouble such a thing portended. He hoped by his expedition northward to obtain full knowledge of what the Indians intended to do. The plan for a foray into Shawnese territory was strenuously opposed by Calloway,[16] the ranking officer in the little garrison. But military forms set lightly on the Kentuckians and on the first of August Boone, at the head of nineteen men, set out for the Ohio. Among the number was Kenton, who had accompanied Clarke to Kaskaskia and had come back to Harrodstown with dispatches. He served as a scout for the company. When but a few miles from their destination Kenton saw two Indians on one horse riding along in great glee. Now Kenton enjoyed taking a scalp as much as did the fiercest Wyandot. So, reckless of alarm, he fired and both Indians fell. Kenton ran forward for the much coveted scalp, and while engaged in that lawful industry, suddenly found himself surrounded by Indians. Fortunately his companions had heard the firing and hurried up in time to relieve him of a situation that was fast growing embarrassing. After this Kenton and Montgomery, reconnoitering, found the Indian village deserted. Boone interpreted this to mean that the inhabitants had joined the Indian expedition to Kentucky; he

---

[16] *Autobiography of Daniel Trabue.*

straightway changed his course and hastened with all possible speed back to Boonesborough. Finding the enemy's trail, he cautiously followed it, and, passing them in the night, he arrived safe at the fort on the seventh of August.[17]

On the eighth the Indians appeared. They numbered nearly three hundred men. Of these ten were Canadians, and the whole force was under the command of Fontenoy de Quindre, an "Indian officer" in the British service.[18] English and French colors were flying over this motley force, and the Indians were painted in all the colors of war. The army, for it deserved the name, had crossed the Ohio at Limestone Creek and had penetrated into central Kentucky by way of the Lower Blue Lick. They approached the fort from the north and crossed the Kentucky at the ford a little below the town. Then, without any haste and without the slightest effort at concealment, they moved around and took up their position on the south of the fort and near the hills. From the time they crossed the river the garrison had been watching their movements in silence. Not a shot was fired on either side; the garrison was so weak that it was absolutely necessary to save their ammunition, and the Indians were hoping to get possession of the fort by peaceful methods. They were still strong in their faith in Boone and heartily believed that he would surrender the fort to them at the earliest opportunity. Blackfish and Moluntha [19] were present in

---

[17] Kenton and Montgomery stayed behind for a last shot at the Indians, and when they finally reached the fort they found themselves locked out.

[18] It must not be forgotten that these "Indian officers" were white men and were so called because they always commanded Indian troops. Like De Quindre, they were usually French.

[19] Blackhoof, soon to be a renowned chief, was also present.

command of the Shawnese; it will be remembered that the former was the adopted "father" of Boone.

The first move on the part of the Indians was to request a parley with Boone. For this purpose they sent a negro slave [20] named Pompey to the fort to ask for him. Pompey went to within one hundred and fifty yards of the fort and, mounting a stump, yelled "hello." Although the men within the fort well knew what he wanted, no answer was made until he had repeated his summons several times. Then Boone condescended to look over the palisade and asked him what he wished. Thereupon Pompey delivered his message that the Indians wanted to have a conference with the chief men of the fort. They had sent word that if Boone would come out they would not hurt him. When Boone reported this message to the men within, there was much division of opinion in regard to the advisability of the conference. Boone put an end to the hesitation by declaring his purpose to go. He went confidently out from the fort to the place where Pompey was standing. The latter spread an Indian blanket on the ground [21] and Boone sat down on it, surrounded by the Indians who had now come up. To the Indian demand for a surrender he replied, as was the fact, that he was no longer the commander. He asked for time to consult the commanders, and it was given him. In the second conference he was accompanied by Calloway and Smith,[22] while the Indians were represented by De Quindre, Blackfish and Moluntha.

---

[20] Other authorities say that the request was delivered by two Canadians. McAfee in his *Life and Times,* gives the incident as above.

[21] *Shane MSS.*, Vol. I, p. 40.

[22] Smith was dressed with a view to impress the Indians. He wore a macaroni hat with a long ostrich feather in it and had also arrayed himself in a red coat.

The meeting between Boone and his "father" must have been an embarrassing one. Blackfish reproached Boone with running away and charged him with killing his son across the Ohio a few days before. Boone answered that he had not even been there. The settlers were urged to surrender, Blackfish saying he had brought along forty pack horses in order to carry them off easily. This offer seems to have been made by the Indians in good faith and as a result of a suggestion made by Boone while he was living a captive among them. The Indians were also undoubtedly sincere in their promises to carry the garrison off without injury. These facts were well understood by Boone, and so, either in jest or sincerity, he affected to be well pleased with the proposition. He asked, however, for two days for consideration, saying that it was necessary to consult the men within the fort. This request was promptly granted and the conference came to an end.

When Boone returned to the fort and related to the garrison what had been said in the conference, their decision was unanimous against surrender. They had no such confidence in Indian promises as Boone had. Feeble as was the fort, they far preferred the chances of war to those of captivity. They decided, however, to defer their answer for the full two days, and in the meantime to strengthen their position in every way possible. Thereupon was to be seen a spectacle unique in Indian warfare. While three hundred warriors were encamped in easy rifle shot, the pioneers went leisurely out and drove in their cattle without the slightest molestation. The men went freely about their work repairing the fort and making firm its gates, while the painted savages sauntered curiously around or looked on indifferently. The Indians, in fact, had no thought but that Boone would surrender the fort; they could not bring themselves to believe that the Big Turtle would turn against his adopted people. Moreover, they were greatly in earnest in wanting to take all the people prisoners; they wanted the promised bounty. But at the end of the allotted time Boone gave his answer that the garrison was unwilling to surrender and was determined to defend itself to the utmost.[23] To say that the Indians were chagrined at this would be putting it mildly. They saw their bounty money slipping away from them and their hopes fast fading of regaining Boone. To commence hostilities would be to lose all; they asked for another conference, repeating that they had instructions from Hamilton not to hurt the men, but to take them prisoners. They proposed that nine representative men from the fort should meet De Quindre and the Indian chiefs at the springs some sixty yards from the fort to discuss terms. They gave the usual promises of protection to the envoys from the fort.

When Boone reported this proposal to the men, an altercation arose that well-nigh came to bloodshed. Calloway opposed it with all his power as a fool-hardy adventure. He was becoming more and more suspicious of Boone's loyalty and feared treachery if they should go outside the fort. Boone for his part urged that the con-

---

[23] Boone's answer as recorded by Filson has quite a different sound from that with which McAfee credits him. The latter represents him as saying that all but a few were ready to surrender, and that he would try further to influence them. McAfee says that Boone went alone to the Indian camp, and while there arranged for the meeting at the springs. The truth probably is that a great many conferences were held with the Indians on this subject before the details were arranged. Boone's conduct during the siege later became a matter of much controversy, and in all probability the reports even of the eyewitnesses were colored by their personal feelings toward the old pioneer.

ference [24] be held, if for no other reason than to gain time. After a violent dispute, Boone prevailed, and it was decided to hold the conference. Daniel and Squire Boone, Richard and Flanders Calloway, W. B. Smith, Stephen and William Hancock and William Buchanan were chosen to represent the fort.[25] Calloway, though going to the conference, had lost none of his suspicions; he ordered the garrison to keep the guns trained on the Indians' representatives [26] and to be ready to fire at the first indication of violence. He also told the women of the fort to put on men's clothing and show themselves above the ramparts so as to make the Indians believe there was a large garrison within. Whether or not the Indians were impressed by this ruse is nowhere recorded. The treaty began on the morning of the tenth and lasted all day. While it was in progress the actions of both parties were of the friendliest. If the Indians meant treachery, no indication of it came to light. Squire Boone took occasion to inform some of the Indians that a huge army under Clarke was on the way from Virginia to relieve the fort. As the Indians knew that Clarke was in Illinois, they must have had, if they believed the story, a highly complimentary notion of that worthy's ubiquity. During the conference Blackfish wandered around the fort and surveyed it leisurely and curiously. Finally the treaty was arranged to be signed the next morning and the commissioners withdrew. Just what the provisions of this strange treaty were is not fully known. It, at least, made provision for annexing Boones-

---

[24] If, as Filson says, Boone had given so defiant an answer such a little while before, it is difficult to account for his attitude at this time. The McAfee account here is in all probability the true one.

[25] Rancke, *Boonesborough*, p. 87.

[26] *Shane MSS.*, Vol. II, p. 75. There were eighteen Indians at the conference.

borough to the dominions of his most Gracious Majesty and provided that the garrison should take the oath of allegiance to him and become British subjects.[27] The next morning Boone, accompanied by five of the representatives, repaired to the meeting place to sign the treaty. As they drew near the place Boone noticed that the trusted chiefs of the day before had been replaced by strange warriors. He spoke of it to Blackfish, only to meet with a denial. Nothing happened amiss, however, and the treaty was signed by both parties. Then the Indians offered their hands in token of amity, and the white men gladly received them. However, as the Indians far outnumbered the whites, and they all insisted on shaking hands, it resulted in each of the white men being grasped by two or more Indians. So far there had been no signs of treachery. But Calloway, not liking the looks of things, jerked away from the detaining hands and ran for the fort.[28] The others did likewise, and a "dreadful scuffle" ensued, the Indians making great efforts to hold Boone. When the garrison saw the disorder, they lost no time in firing on the Indians, and the fire was returned by a party of concealed warriors. Thus exposed to two fires, the treaty-makers hurried to the fort and succeeded in reaching it with no one wounded except Squire Boone.[29] Whether this was due to the amazingly poor marksmanship of the Indians or to their reluctance to harm their prospective prisoners does not appear.

---

[27] Draper, MSS. *Life of Boone,* Vol. IV, p. 224.
[28] Another tradition gives John South as the first man to break away.
[29] One commissioner was unable to reach the fort and was compelled to remain hidden behind a stump until the darkness made it possible for the garrison to let him inside.

It is by no means settled that the Indians were acting in bad faith in taking the hands of the white men. Rather is it to be believed that the lamentable outcome was a result of the panic on the part of Colonel Calloway. He was constantly expecting treachery from the Indians and would be quick to take alarm at a situation such as this. On the other hand, there were many reasons to believe that the Indians were sincere. If they had meditated treachery, they had had several, and better, opportunities before. Only the day before they had had nine men in their power and did not offer to molest them. They had not attempted violence at their first conference. They had allowed the settlers, on several occasions, to drive their cattle into the fort and, finally, they could but know that they were under the rifles of the garrison and that any violence on their part meant death to themselves. From these considerations, it remains at least an open question whether the trouble at the spring was due to treachery on the part of the Indians or a panic on the part of the white men.

Whatever had been the nature of the Indians' former actions, there could be no doubt about their hostility from this time forward. Having secreted a chosen band near the Kentucky River, the others broke up camp in wild confusion and ostentatiously pretended to retreat, evidently hoping that the garrison would come out and pursue.[30] This, however, was the one thing above all others that the men would not do. They suspected a trap and held themselves steadily in the fort. Then the Indians returned and began a fierce attack, which they kept up almost without cessation for nine days.[31] The fire of the

---
[30] McAfee, *Life and Times*.
[31] Indian sharpshooters on several occasions fired into the fort from the hills behind and those across the river. *Shane MSS.*, Vol. I, p. 44.

Indians was, however, of little effect and that of the garrison seems to have been but little better. Not content with rifle fire, the garrison brought out a wooden cannon bound around with a wagon tire and prepared to use it. They loaded it with twenty or thirty-ounce balls and fired at a group of Indians.[32] So great a terror was inspired in the Indians that it was fired again. But this time it burst and the loud report so alarmed the Indians that they "skampered perdidiously" and did not dare during the remainder of the siege to gather together in groups.[33] Oftentimes the Indians would taunt the garrison and defy them to shoot their big gun again; to this the usual reply was that it was not worth while to shoot it at single Indians. Great efforts were made by the Indians to undermine the fort. They began digging under the river bank and mined to within fifteen or twenty steps of the fort. The mines approached so nearly that the white men and the Indians could hear each other digging. When the Indians had mined close to the fort they made constant efforts to throw torches and firebrands on the roofs of the cabins.[34] Fortunately, however, there had been heavy rains [35] for several days and no damage was done, as the roofs were too damp to ignite. The constant raining made mining a very disagreeable business, and the Indians, tiring, abandoned it. There was the additional reason that they feared lest the pioneers might place their cannon in the countermine and fire through the thin intervening walls. Finally,

---

[32] *Autobiography of Daniel Trabue.*

[33] Squire Boone before the siege had made two of these rude swivels, but one had already burst. *Shane MSS.*, Vol. I, p. 40.

[34] At one time the house formerly occupied by Henderson was set on fire, but the blaze was extinguished by knocking off the shingles.

[35] The accounts of both McAfee and Trabue make it plain that if it had not been for the opportune rains the garrison would have been compelled to surrender.

fully disheartened, the entire force, on the twentieth of August, after destroying all the property they could find exposed, raised the siege and began a retreat. Weakness and fear of treachery prevented the garrison from pursuing. As an evidence of poor marksmanship and an overabundant supply of ammunition, the settlers, after the siege, picked up some one hundred and twenty-five pounds of bullets near the fort. The garrison had lost but two killed and four wounded; the Indians had two killed and three wounded.[36]

Only a few days after the raising of the siege a company of eighty men came into the fort from the Holstein settlements.[37] No attempt at resistance was made either from Harrodstown or Logan's during the siege. The former, in fact, was wholly ignorant that the fort was being besieged. They did not learn of it at all till after the siege had been raised when, surprised because they had received no communication from Boonesborough for so long a time, they sent messengers to see what was wrong, and only then learned of the peril through which the fort had lately passed. Logan's had been expecting a siege the same time as Boonesborough, but though the Indians appeared around the fort, killing and driving off the cattle, no actual attack occurred. Small as their own garrison[38] was, they had sent men to Boonesborough when

---

[36] Butterfield, *Clarke's Conquest of the Illinois*, p. 199. It is impossible to reconcile the Indian account of their losses with that usually given by the Kentucky historians. Butterfield's statement is derived from the Haldimand Papers and is undoubtedly correct. As a rule the Indian officers were very accurate in reporting their losses—and gains—to the Canadian headquarters. Among the Indian dead was the negro slave Pompey.

[37] Rancke, *Boonesborough*, p. 104.

[38] McAfee, *Sketches of the First Settlements in Kentucky*. There were twenty-four men at Logan's. Logan himself went to the lick to drive in the cattle and was gravely wounded by the lurking Indians.

they heard that it was threatened, and for this reason the fort could possibly have been taken had the Indians attacked it in force. After the Indians had withdrawn from before their own walls, they feared attack from those before Boonesborough.[39] On one occasion, when the feeble garrison was anxiously manning the walls, they saw a considerable force approaching from the direction of Boonesborough, and they hastened to prepare themselves for the expected attack. Logan was confined to his bed by wounds and the garrison was almost exhausted.[40] But the approaching force [41] proved to be their own men returned from the siege of Boonesborough, and as soon as they were recognized, both sides gave themselves up to the wildest rejoicing.

The aftermath of the siege of Boonesborough is worthy of record. The feeling against Boone for his promises to the British and Indians and for his conduct during the siege was bitter, and particularly so on the part of Calloway.[42] A meeting of the militia officers was called at Logan's, where Logan was confined by his wounds, and Boone was court-martialed for treason. Calloway charged that at Lower Blue Licks Boone had been found hunting ten miles away from his companions and that he had surrendered them unnecessarily and against their will. He

---

[39] *Autobiography of Daniel Trabue.*

[40] During this trouble the garrison had built a tunnel of some length from the fort to the spring outside. A messenger, Martin, was despatched to the Holstein for help.

[41] These men, as well as a few from Harrodstown, had been sent to Boonesborough when the siege was expected. They remained within the fort throughout the siege. A Boonesborough hunter, Patton, caught outside the fort by the coming of the Indians, lingered near until at the final assault, thinking the fort captured, he bore the news to Logan's. *Clarke MSS.*, Vol. XXVI.

[42] Flanders Calloway had married the daughter of Boone, and there were probably family reasons for the bad feeling between the Boones and Calloways. *Shane MSS.*, Vol. I, p. 27.

further charged that Boone had entered into treasonable agreements with Hamilton for the surrender of the Kentucky settlements. Boone, in answer, justified his conduct at the Lower Blue Licks and affirmed that, in making such promises to the British at Detroit, he had only meant to deceive them. The court adopted Boone's side of the question and gave him an honorable acquittal. He shortly became a major in the militia. Calloway and Logan were greatly displeased with the verdict, but it was a popular one with the people. Boone soon returned to North Carolina, whither his family had gone after his capture by the Indians. He did not return until the fall of 1779.[43]

The latter half of the year 1778 was much quieter than the first. Although straggling bodies of Indians made desultory attacks around the forts, there was no longer any great peril. In September a party of white men going from Harrodstown to Logan's was fired upon, but no damage was done. A corn-shelling party sent out from Harrodstown under Colonel Bowman fared somewhat worse; fired upon from a canebrake, they lost seven men before driving off their assailants. Calloway went to Virginia the last of the year and brought back a great supply of ammunition, conveying it over the long road on some forty pack horses.

There came in November a melancholy suggestion of Transylvania in an act of the Virginia Legislature relating to Richard Henderson and his associates. An act was passed formally annulling their purchase from the Cherokees, but giving them two hundred thousand acres of land at the mouth of Green River. In the troubled times of the last two years Transylvania had almost passed out of memory in Kentucky.

---

[43] Thwaites, *Life of Boone*, p. 167.

GROWTH AND EXPANSION.

WHILE Boonesborough and the other Kentucky settlements were fighting the Indians hand to hand, Colonel George Rogers Clarke, several hundred miles away from the danger zone, was waging a bloodless warfare against a somnolent enemy.[1] Kaskaskia capitulated with a readiness highly suggestive that its submission at that time was caused only by a lack of earlier opportunity. Sixty miles up the Mississippi the inhabitants of Cahokia, influenced by the entreaties of their friends at Kaskaskia, surrendered without a struggle to a small force under Captain Bowman, sent from the latter fort. Here, as at Kaskaskia, no casualties resulted unless, perhaps, to the vocabulary of the excitable French. Kaskaskia submitted to a regiment; Cahokia, to a company; Vincennes, to a priest. The absence of a commander, the influence of Father Gibault and the indifference of the inhabitants brought about the surrender of Vincennes entirely unmenaced by arms. This succession of triumphs was rudely and ingloriously broken when Governor Hamilton moved down from Detroit and retook Vincennes. There being no alternative but to capture or be captured, Clarke promptly moved to the lately lost fort and, after terrible privations, reached, surprised and captured it. The "great hair buyer" himself was sent a captive to Virginia as a concrete testimonial to the activity of Clarke's army. Clarke, after a campaign of less than one year, held the Illinois country and looked with covetous eyes toward Detroit.

---

[1] Butterfield, *Clarke's Conquest of the Illinois*. *Passim*.

Before setting out for Vincennes, Clarke had reorganized his little army and sent, under Captain Linn, back to Kentucky such of his militia as did not care to re-enlist. Linn was instructed to return to the Falls and erect there a fort with whatever men he could induce to stay. A stockade had been built there on Corn Island by Clarke himself the preceding spring; this stockade, to which a few families were still clinging, was removed to the mainland, enlarged and called Fort Nelson at first, but later grew into the city of Louisville. Fort Nelson quickly became a position of importance.[2] There were now four posts in the Kentucky country sufficiently strong to resist Indian attack: Harrodstown, Logan's, Boonesborough and Fort Nelson became centers of population and cities of refuge. To these four places the settlers fled in times of danger and from them in peaceful times they went forth to establish new forts or reoccupy the old. From Fort Nelson, in the spring of 1779, there went out colonies to establish forts and stations in the vicinity. On Beargrass Creek, ten miles from the Falls, they located Lynn's Station; Brashear's Station was placed at Floyd's Fork and Sullivan's, only five miles from the Falls.

Harrodstown was also expanding. A company, headed by Robert Patterson, founded and named Lexington, and Isaac Ruddle led a party to Hinkston's old settlement on the Licking and built the ill-fated station that bore his name. Martin's was erected in the same neighborhood. Grant's and Todd's were weak stockades abandoned before a year. From Saint Asaph were established Whitley's, Worthington's, Field's and Pittman's. From Boonesborough, Floyd settled on the Beargrass and Squire Boone

---

[2] For a description of the fort, see R. T. Durrett in the *Courier-Journal* of August 2, 1883. It contained fifty-two cabins.

near by on Clear Creek; Strode settled across the river from Boonesborough in what was later Clarke County. One or two important stations were built by parties from across the mountains. The most noted of these was Bryant's, a little northeast of Lexington. It was settled mainly by North Carolinians, and there were two brothers-in-law of Boone among its founders. The McAfees returned from Virginia and reoccupied their old cabins on Salt River.

The establishment of so many new stations indicated a rapidly increasing population. The number of inhabitants was, in fact, growing daily. The report of Clarke's success in the Illinois country was being spread abroad in the backwoods of Virginia and North Carolina, and the frontiersmen, having long desired to move into Kentucky, easily satisfied themselves that henceforth life there would not be imperiled by Indian war. How vain was this reflection the events of a few years made greatly evident. But for a time the people rushed into Kentucky. The country that only a few months before had excelled a wilderness only by three forts, began to take on the aspect of a settled country. Stockades sprang into existence in the midst of the forests and the land was fast being cleared for the crops of corn. All central Kentucky, both north and south of the river, was dotted with stations. Ruddle's on the north, Fort Nelson and McAfee's on the west, and the mountains on the south marked the limits of the new domain. So many stations were built, so great was the immigration and so safe seemed the country from all foes that before the year was out Virginia dismissed her militia, locked up the commissaries and left Kentucky to shift for herself.[3]

---

[3] *Autobiography of Daniel Trabue* in Draper MSS.

The year 1779 is a notable one in Kentucky history in one respect: it was the first time the white men attempted to take the offensive against the Indians. The marauding bands that beset the Wilderness Road and the banks of the Ohio did a profitable business at the expense of the immigrants to Kentucky. They were persistent enough to annoy, while not strong enough to imperil, the settlements. A more patient people than the Kentuckians would have grown restive under continual worry. When they decided to take revenge they were at no loss where to look for the foe; no other than a Shawnee would wage such a war. The invasion of the preceding year was also a bitter memory. The military authorities decided to carry the war to the enemy.

The objective point was Old Chillicothe on the Little Miami, some sixty miles from the Ohio. Colonel John Bowman, the county-lieutenant, took the initiative by notifying the settlers that immediately after they had finished planting their corn they should rendezvous at the mouth of the Licking for an expedition northward. This particular time was selected for the expedition because there were present in Kentucky then some seventy men from the Monongahela country, and it had been ascertained that their aid could be secured for the attempt. These men had been in Kentucky prospecting for land and were now on the point of returning home. Captain Harrod undertook the task of recruiting them at Fort Nelson and leading them to the appointed rendezvous. The Boonesborough contingent, consisting of twenty or twenty-five men, was led by Captain John Holder. Those of Saint Asaph and vicinity were under the command of Logan, who was Bowman's chief lieutenant. Levi Todd headed a company recruited from Bryant's and Lexington; Lieutenant Haggin commanded the little band from Martin's and Ruddle's, while the McAfee and Harrodstown men were led by Captain Harlan. Bowman, by virtue of his commission as county-lieutenant, was the commander-in-chief of the little army, with Logan second in command, and Major Bedinger, adjutant and quartermaster. After crossing the Ohio the army marched in three divisions under Logan, Holder and Harrod. The Indians' trail was found opposite the mouth of the Licking, and, advancing cautiously, the expedition arrived at Chillicothe undetected.

The progress so far was clear and decisive; from this time forward it was confusion worse confounded. It is, in fact, a great tribute to the capacity for confusion shown by the historians of Kentucky to be able to admit that their accounts of the battle are more obscure than the battle itself. It is comparatively certain that the army reached the Indian town about dark, and, finding the Indians unsuspecting, determined to attack at daybreak.[4] Logan, with one-third the force, moved to the left to encircle the town, and Harrod with his division passed to the right; Holder remained in front. A premature shot from one of Holder's men disclosed the presence of the white men and the battle began in confusion. The Indians collected in a big cabin near the center of the town, and the white men, taking possession of the other cabins, pushed forward till they were within seventy yards of the Indians' position. Here they were held determinedly at bay. The fighting continued until ten o'clock, by which time the white men had lost nine men, had burned from twenty to forty cabins and had stolen,

---

[4] Bradford, *Notes on Kentucky,* p. 46.

or regained, one hundred and forty-three horses. But the Indians, far outnumbering them, began to employ flank movements that promised to result in the speedy destruction of the Kentuckians. All this time, Logan and Holder had been fighting hard and waiting for the expected aid from Harrod's Monongahelians. But the Monongahelians refused all obedience and gave themselves up to plundering the camp; they could not be induced to go to the aid of the hard-pressed Kentuckians. Bowman, seeing that the Kentuckians were in danger of being surrounded, and not being able to compel or persuade the Monongahelians to advance, ordered a retreat. The order came as a complete surprise to Holder and Logan, who knew nothing of the conduct of the Monongahelians and were under the impression that everything was going favorably to the white men; nevertheless, they obeyed. The retreat began in good order, with the men falling back slowly and deliberately. The Indians at first were too much relieved to press the pursuit, but recovering their spirits after the Kentuckians had gone some ten miles, they rushed furiously against the retreating column and poured in a rapid and misdirected fire. The officers, in the face of a growing panic formed their men in a hollow square and stood at bay. But the Indians wisely refused to come to close quarters, and the white men were compelled again to retreat. The renowned Blackfish had fallen and Red Hawk led the warriors.[5] He persisted in the policy of hanging on the rear of the Kentuckians and continually hampering the retreat. These galling tactics would have ultimately resulted in the destruction of the invading force but for a bold expedient of the officers; Logan, Harrod

---

[5] Red Hawk was also killed in the course of the day.

and Bedinger headed a cavalry charge that scattered the Indians and rendered safe the remainder of the retreat.[6] The force crossed the Ohio and dispersed to their homes.

No loss of any moment was received on this expedition, and the Indians suffered far more than the white men. But the moral effect of the retreat was incalculable. It was the first attempt Kentucky had made to invade the enemy's country, and, notwithstanding the damage done to the enemy, the enforced retreat gave it all the appearance of a defeat. And as a defeat it was considered by the settlers themselves; they could only see, as a recent historian has put it, that Blackfish had "smitten them hip and thigh." In their resentment they looked around for a scapegoat among their officers, and finally fixed on Bowman to fill the position. The story was put in circulation that Bowman failed to support Logan in the battle, had remained inactive while it was fought and had ordered a retreat at the moment of victory.[7] This delectable bit of mythology does as little credit to the intelligence of its fabricators as to that of the historians who accepted and recorded it. Bowmen was an old and tried Indian fighter; he had come to Kentucky as a leader of the Virginia militia and had proved himself in many an engagement since. No one was less likely to remain inactive during the battle than he. In regard to the retreat, an analysis of the battle will plainly show that it was a choice between retreat or annihilation, and Bowman wisely decided upon retreating. The credit of the defeat may be given to the

---

[6] Bedinger MSS., pp. 19-80.
[7] Historians have as a rule followed McClung's "Sketches" in recording the battle. The character of these sketches is such as to justify no one in following them unless confirmed by other authorities. Such an agreement, however, would rather tend to discredit the authorities than to confirm McClung.

seventy Monongahelians who refused to obey Bowman's order to advance. Logan's impetuosity in the early part of the battle had carried him into a perilous situation, but his lack of judgment then was lost sight of in the remembrance of his heroic conduct during the retreat. Unjustly, but very effectively, public opinion enforced the retirement of Bowman, who was, after all, but an "outlander." Logan's reputation was not injured by the failure.

Notwithstanding Bowman's defeat, the immigration to Kentucky continued as rapidly as before. The Indians, indeed, had been too severely crippled to send any considerable force into the country; only small parties continued to infest the roads and cut off the people as they came in.[8] There were many isolated conflicts with these during the year, but none of enough moment to merit narration. But a far worse foe than the Indians was now to be encountered; it was the terrible winter of 1779. This was the longest and coldest winter that the Kentuckians had ever experienced.[9] It began the first of November and continued until February 20th. During all that time the ground was covered with snow and ice several feet deep, and the rivers were frozen solid to the very bottom. The brute life of the land was practically exterminated, and only a few of the domestic animals lived through the winter. Men and women died by the score for want of food, and the survivors were reduced to the extremity of eating the horses and dogs that had perished from hunger. The population of Kentucky at this time was for the most part living in isolated cabins, and communication was difficult. The commonest articles of food could be secured

---

[8] Notwithstanding the destruction of the corn, it grew again into a good crop. *Statement of Joseph Jackson,* Boone MSS., Vol. XI.
[9] *Autobiography of Daniel Trabue.*

only at enormous prices. The bitter winter affected the incoming settlers most cruelly of all. Traveling was reduced to two or three miles a day, and many parties were unable to pass the mountains and were forced to spend the winter in camp.[10]

The Virginia Assembly in its May session had passed several acts that were of importance to Kentucky. One of these acts provided for a ferry over the Kentucky River.[11] It was to be established at Boonesborough and was put under the charge of Richard Calloway. The provision for this ferry, although insignificant in itself, is of importance as showing the drift of settlers to the north of the Kentucky and the gradual settling of the land. It was probably the first public ferry west of the Alleghanies. The same Assembly had passed an act establishing a pack horse road to Kentucky by way of Cumberland Gap.[12] Two men were appointed to mark this road and it was designed to facilitate immigration into the western lands. Boone's old trace which he had blazed for Henderson was utilized and was eventually improved until it became the most serviceable road in the west. Still another act of the Assembly concerned itself with the military condition of Kentucky.[13] For the better defense of her westernmost county Virginia enacted that two battalions of militia should be enlisted. Each battalion was to consist of ten companies and each company of fifty men. The men were to be enrolled for nine months and to receive pay from Virginia. But perhaps the most important of the acts

---

[10] *Shane MSS.*, Vol. I, p. 129.
[11] Hening, Vol. X, p. 196.
[12] *Ibid.*, p. 143. Calloway and Evan Shelby were appointed to mark this road, but Shelby refused to serve, and Captain Kinkead was appointed.
[13] *Ibid.*, p. 135.

passed at this session was the land act, establishing a Court of Land Commissioners to adjudicate claims under the Virginia Land Law.[14] By the provision of this act practically all the land claims in Kentucky were validated and the settlers were given an opportunity to buy greater tracts on credit. It was a most liberal law, and the evils that arose from it were due to lax administration and not to the law itself. It played a great part in the bringing of settlers to Kentucky. So great, indeed, was the rush of immigrants to Kentucky and so imperfect were the methods of surveying that the danger became great that conflicting claims would be recorded. The Commissioners appointed for the adjusting of claims hurried to Kentucky and began their work. There were four members of this court, William Fleming, Edmund Lyne, James Barbour and Stephen Trigg. It is noticeable that none of these were natives of Kentucky, but were all appointed from Virginia. The court met October 13th, at St. Asaph, where John Williams was appointed clerk and a multitude of claims were passed upon. A future Governor, Isaac Shelby, enjoyed the honor of presenting the first claim. On the twenty-sixth of October the court, out of accommodation, removed to Harrodstown, on November 16th to Louisville, December 18th, to Boonesborough, and on January 3d, to Bryant's Station. Over three thousand claims were presented during the first year of the court's existence.[15]

The year 1779 came to a close with a disaster that served to warn the Kentuckians that their land, after all, was but a frontier country, and that their enemies had not lost their vigilance. Colonel David Rogers, a member of

---
[14] *Ibid.*, p. 18.
[15] *Clarke MSS.*, Vol. X, p. 368.

the Virginia Assembly, had been sent by Governor Henry down the Ohio and Mississippi to New Orleans to bring back some goods that had been deposited there for Virginia.[16] He was also carrying instructions to Clarke in the Illinois country and expected to be escorted homeward by a military guard. He accomplished his mission successfully and started on his return to Fort Pitt in the fall of 1779. He had three keel boats laden with stores and had nearly one hundred men on board. As the three boats reached the great sandbar, some three miles below the mouth of the Little Miami, the men on board were surprised to see a vast number of Indian-laden rafts shoot out from the mouth of the Miami into the Ohio. These were a party of Indians returning from a hunting trip and they were under the leadership of the so-called renegades, Elliot and the three Girtys. Rogers, thinking himself unseen, promptly landed his men, in the hope of ambushing the Indians. As it proved, however, the Indians had observed him, and scarcely had the white men landed when they found themselves surrounded by several hundred Indians. Only about ten men escaped to their homes. One boat with five men aboard escaped by pushing into the current and drifting down to the Falls. In a desperate effort to break through the enemy's line, Captain Benham was so wounded as to be unable to walk, while a companion, Watson, had both arms broken. Each, however, lay concealed until the Indians withdrew, when, discovering each other, they both, by utilizing one pair of legs and a single pair of arms, managed to sustain life until a chance flatboat rescued and carried them to the Falls. This disaster occurred October 3d, and the magnitude of it cast gloom over the closing days of 1779.

---

[16] Butterfield, *History of the Girtys*, p. 110.

HISTORY OF PIONEER KENTUCKY

Yet the immigration of 1780 broke all previous records. The Ohio River route was now being utilized as well as the better known way through Cumberland Gap. This route, being along the borders of the Shawnese, was the more dangerous of the two, and there were innumerable outrages committed on its waters and along its banks. The use of it tended greatly to the upbuilding of northern Kentucky. Heretofore settlements had been slow to move out of the Bluegrass; now Fort Nelson, from its position at the Falls, began to be the goal of immigration. In the spring of 1780 three hundred boatloads of immigrants landed at the Falls. Many of these remained at Fort Nelson, but many also ventured to establish independent stations along the Beargrass. Notable, too, was the change in the character of the immigration. The previous immigrants had been drawn almost exclusively from Virginia and North Carolina; now over the northern route began to come in the people of Maryland and of Pennsylvania. The increase of people meant, of course, more work for the Land Court. In May, 1780, the county surveyor, John May, opened his office at Harrodstown, and was thenceforth kept busy with the numerous demands for his services.

Virginia's plans of the previous year were, after all, not able to be carried out for the military defense of Kentucky. In May, 1780, the Virginia Assembly decided to send but one regiment of troops to Kentucky, instead of the two provided by the act of 1779. Colonel Slaughter's corps of infantry was designated as a part of the troops that were to be sent to Kentucky. This act of Virginia's in curtailing the military establishment was made necessary by stringent financial conditions. At the same time Virginia directed that her militia in service in Illinois should be withdrawn to Kentucky. This action was taken because of the fact that the paper money of Virginia would not pass current in Illinois, and she had no way of paying her militia there.[17]

Early in the spring of 1780 Colonel Slaughter's regiment arrived at Fort Nelson with one hundred and fifty Virginia troops. The arrival of these made the Falls of the Ohio the best fortified post in Kentucky. Moreover, Colonel Clarke was again in the fort, having returned thither after giving into the hands of John Todd the civil administration of Illinois. But neither Clarke nor the troops were to remain long at the Falls. The Virginia authorities were not yet content with the limits of their State. Annexation had become a contagious disease. Having appropriated Kentucky and possessed themselves of Illinois, Virginia looked longingly toward Canada and the Mississippi. But the renewed activities of the restless Shawnese made any expedition against Detroit out of the question. Nothing was needed to insure the expansion to the Mississippi, save outraging some friendly Indians and violating a well-kept peace. Neither of these troubled the official conscience of Virginia. Clarke was ordered by Jefferson to proceed to the mouth of the Ohio and plant a fort upon the Mississippi.[18] Clarke, accordingly, in the last days of April, descended the Ohio with two hundred men and built a fort about five miles below its junction with the Mississippi. The Chickasaws, not yet initiated into the mysteries of Virginia diplomacy, might well stand amazed at this move. Up to this time they had not molested the Kentucky settlements; when they realized the

---

[17] Hening, Vol. X, p. 215.
[18] It was Jefferson's intention to purchase territory from the Cherokees. *Clarke MSS.*, Vol. I., Jefferson to Martin.

significance of the new fort in their territory, they turned their fury against the exposed settlements in more implacable wrath than the Shawnese themselves.

The Chickasaws were not alone in their disapproval of Clarke's movement; the Kentuckians denounced it from the beginning. Their enemy, they asserted, was at the north and not the west. If Clarke wished to aid Kentucky, let him lead them against the northern Indians, or at least stay and aid them against the invasion they felt was preparing. The placing of a fort on the Mississippi would bring the Chickasaws promptly down upon them. Clarke had made himself unpopular by leaving Boonesborough defenseless while he invaded Illinois, but the success of this expedition had restored him to favor. The new project turned the people once more against him. Kentucky felt that it was being abandoned by Virginia and her officers. The first mutterings were heard against being governed by transmontane authority. Kentucky was sullen, discontented and apprehensive.

Kentucky had good reason to be apprehensive. As the British officers had in 1778 taken advantage of Clarke's absence to send an expedition against Boonesborough, so they lost no time in seizing this second opportunity. While Clarke was at Fort Jefferson, Colonel Byrd, of the English army, collected a motley army of six hundred Canadians and Indians and set out for Kentucky. He had six pieces of artillery with him; these probably were intended as much for inspiring the Indians as for intimidating the Kentuckians. Simon Girty was along in charge of the Wyandots. The army made its way down the Miami River to the Ohio, from which place it was planned to descend upon Fort Nelson. But on reaching the river they found the waters of the Licking at full flood and easily high enough to admit boats. The plans were accordingly changed, and the entire force embarked on the Licking for the interior of Kentucky. Progress was easy until they reached the forks of the river where Falmouth now stands. Here the shallowness of the river made it necessary to land the cannon and haul them overland to Ruddle's, the objective point of the expedition. It was found necessary to cut a wagon road and, consequently, it was not till June 22d that the force appeared before Ruddle's, having consumed eleven days in coming from the Ohio. Nevertheless, the garrison was taken entirely by surprise. It must be remembered that it was an unusually wet spring and much of the country was flooded. The settlers at Ruddle's had no thought that the Indians would attempt to penetrate into the interior of Kentucky while the floods were on. Moreover, they thought, with the other Kentuckians, that Louisville would be the object of attack. Byrd's army found them altogether unsuspecting.

Bryd made known his presence by firing his cannon.[19] The sight of an enemy so numerous dispirited the commander, Ruddle, but failed to shake the fortitude of his men. But after a second discharge of the cannon, Ruddle prevailed on the men to surrender. A written agreement was entered into by Byrd and the Kentuckians, by which the former undertook to ensure good treatment. There is no reason to believe that Byrd was insincere in this, but when the gates were thrown open, the red allies were not to be restrained. Although little murder was done, the Indians took possession of the prisoners and mistreated them in every way that suggested itself to their savage

---

[19] *Clarke MSS.*, Vol. XXIX, p. 25.

fancy. Families were separated, and complaints, if made, were silenced rudely by the club or tomahawk. Ruddle's was at the junction of South Licking and Hinkston Creek and Martin's Station was but five miles away up the banks of the former stream. Thither the Indians, highly elated at their success, hastened their way. Byrd, before approaching the fort, made it plain to the Indians that in case of a surrender the prisoners must be given good treatment.[20] And, in fact, the Indians did observe the agreement at Martin's, rifling the property, but respecting the prisoners.[21] Both these forts having succumbed so readily, many of the Indians were for marching directly on the older settlements and sweeping Kentucky clear of white men. But wiser counsels prevailed. The Indian leaders were satisfied with what they had done, and were not confident of further success if they penetrated into the more settled portions of Kentucky. Byrd urged that the Licking was rapidly falling and there was need to take their cannon out of the country before the alarm was spread. The tradition that Byrd refused to go further because of the inhumanity of the Indians may safely be dismissed as idle fancy. It is not reasonable to suppose that an officer so well acquainted with the Indians as to be trusted with the command of them on an important expedition could have been so ignorant of their customs as to feel shocked at their recent behavior.

After the fall, then, of the two stations, Byrd's entire army retreated to the site of the present Falmouth. At this place the army divided into two sections; some were content to go home slowly, while others preferred a more rapid retreat. The other settlements did not remain long

---

[20] Butterfield, *History of the Girtys*, p. 115.
[21] In all, Byrd took 129 prisoners at the two forts.

ignorant of Byrd's expedition and its success. On the first night after the British force divided at the forks of the Licking, one of the prisoners of the Indians, John Hinkston, escaped, and, after much wandering about, reached Lexington and told of the fall of the two stations. Kentucky, roused and stung by the double defeat, turned her thoughts to retaliation. A clamor arose for an expedition against the Shawnese.

Meanwhile Clarke had marched from Fort Jefferson to the relief of Cahokia, which was menaced by a British force, and learning there that Byrd was marching against Kentucky, he hastened to Louisville with what men he could spare and began preparations for a retaliatory expedition against the Shawnese. Clarke and the Virginia authorities had had in mind such an expedition since the first of the year.[22] In January, Jefferson had written to Clarke that he expected him to invade the Shawnese territory some time in the summer; a little later he informed him that, in addition to his own force, there was preparing another expedition to march from Fort Pitt and co-operate with him. But this second expedition had to be given up, and by June it had been practically decided that the Kentucky force would not be raised until the following year. In the meantime the Kentuckians had been growing more and more eager for such an enterprise. In March, 1780, Richard Henderson spent some little time at Boonesborough trying to collect provisions for his proposed settlement on the land given him by North Carolina near Nashville. When he finally set out down the Kentucky River on the way to his new home, the Boonesborough people took occasion to send by him to Clarke a petition ask-

---

[22] *Clarke MSS.*, Vol. L. Correspondence of Jefferson, Clarke and Brodhead.

ing that the latter lead them against the Shawnese.[23] As Henderson passed down the river the inhabitants of Bryant's and Lexington put in his charge similar petitions to Clarke for the invasion, expressing their confidence in the "great guns" that Clarke had at his command. These petitions were delivered to Clarke at Louisville before he set out for Fort Jefferson, but he was unable to act upon them. However, they confirmed him in his resolution to invade Ohio at the first suitable opportunity.

Thus it happened that when Clarke returned to the Bluegrass he found no trouble in getting the people enlisted in the expedition that he for so long had had in mind. He sent throughout the settlements a proclamation of his intended enterprise and appealed to the people to rally to its support. He called for a general rendezvous at the mouth of the Licking. Nearly one thousand men gathered at the appointed place August 1st; among these were the State troops that had previously come from Virginia with Slaughter.[24] Clarke, as commander of this force, divided it into two divisions under the leadership of Colonel Linn and Colonel Logan. The army tarried a few days at the mouth of the Licking, built two block houses and then, with Simon Kenton as guide, set out for the Shawnese towns. There was little likelihood that Kenton would lose his way; he had been over the ground a score of times in forays and horse-stealing expeditions. Here two years before as an unlucky sequel to a horse-stealing adventure of more than ordinary flagrance, he had been captured, forced to run the gauntlet and finally tied to a stake to be burned. This interesting event was prevented only by the interference of his old friend Girty.

[23] *Ibid.*, Vol. L.
[24] *Clarke MSS.*, Vol. XXVI, p. 101.

Such incidents were not calculated to make him forget the country. As they marched a road had to be cut for the artillery, and it was the sixth of August before they reached the Indian towns. They found the towns deserted and they lost no time in applying the torch to the houses. The orchards and corn were cut to the ground. After this martial and civilized pastime had been exhausted, the army passed on to Piqua on the Big Miami. Here, however, the Indians made a stand and held their own until the use of cannon compelled them to retreat. The loss of the white force was fourteen killed and thirteen wounded; the Indian loss was triple this, but they managed to carry off their dead in the night. More than eight hundred of well-cultivated corn was destroyed.

The Kentuckians hoped by this expedition to prevent further invasion of their country. They argued that the destruction of the villages and cornfields of the Indians would render them destitute and helpless; it was so late that no further crops could be raised that year and suffering must result during the winter. This reasoning was as fallacious as it was ingenious. The Indians could rebuild their cabins in a few days' time. They were not dependent on their cornfields for supplies. The British in Canada would see to it that their red allies did not want; they would not risk disaffection by a failure to afford supplies. The next spring the Indians would rebuild their cabins, replant their cornfields and take up their guerrilla warfare against Kentucky with a ferocity only increased by the destruction of their property. Kentucky was destined to have peace only when the Indians themselves were appeased or their British aid withdrawn.

The raising of one thousand troops for this expedition shows plainly how great had been the immigation during the year. Desire for Kentucky land was not the only motive these people had in crossing the mountains. Over on the seacoast the British were beginning to carry the war into the south. The dread of their coming drove many families over the Cumberlands; they preferred to encounter the Indians rather than the British. Many royalists, too, fled to Kentucky rather than stay at home and be compelled to oppose the British. Neither royalist nor patriot was much inclined to settle in Kentucky; as soon as they thought the dangers passed at home they returned. A worse class of settlers and one that Kentucky could well have spared were the land speculators. The looseness of the land laws made it possible for speculators to take up immense tracts without the formality of seeing them. The warrants for these, readily obtained, they industriously sold to the prospective settlers. The warrants were issued by Virginia. But neither Virginia nor the settler knew whether they represented actual land or not. The proud possessor of them, on reaching Kentucky, often found the land entirely fictitious or possessed by some one else. The speculators became experts also in Indian signs. An Indian scare always resulted in many people leaving the country and selling their holdings for whatever they would bring. It was the policy of the speculators to manufacture as many Indian scares as possible in order to buy up the lands cheaply. Such tactics were later to bring results of great moment to Kentucky.

Virginia had not been unmindful of this great growth in her western domain. In November, 1780, the Virginia Assembly passed an act dividing Kentucky into three

---

[25] Hening, Vol. X, p. 315.

counties.²⁵ North of the Kentucky River was Fayette County; west of the same river was Jefferson, while the residue received the name of Lincoln. Each county had a completely organized government similar in detail to those of eastern Virginia. It is to be noticed that in the creation of these three new counties, the time honored name, Kentucky, disappeared. For a little while there was no "Kentucky," but the name survived in the speech of the people and came to life in a few years as the name of a court. This creation of more county units was necessarily accompanied by a better and more complete organization of the militia. Kentucky was expanding and growing, but the peril from the Indians was increased rather than lessened by the fact; there was now both more at stake and the foe was better organized than ever before. Kentucky had need of her militia. Logan commanded in Lincoln County, Floyd in Jefferson, and Todd in Fayette. Daniel Boone was second in command under Todd, Trigg under Logan and Pope under Floyd. All these men were tried fighters and tested leaders. In their hands Kentucky had reason to believe that the long-desired peace would come to her borders.

When Kentucky County was established in 1776 her southern boundary was fixed at the northern line of North Carolina. This would have been eminently definite had any one known where the said northern line was located. Neither Virginia nor North Carolina had more than the vaguest idea of the boundary between their territory beyond the mountains. But as Tennessee and Kentucky began to be filled with actual settlers, it became increasingly important that the line should be determined. Accordingly, in the latter part of 1778 Virginia had appointed a commission to act with one selected by North Carolina to survey the line to the Ohio or the Tennessee.[26] At the head of the Virginia commission was Dr. Thomas Walker, while the North Carolina men were under the direction of Richard Henderson.[27] Walker had led the first exploring party into Kentucky and Henderson had established the first colony within its borders. Their names were reminiscent of a time even then fast fading from memory. The commissioners were to follow the parallel 36° 30′ until they ran into the Tennessee, the Ohio or the Mississippi. Jefferson suspected that the line would strike the Tennessee first, and he instructed Walker that in that emergency he should go down the Tennessee and the Ohio and ascertain the latitude of the junction of the Ohio and the Mississippi.[28] It will be remembered that these instructions were given before the building of Fort Jefferson and when the land beyond the Tennessee was yet admitted to be Indian territory. The commissioners met by appointment and began their survey. The prejudice of the surveyors or the inaccuracy of their instruments soon resulted in a difference in surveying. They separated and ran different lines; when they reached the top of the Cumberland Mountains Henderson quit while Walker continued his survey alone.[29] He ran to the Tennessee River and marked his line. Perceiving that the extension of this line would enter Indian territory and would strike the Mississippi, he abandoned the work. Walker's line was subsequently adopted by Kentucky, but at the Tennessee River

---

[26] Hening, Vol. IX, p. 561.
[27] *Laws of North Carolina*, Vol. XXIV, p. 223. William Bailey Smith, John Williams, James Kerr and Orandatus Davis were Henderson's associates on the commission.
[28] *Clarke MSS.*, Vol. L. Correspondence of Walker and Jefferson.
[29] Summers, *History of Southwest Virginia*, p. 699.

it is twelve miles out of course. Kentucky and Tennessee were to engage in many a quarrel over this imperfect boundary; even today the status of the region between Walker's line and 36° 30' is undefined.

The completion of the survey of the southern boundary of Kentucky was not reached until 1780. Coming as it did in the same year as the erection of two new counties in Kentucky, 1780 is a date to be remembered as one in which an important step was taken for the greater stability and orderliness of the government.

In the early part of 1781, Clarke was created a brigadier-general commanding the Virginia troops in the west and having his headquarters at Louisville. Virginia, in taking this action, had designed that neither he nor the Kentucky militia should be idle. Her eyes were still turned to the far-off fields. In the preceding autumn her statesmen had formed a plan for the capture of Detroit and for relieving His Most Gracious Majesty of quite a little of his northern territory. Clarke was instructed to gather by March 15th a force of two thousand militia at Louisville and be ready in the spring to proceed northward.[30] But it so happened that the rendezvous was not made until late in the summer and the expedition never made at all. There were many reasons for this.

The British, in the prosecution of their plan for invading the south were now, thanks to General Green, engaged in an unprofitable war in Virginia. Before Clarke could go west again it became necessary for him to help defend his home. He entered the Continental army and served till the danger seemed averted. Spring had already gone when he at length was free to turn his attention westward. He was to have the aid of the Pennsylvania militia

---

[30] *Clarke MSS.*, Jefferson to Clarke, January 19, 1781.

as well as of his own State. Colonel Laughrey was to command them and meet him at Wheeling. The rapidity of Laughrey's movements may be inferred from the fact that, although Clarke did not reach Wheeling until July, he found Laughrey not yet arrived. Clarke reached Wheeling with a respectable force, but their wholesale desertion warned him to proceed. He hastened on to Louisville. Laughrey reaching Wheeling and finding Clarke gone, sent five men ahead to overtake Clarke and tell him that they needed supplies. The five were captured by the Indians and disclosed Laughrey's plans and his weakness. Laughrey was ambushed at Island No. 54; sixty-four of his men were killed and forty-two made prisoners.[31]

Clarke, disappointed in Laughrey's aid, could not succeed in raising the Kentucky militia. The Kentuckians firmly and disrespectfully refused to go against Detroit. Clarke had alienated them by his Illinois campaign, his establishing of Fort Jefferson and by a late regulation requiring the militia to serve on board a patrol boat he had established on the Ohio.[32] The settlers were willing enough to fight Indians, but were not ardent over the prospect of rowing a heavy boat up and down the Ohio on the very meagre chance of encountering a foe. The boat soon ran ashore at the mouth of the Beargrass and suspicion was not lacking that the stranding was encouraged by the crew. Kentucky, in truth, had enough and more to do in engaging her land foes. In March, Captain Tipton, Captain Chapman and Colonel Lynn were killed in the Beargrass, and Captain Whittaker, attempting to avenge the loss, was ambushed and lost heavily. In April,

---

[31] *Clarke MSS.*, Vol. X, p. 513.
[32] *Clarke MSS.*, Vol. XXIX. Deposition of John Mitchell. This boat had seventy oars and was equipped with cannon.

while Squire Boone and the inhabitants of his station were removing to Louisville, they were attacked and scattered by the Indians. Colonel Floyd, with thirty mounted men, attempting to retaliate, was himself ambushed and lost one-half his force. McAfee's Station and Montgomery's had both been attacked and suffered great loss. Kentucky did not need to look to Detroit for trouble.

Added to Laughrey's defeat and the attitude of Kentucky came the news that the Chickasaws had risen, were besieging Fort Jefferson, and would certainly take it unless Clarke hurried to its relief.[33] Clarke lost no time in starting; when he arrived he found that the Indians were led by a Scotchman named Colbert and had attempted more than once to storm the fort. Only the use of cannon had prevented the loss of the post. The siege had been going on for several days before Clarke's arrival and continued a few days more. The Indians, however, ultimately became disheartened and retired. Fort Jefferson was abandoned soon after; it should never have been occupied.

Such were the events that prevented Clarke from carrying out his long-cherished desire for an expedition against Detroit. It was, perhaps, as well for the American cause and his own fame that he was not enabled to begin it. The conquest of Detroit would have been a far different undertaking from that of Kaskaskia and Vincennes. The two latter posts had been feeble and indifferent or friendly, but Detroit was hostile and manned by Englishmen. The capture of it would have called for the best efforts of a great general and an enthusiastic army. That Clarke, supported by a rabble of disgruntled frontiersmen, would have encountered great obstacles goes almost with-

---

[33] *Cal. Va. St. Papers,* Vol. I, p. 882.

out saying. Clarke resigned himself to the inevitable and proceeded to utilize his energies in fortifying Fort Nelson. His success in this only rendered him more unpopular in Kentucky, where a strong and insistent demand was being made that forts should be built to protect the Licking and the Kentucky rather than the Beargrass. By advice of the Virginia Council in June, 1780, frontier forts in the west were to be built at the mouth of the Kanawha, the Big Sandy and the Licking. For the garrison of the fort on the Licking, fifty men were to be raised from Kentucky and Colonel Crockett's regiment was to march thither from Virginia. In all there were to be one hundred and fifty men in the fort and Clarke was to have the chief command as in all western matters. In September, Crockett received orders to proceed westward, but the fort on the Licking was never built. Much to the disgust of the Kentuckians, Clarke gave his entire time to fortifying Louisville, and, either through inability or disinclination, steadily disregarded the clamor of the Kentuckians for the building of the other forts. While this controversy was going on as to whether the land should be protected from the ever-present Indian or the remote Englishman, the Revolutionary war came to a sudden and unexpected close. Yorktown put an end to Clarke's plans, defensive or offensive, against the British, and rendered the Kentuckians, so they vainly thought, secure against Indian war for the future. Kentucky had taken little interest and less part in the Revolution. The Kentuckians cared little, probably knew little, of the merits of the dispute; they were seemingly as little concerned with the results. They were Kentuckians first and Virginians afterwards. They were intensely interested in rendering their own homes safe from the Indians, but were profanely unwilling to fight England for the sake of an abstraction. When Clarke conquered the Illinois, only a handful of Kentuckians were with him; when the frontiersmen engaged Tarleton at King's Mountain, Kentuckians were conspicuously absent. But no leader, no matter how mediocre or unpopular, ever proposed an expedition against the Shawnese and failed to find enthusiastic support among the Kentuckians. The question of defending Kentucky and of repulsing or destroying her Indian foes was a vital matter among the pioneers. They were absorbed in Kentucky; no foreign affair, no matter how important in itself, could be appreciated among them as long as their own homes were endangered. A clear conception of this fact will do much toward rendering plain the seemingly inexplicable actions of the Kentuckians of the next decade.

THE YEAR OF SORROWS.

THE surrender of Cornwallis at Yorktown in October, 1781, actually closed the Revolution in the seaboard States. There followed a year of truce, during which both combatants rested on their arms, exhausted by past endeavors and hopeful of a lasting peace. For seven miserable years and more the colonists along the Atlantic had striven desperately, body and soul, against foreign invaders and domestic foes. In the course of that time they had, after infinite striving, succeeded in keeping their land inviolate and themselves a nation; they had captured two armies on land and well-nigh shipwrecked the power of England on the sea. They had done more. They had struck at and destroyed in New York the powerful Iroquois Confederacy which had clung so long and faithfully to the English. Yet they had not come unscathed from the contest; towns had been burnt and countrysides harried by their enemies. There had been Camdens and Valley Forges without number. Their soldiers had gone into the war destitute and emerged with conditions unimproved. The credit of the nation was destroyed and treason was abroad in the land. Surely if past misfortunes were any indication of deserts to come, the Atlantic States merited, as they secured, a time of peace and of prosperity.

But the time that brought peace to the eastern States brought little but disasters to the transmontane lands. Kentucky had remained careless, if not indifferent, while the eastern States were fighting for existence; it was perhaps no more than fitting that now while the remainder of the land was given an opportunity for rest, Kentucky must needs struggle, unaided, for her life. The British, by reason of Cornwallis' surrender and the extermination of the Iroquois, were utterly unable to strike, even had they wished, at the Tidewater countries; they were better prepared than ever before to carry the war into Kentucky. They had clinched their hold on Canada and tightened their grasp on the northwest posts. From these positions they enjoyed and used every opportunity for inciting their Indian allies against Kentucky. The time, moreover, was opportune, for the Indians of Ohio and Indiana were alarmed by the prospect of peace and fearful for an accounting for past misdeeds. They readily lent themselves to the urgent plans of the English Governor of Canada, and so while the seaboard States were joyous in expectation and possession of peace, Kentucky, alone, was approaching the valley of the shadow.

Moved by the urgings and even the pleadings of the English, the Indians of the northwest, in the winter of 1781-82, planned for a grand assembly to mature plans for a joint expedition against Kentucky. The assembly was to meet in the summer at the Shawnese capital of Old Chillicothe and was to be attended by the chiefs and warriors of all tribes under the British influence; Shawnese, Mingoes, Delawares, Wyandots, and Pottawattomies were to be there from the north of the Ohio, and even the Cherokees from distant Tennessee were represented. In all the efforts to unite the Indians for this expedition, the Shawnese, as the most inveterate enemies of the Kentuckians, had taken the lead. All during the winter their runners were kept busy visiting the different tribes and urging upon them the necessity of prompt and decisive action. Such an appeal could not fail of success among the Indians; not a tribe of them but had good reason for hating the Kentuckians.

So the Shawnese found themselves leaders in a movement second only to that of Pontiac. All tribes were to meet at Chillicothe in August and march against Kentucky.

But neither the passions of the Indians nor the impatience of the English disposed them to wait until August to begin the war. A party of twenty-five Wyandots started on the warpath early in the spring. They crossed the Ohio River and made their way rapidly toward central Kentucky, appearing before Strode's Station on the first of March. Strode's was a small station of some thirty cabins settled entirely from Boonesborough and serving as an outpost of the older fort from which it was distant about ten miles. A part of its garrison at the time of the attack was gone to Boonesborough to help ward off an Indian attack that never came, but there happened to be within the fort several hunters from a neighboring post. The Indians, surprising the fort, succeeded in killing two men, but were unable to accomplish anything more. After a thirty-six hour siege, having destroyed all the sheep and cattle, they departed in high spirits just a few hours previous to the return of the men who had gone to Boonesborough. The garrison, being too weak to pursue, had to content itself with burying the dead. The Indians pursued their way eastward and crossed the Kentucky several miles above Boonesborough. By accident or design one of the rafts on which they crossed the river was allowed to float down the Kentucky and was detected by the Boonesborough men on the nineteenth as it drifted past the fort. To them it was an ominous sign, indicating that Indians were near and in considerable numbers. They lost no time in sending word to Colonel Logan at Saint Asaph that trouble was brewing for Lincoln County. Logan, upon receiving the news, dispatched fifteen men to Estill's Station, with the injunction that Estill should take forty men and search for the Indians. Estill, in obeying these orders, left his own fort defenseless. Hardly had he started on his search before the Wyandots appeared around the fort, caught outside and killed one of the women and captured Monk, the negro slave of Captain Estill. Prodigious lying on Monk's part led the Indians to believe that the fort was well manned; they withdrew in some trepidation, taking Monk along. Immediately two boys were sent out from the fort to find Estill and tell him what had happened. Estill, hearing this report, set out in hot pursuit with twenty-five of his men. On the morning of the twenty-second of March he overtook the Indians near the site of the present Mount Sterling.

The struggle that followed has become a memorable event in Kentucky history under the name of "Estill's defeat."[1] It was in fact more than defeat; it was annihilation. When Estill came up with the Indians they were just crossing a branch of Hinkston Creek known as Small Mountain Creek. As the white men came into view a sharp command from the Wyandot chieftain sent his followers quickly to cover and the battle began with the stream separating the opposing forces. The struggle was over a densely wooded field of eight or ten acres, and the method of fighting was one well suited to each side; it was from the beginning "every man to his man and every man to his tree." The numbers were equal of each force, but at the beginning of the fight Estill thought it expedient to detach Lieutenant Miller with six men to guard the horses. These took their station in the rear while the remaining eighteen pressed on against the Indians. The thick for-

---

[1] *Boone MSS.*, Vol. XIII. Depositions of Joseph Proctor, David Lynch and Hazelrigg.

ests intervening soon made it impossible for Miller to understand how the battle was going. The contest was stubborn and desperate. The Wyandots fought with their characteristic fierceness and resolution, and under the direction of their chief executed a daring flank movement at the most critical moment of the battle. Their flanking party came upon Miller and his men as they were unsuspectingly guarding the horses in the rear. The seven white men fled precipitately and ingloriously from the field. The battle now became a slaughter and ended in the death of Estill and all but five of his men. The same number of Indians remained alive, and with the withdrawal of the white men these, sullen and weary, set out on their long way home.

The effect of this battle was indescribable. Kentucky had never before been invaded by Indians capable of fighting so determinedly. The Kentuckians had tried the mettle of the Wyandots and had to acknowledge defeat. Henceforth the very name spread terror over the land. The white dead had been left with the Indians, and Kentucky felt keenly the disgrace of this. Previously they had despised the Indians; henceforward they were compelled to dread. Miller and his companions were held up to public obloquy, but to a dispassionate enquirer their actions appear far from disgraceful. They had no way of knowing the fate of Estill and his men. The advance of the Indians indicated that the van of the white force had been destroyed. In such an event, it was certain death for them to stand their ground. It would have been of more than human courage to do otherwise than flee. Apparently, too, the Wyandots had satiated themselves with fighting, for only a few minor depredations followed

Estill's defeat. During June and July Kentucky was unvisited by hostile Indians and the country enjoyed a short and delusive quiet. It was the calm that comes before a storm; the two months' cessation of hostilities was necessitated by the preparations of the Indians for their proposed expedition against Kentucky. The tribes met at Old Chillicothe during the first days of August and aroused by every device known to Indian savagery the passions of their warriors for the work in hand. Ths Wyandots, in fact, needed no encouragement; it was to be with them a matter of revenge. For in the spring of the year an expedition sent out from Fort Pitt had ruthlessly and in definance of the laws of God and man slaughtered the Moravian Indians of the Wyandots living on the Sandusky River. A second marauding expedition had fallen into their hands, and its leader, Colonel Crawford, had been burned after horrible barbarities. These things had roused the wrath and inflamed the passions of the Wyandots. Their white leader, Simon Girty, took a prominent part in the deliberations, if such they can be called, at Chillicothe. In an oration, second only in beauty and intensity of feeling to that of Logan's, he recited their wrongs and invoked their vengeance. Captain Caldwell of the British service was in command of the force that finally got under way for Kentucky; Moluntha commanded the Shawnese and Girty went along as interpreter and quasi-commander of the Wyandots. Caldwell had with him some thirty picked rangers, and his total force numbered about three hundred men. He moved down the Little Miami, crossed the Ohio, and made his way into Kentucky over the route used by Byrd two years before.[2]

---

[2] De Peyster to Haldimand, *Clarke MSS.*, Vol. X, p. 635.

What was the power of Kentucky to resist an invasion so formidable? The highest officer in the land was Brigadier-General Clarke, at that time with headquarters at Louisville. But he was thoroughly disgruntled over the failure of his Detroit campaign and remained sullenly aloof from things Kentuckian. His indifference, in truth, was so great as to merit and receive the sharpest of reprimands from the Governor of Virginia before the close of the year.[3] Of the three counties of Kentucky, John Todd commanded as county-lieutenant in Fayette, John Floyd in Jefferson, and Benjamin Logan in Lincoln. All these men were commanders of proven ability, but there is some evidence to indicate that there was not complete harmony among them. They had differed in regard to the location of the forts to be built by Virginia for the protection of Kentucky and to the advisability of the expedition against Detroit. The superior reputation of Logan as an Indian fighter did not, perhaps, increase his popularity with his brother officers. Logan, moreover, as senior colonel was the ranking officer in any joint enterprise. The military strength of Kentucky, as ascertained the previous summer, was 1,236, of which number Jefferson furnished 354, Lincoln, 732 and Fayette, 150.[4] In all probability the Kentucky militia, in August, 1782, did not number more than 1,500. No such number, however, could be gathered together at any one time for a definite purpose. The Kentuckians, as their leaders, were divided among themselves in regard to Virginia's war policy and the merits of their commanders.

Such was the state of Kentucky when Caldwell crossed the Ohio with his force of Indians and rangers. Passing

---

[3] *Clarke MSS.*, Vol. LII, Harrison to Clarke, October 17, 1782, p. 50.

[4] Floyd to Clarke, *Clarke MSS.*, Vol. LI, May 22, 1781, p. 53.

down the Licking River until he was near Ruddle's Station, he, at Mill Creek, turned his course toward central Kentucky, and, after detaching a part of his force to distract the attention of the other forts, led the main body of his men to Bryant's Station, about five miles from Lexington, and placed them in hiding around it on the night of August 15th. Meanwhile the subordinate force had been doing its work well. On the tenth it had raided Hoy's Station in what is now Madison County, and had carried off two boys, one of whom was Hoy's son.[5] They then retreated slowly and insolently toward the Ohio, with the hope that a force would be collected for pursuit, and thus leave fewer men to guard Bryant's. Their expectations were realized. Captain John Holder in hot haste set out from his own station, and gathering volunteers as he passed Boonesborough, Strode's and McGee's followed rapidly with a force numbering sixty-three men. He reached the Upper Blue Licks on Licking River just as the Indians were disappearing in the distance on the trail to the Lower Blue Licks. Holder, in spite of his precautions, ran into an ambuscade a mile below the Licks, and the defeat that followed is commemorated by the name—Battle Run—given to the stream near which the Indians were overtaken. After a period of confused and desperate fighting, Holder managed to extricate his force with but one man killed and three wounded. His retreat across the Licking left the Indians in possession of the field and added one more defeat to the already long list of the year's disasters.

The news of Hoy's Station and Battle Run reached Bryant's a little before the Indians encamped around it,

[5] *Shane MSS.*, Vol. II, p. 245.

and, as Caldwell had hoped, the garrison began at once making preparations to march to the aid of their neighbors. All the night long, while the Indians lay hidden around the fort, the garrison of forty-four men was kept busy within making preparations for an early start next morning. Had Caldwell known of this he would have bided his time until the force had departed and had left the fort bare of defenders. But he had miscalculated and was under the impression that the relief company had already marched. So, when at sunrise one of the negro slaves, Jim, made his appearance he was fired upon and the shots made known to the garrison that the fort was invested.[6] There was no further talk of marching; the men settled themselves grimly for the struggle before them. Yet the Indians, as often, did not choose to show their strength. Two men on horseback were sent out from the fort to seek help from Lexington and the Indians allowed them to depart unmolested; nor was any injury done to the women who went out and milked the cows nor to the negroes who carried in the water from the spring. The Indians, evidently, had no intention of unmasking their forces for the sake of capturing a few women or negroes. Elijah Craig who was in command of the fort determined to decoy the Indians into an attack; he sent thirteen men about eight o'clock into the lane beside the fort to draw the fire of the Indians whom he suspected of being in ambush there. The Indians fired upon the men and immediately there was a rush to storm the fort. But a terrific fire from the alert garrison forced them to retreat in confusion. For the remainder of the day they contented themselves with burning the

---

[6] *Boone MSS.*, Vol. XIII. Deposition of Joseph Fisklin, p. 74.

stables and keeping up an uninterrupted yelling and firing from a safe distance. In the meantime the two messengers sent to Lexington returned with the news that they had found, on reaching Lexington, all the available men there already on the road to reinforce Holder, that they had overtaken them on the march and induced them to turn back to the relief of Bryant's. The Lexington men, in fact, followed close on the messenger and appeared near the fort at about one o'clock. In order to enter the fort it was necessary for them to pass through a cornfield down a narrow lane. In this cornfield the Indians lay in ambush silently until the entire mounted force was encompassed. Then they began a furious but ill-aimed fire. But the Lexington men forseeing such an event, had at the first report spurred their horses to full speed and by dint of hard riding and rare good fortune managed to reach the fort without an injury. The garrison, not daring to open their gates, took them bodily, horses and riders, through their cabin doors. Meanwhile, some half dozen horsemen from Boonesborough and about thirty footmen from Lexington came up and hearing the firing made for the lane. They quickly found themselves confronted by Indians in overwhelming numbers but with empty guns. This latter fact gave the white men an opportunity to escape and they took it in the swiftest and most informal manner. All escaped but six.

After the arrival of the Lexington men within the fort, the Indians made little effort to force the fighting but contented themselves with random firing and yelling of the most astounding fashion. As the afternoon wore on they killed all the cattle they could collect and made a great feast. About dusk Simon Girty cautiously advanced to within a few yards of the fort, and prudently sheltering himself behind a long stump asked for a conference. This request was carried to Captain Craig who without leaving the fort inquired of Girty what he wanted. The substance of Girty's reply was a demand to surrender—a proceeding which Craig promptly refused to consider. Girty continued to urge a surrender, mentioning that he had six hundred Indians and was expecting artillery. In concluding he gave his personal guarantee that in case of surrender none of the garrison would be mistreated and mentioned his name asking if the Kentucky people did not know him. To this question Aaron Reynolds replied that Simon Girty was well known in Kentucky and that he himself had two worthless dogs, one of which he had named Simon and the other Girty on account of their striking resemblance to the moral character of that worthy. At this badinage Girty pretended to be, and perhaps was, much offended. He insisted that such an awful crisis should not be made light of. Reynolds interrupted to explain that if Girty or any other men came too near the fort the white men purposed to punish them with switches, of which commodity they had secured a great amount for this particular purpose. An end was put to this singular interview by an audible request from Reynolds to Craig for permission to try a shot at Girty. The latter lost no time in withdrawing.

It was evident to the Indians that no advantage would result from a longer investment. They decided to try the tactics of Hoy's Station and retreat in the hope of ambushing the white men if they pursued. So early in the night the whole force, thirty or forty, noisily withdrew. Toward daybreak all the others departed and the garrison coming cautiously out the next morning found only their campfires and the remnant of their breakfast. In a siege of twenty-four hours the Indians had lost five killed and two wounded, four of the garrison had been killed. Three hundred hogs, one hundred and fifty head of cattle, and many sheep had been destroyed; a number of horses had been stolen, the potatoes and corn destroyed. In itself the siege of Bryant's Station was of small moment; its importance is due to the fact that it was one link in the chain of disasters beginning with Strode's Station and culminating in the catastrophe of Lower Blue Licks.

As was usually the case, many legends sprang up after the investment was ended. The choicest of these, perhaps, is that which relates to the carrying of water during the siege. The tradition goes that the water was brought in by the women as the result of a shrewd surmise on the part of the garrison that the Indians would not fire on them. Each succeeding historian has added to the fable until it bids fair to crowd out all the other events of the day. As a matter of fact the story is pure fiction and has no support from contemporary authorities. Equally imaginative is the fear caused the settlers by Girty's threats. There were more than sixty men in the fort when Girty demanded its surrender and it would have been extremely difficult to find in Kentucky sixty well-armed men timid enough to feel dismayed at the threats of an intemperate Irishman. Under the facile touch of the Kentuckians the number of Indians at Bryant's Station has increased as remarkably as did

Falstaff's opponents in buckram suits; we are repeatedly assured that there were five or six hundred Indians around the fort. By Caldwell's own report he had but three hundred men with him when he crossed the Ohio and if we make allowance for the men sent to Hoy's Station and for deserters it is improbable that he reached Bryant's with many more than two hundred.

All during the day following the siege the relief forces kept coming into the fort. Colonel Levi Todd had led the seventeen men who had made their way into the fort through the opposing Indians.[7] In the evening of the next day, Colonel John Todd, Colonel Trigg and Major McGary arrived with one hundred and thirty militia from Lincoln and Fayette.[8] No aid, because of distance, was attempted from Jefferson, but Colonel Logan was busily engaged in getting out the militia in full force in Lincoln. A council of war was held on the night of the seventeenth, and immediate pursuit of the enemy was decided upon, notwithstanding the protests of McGary and others. One hundred and eighty-two men on horseback left the fort early on the morning of the eighteenth and marched swiftly over the trail that the Indians had rendered suspiciously evident. Colonel John Todd was the ranking officer of the little army and of the entire force over one-third were officers. They were well mounted and as there was no difficulty in keeping the trail, the march was rapid. By early afternoon they had reached the banks of Hinkston Creek near the present site of Millersburg and saw that the Indians had built their campfires there the night before. By night they

---

[7] He himself, however, being on foot, was unable to get in.
[8] Todd to Todd, *Cal Va. St. Papers*, Vol. III, p. 333].

had covered thirty-three miles. They went into the camp for the night near the Licking River; the Indians were encamped only four miles away; neither force knew that the other was near.

A short march the following morning brought them to the banks of the Licking. As they came to the edge of the stream they could see on the opposite side the stragglers of the Indian army dissappearing over the hill.[9] Evidently the enemy was at hand and the longed for encounter of white man and Wyandot was imminent. In the presence of danger the leaders were sobered and halted their troops for a consultation. The march had been impetuous and disorderly, the hearts of the Kentuckians were hot for revenge, and they meant to attain it at all hazards. Yet for all their ardor none knew better than they that in a planless encounter every chance favored their enemies. It was, moreover, increasingly evident that the Indians were acting on a well-calculated plan. They had retreated slowly, covering in two days the distance that the hot-headed Kentuckians had traversed in one. They had left so many signs of their passing that all the white leaders knew that they were courting pursuit. Finally, they had allowed themselves to be overtaken at a place the most suitable for their style of fighting. These things influenced Todd to call a halt.

The location was as well known to Boone as was Boonesborough itself. In the council he explained the nature of the ground and predicted an ambuscade along the ridge that rose from the river. He counseled crossing the river up stream and so flanking the Indians.

---

[9] Logan to Harrison, *Cal. Va. St. Papers*, Vol. III, p. 280.

HISTORY OF PIONEER KENTUCKY 191

Boone's advice was not to be disregarded, and two horsemen were sent across the river and along the ridge to discover, if possible, the suspected ambush. They returned and reported that the Indians had retired and were no longer to be seen. When the white men heard this, there was no restraining either officer or man; they spurred their horses into the river and splashed their way tumultuously to the other side. The advance, however, was not without method. It had already been decided that when the enemy was encountered an advance guard should attack on horseback and the others dismounted should rush up and finish the work when the Indian lines were broken. The foot soldiers were to separate into three divisions of which Boone was to command the left, Trigg the right and Todd the center. Harlan, McGary and McBride were to lead the advance.

With this arrangement the Kentuckians advanced up the ridge in good order.[10] The advance guard had come within forty yards of the place where Boone had predicted an ambush would be made when they received from the hidden Wyandots a volley so furious that all but three of the Kentuckians fell. The battle was now on and in spite of the surprise of the advance, it went at first not unfavorably to the white men. Boone on the left fighting heroically drove back his enemy by sheer force of valor. But Todd and his men had been caught in the open and were annihilated; Trigg on the right had been outflanked. As Boone was coolly going about his work of destruction he suddenly perceived that the right was being doubled back and that the Wyandots were surrounding him. There was no further thought

---
[10] Boone to Harrison, *Cal. Va. St. Papers,* Vol. III, p. 275.

of advance nor was there any order given to retreat. Out of that flaming wall of fire the Kentuckians broke desperately, each man for himself. As they turned, the Wyandots broke from cover, threw away their rifles and prepared to finish the work with the tomahawk. The retreat became a rout; the rout a slaughter. The Indians took possession of the horses and rode to and fro among the Kentuckians striking with the tomahawk until their insensate souls were satiated with killing. They pursued to the very brink of the water and were only prevented from crossing by a terrible fire from a group of men who had been rallied on the other side by Benjamin Netherlands. The Kentuckians made their way where-ever and whenever they could across the river and reaching the other side, without waiting for consultation, plunged panic-stricken into the forest and each for himself made for the nearest station.

The battle had lasted about five minutes and sixty-six men had fallen of the pioneers. Four were captured. The Indians had lost ten men and a French leader, Le Bute. Todd, Trigg, Harlan and McBride were among the slain. No such calamity had ever before befallen Kentucky.

Meanwhile Logan had raised the Lincoln militia and had advanced to Bryant's; Colonel Todd was already a day's march on his way. Logan learned with dismay of the headlong pursuit and hurried with five hundred men to anticipate the slaughter he feared. He had advanced but a few miles from Bryant's when twenty-five fugitives were encountered; from these the details of the awful conflict were learned. At this news Logan halted his men and throwing out scouts far in advance, waited throughout the long dismal day while the fugitives kept coming into camp. Toward night he turned and went back to Bryant's. The news had already reached the fort and the ensuing hours of desolation are not to be described in words. Here while the stricken families lamented and strong men seemed shocked into listlessness, Logan waited. On the twenty-fourth, with five hundred men, he began his march to the Lower Licks, but when he reached the battlefield the Indians were gone. The mutilated bodies of the dead were collected and given a common grave. Nothing else could be done. Logan returned to Bryant's and the battle of Lower Blue Licks passed into history.

In the thoughts of pioneer Kentuckians the battle of Lower Blue Licks was the most portentous thing of their lives; those who took part in it never succeeded in forgetting its horrors.[11] In after years it was talked over around the firesides and its incidents were magnified a thousand times.[12] But the topic in which the pioneer mind most delighted was the problem presented by the defeat—what caused it? The Kentuckians were slow to admit defeat in a fair fight. They found balm for their wounded pride in magnifying the strength of the enemy and stressing the fact of an ambuscade. As in the case of Bowman's defeat a scapegoat was sought for and found in the person of Major McGary. The story was put in circulation that McGary had seditiously incited the men to cross the river by his taunt that all who were not cowards should follow him. This action accorded well

---

[11] The letters of the commanders and survivors of Lower Blue Licks are admirably grouped in the appendix to Colonel Young's *Battle of Lower Blue Licks*.

[12] In Cuming's Tour it is related that 2,000 white men took part in the battle and that of these 600 were killed.

with the character of the hot-headed McGary and the story was not long in finding a place in history. That McGary uttered the words attributed to him is not at all improbable; but that they had any such effect on the Kentuckians as tradition relates, it is scarcely possible to believe. Boone, Levi Todd, Logan and Clarke all made reports of the battle and none of them mention McGary in any such role. It is not plausible that if McGary's conduct had been so reprehensible, he would have escaped censure at the hands of these men. Their silence is significant. Moreover, there is much evidence to show that McGary was throughout for caution, but that when fighting became necessary he did it with his accustomed vigor and resolution. Forty years after the battle a doubtful author gave the statement of an unknown gentleman that McGary had admitted to him his fault. History will not permanently accept as true the story of a witness so doubtful. There is no respectable evidence to prove that McGary was in any way more than his comrades responsible for the great calamity.

The truth is that the Kentuckians were outgeneraled and outfought. They had no one to blame but themselves. In the Wyandots they found an enemy far superior to the other Indians in craft and resolution. Their operations during 1782 had completely baffled the settlers; they had kept the white men divided while they roamed almost at will through the country. When encountered they showed a disposition for hand-to-hand fighting that amazed the pioneers. In half a dozen conflicts they had shown themselves superior to their white antagonists. They had *not* ambushed the settlers at Lower Blue Licks in any real sense of the word. The

Kentuckians had *not* gone into the battle in confusion, but with plans already made. The number of the Wyandots was *not* largely in excess of that of the whites. The battle was decided when, after the first fire, the Wyandots threw away their rifles and with only their tomahawks rushed in hand to hand. Excuses notwithstanding, the Kentuckians had met their match— and more.

Simon Girty has suffered at the hands of the historians less only than McGary. Among the early writers he was credited with the command of the Indians around Bryant's and at the Licks. Modern writers show a tendency to represent him as an ignorant renegade entirely without authority. All picture him as a monster of depravity. There can be no question now as to who was in nominal command around Bryant's. The testimony of the Haldimand Papers is incontestable that it was Caldwell. But the reports of the Kentucky leaders make it plain that the real commander was Girty. His official position, it was true, was only that of interpreter, but as an adopted child of the Wyandot tribe he wielded enormous power and influence. There can hardly be a doubt that Girty was the leading spirit in the campaign. It must be remembered that nearly all Caldwell's Indians were Wyandots.

The character and reputation of Simon Girty have been variously distorted to suit the views of Kentucky historians. He was bad enough, in all truth, but by no means the monster of depravity he is usually represented. Born of Irish parents in the most abject poverty and the most immoral environment, he could hardly have escaped being what he was. He had been reared among the Indians and was conscious of no disgrace when he finally cast his lot among them. He was no traitor. He would have been one had he taken any other side than he did. He was wildly intemperate and, drunk or sober, endowed with a reckless courage that made his name a proverb in the west. His nature was not essentially cruel and he acted often from noble impulses; he saved Kenton from the stake and tried to save Crawford. His conduct must always be viewed as that of an Indian, for he was Indian more than he was white. He was not, as is so often stated, hated or despised by the Kentuckians. There is some evidence that he was personally popular among them. White Indians were not uncommon then and inspired no such feeling among the pioneers as among later generations. Had Girty been hated by the Kentuckians, he would hardly have dared to come within five yards of the fort for a conference. His asking if the Kentuckians knew him showed his consciousness of the feeling toward him.

Aside from the question of Girty and McGary there is the additional problem of dissension among the leaders of the Kentuckians. That such dissension existed is clearly shown by the language used by the different writers after the battle. McGary in a letter to Clarke openly charged that Todd wished by an early pursuit to rob Logan of the credit for the expected victory. Logan reported to Harrison that the pursuit had been rash, and indirectly he blamed the other leaders. After the battle Boone and others wrote to Harrison, blaming Clarke for inactivity; Clarke wrote to Harrison, censuring the leaders—and Todd in particular—and Harrison finally sent Clarke a most cutting reprimand for his conduct. Logan did not escape suspicion. The question was asked why he was so dilatory in his movements. He did not reach Bryant's till the enemy had been gone twenty-four hours and twelve hours later had advanced but five miles. His delay of four days in marching to the battlefield is inexplicable. The most accommodating of enemies could not have so long awaited his convenience.

The aftermath of the Licks was more comforting to the pride of Kentucky. Lashed into action by the rebukes of Harrison, Clarke in November essayed to revenge the disaster that he should have prevented. In a meeting of the officers held at the Falls shortly after the battle, it was decided to invade the Indian country. The militia was to gather at Bryant's under Logan and at Louisville under Floyd. The two divisions were to meet at the mouth of the Licking, and under the command of Clarke proceed against the Indian towns on the Great Miami. More than one thousand men gathered at the appointed rendezvous and moved into Ohio. A straggling Indian discovered the advance and gave the alarm; the Indian towns were deserted when Clarke arrived. He burnt the towns and sent Logan to perform the same kind office for the British post at the head of the Miami. Then, having taken ten scalps, seven prisoners and regained two captives, the army of one thousand men returned somewhat ingloriously to Kentucky.

THE STRUGGLE FOR AUTONOMY.

FOR Kentucky the year 1782 had ended, as it began, in bloodshed. But beginning with 1783 it may fairly be said that a new era was ushered in. Previous to this, the thoughts of the Kentuckians had been directed almost exclusively to matters offensive and defensive against the Indians; subsequently things political and economic occupied the greater part of their attention. For with the carnage of Blue Licks the energy of the Indians seemed to perish wholly and Kentucky was destined not again to be visited by hostile war-bands of any great size. At the same time the population was growing apace, towns began to spring up, forts were gradually abandoned for farmhouses and the entire country took on the appearance of a long-settled community. In these unwonted times of peace the people were at leisure to meditate on and discuss their government, to criticize its defects and to formulate plans for its improvement. Politics, not war, was to occupy the center of the stage for a decade. With 1782 the Heroic Age of Kentucky history may be said to end. Of the great names of earlier days Logan's alone remained undimmed. Clarke was sinking into a drunkard, Todd had fallen in battle, Kenton, Boone and Harrod had remained hunters or become unsuccessful farmers. Floyd was soon to find a grave. New names were to be found in the place of old; new interests were come in essentially different from those of the last decade.

By the articles of peace signed in November, 1782, the status of Kentucky was confirmed rather than determined. Whatever the paper stipulations might have been, by no stretch of the imagination can we conceive the Kentuckians permitting themselves to become French, Spanish or English. The Mississippi did not become the western boundary of the young nation merely by treaty; the retention of the west was the necessary result of aggressive settlement beginning when Boone blazed the way along the Wilderness Road. Had the treaty of Paris left the transmontane lands nominally Spanish or English, the western settlers could have been depended upon to violate it swiftly and effectually. England, at least, knew this fact well and the other nations could hardly have been ignorant of it. Nothing done at Paris could affect the destinies of the Kentuckians; their future was not a matter of diplomacy; they were Virginians and could be changed by no power but themselves. No sentiment need be wasted on the generosity or shrewdness that extended the United States to the Mississippi; the diplomats merely recognized an unalterable *status quo*. Within the next few years there was much talk in Kentucky about a union with Spain; it was an evidence of discontent rather than an earnest of intention.

Of much greater moment to Kentucky was that article of the treaty providing that England should surrender her posts in the Northwest. This more than anything else secured for Kentucky a cessation of Indian attacks. It would perhaps be no exaggeration to say that nine-tenths of the Indian depredations during the Revolution were instigated from these English posts in the Northwest; their surrender, or the promise of it, meant that henceforth the Indians themselves must plan and support their expeditions. It is significant that Kentucky was not again invaded by Indians in any considerable number. The Indian depredations had been planned by British brains, financed by British money and mitigated by British humanity. The withdrawal of British aid was necessarily accompanied by a cessation of Indian hostilities. Yet candor compels the admission that the Indian warfare against Kentucky has been monstrously exaggerated. The Indians were not, as is so often asserted, the implacable foe of the Kentuckians; the British agents, as the Haldimand Papers abundantly show, were compelled to put forth enormous efforts to rouse the sluggish red men for the warpath. They were always reluctant to cross the Ohio and were induced to do so only by dint of extraordinary expenditures for presents and provisions. Early in their relations with the British they had learned that gifts were the wages of indifference, and their impatience was never so great nor their wrath so savage that they failed to profit by their knowledge. England paid many times over for every effort of the Indians in her behalf. Moreover, the Indians once on the warpath were, for the most part, lukewarm and could rarely be incited to vigorous action. Notwithstanding the volumes that have been written about the Indian atrocities in Kentucky, the country suffered no more therefrom than did Virginia, Massachusetts or many of the eastern States. As far as war between white man and Indian is concerned, Kentucky certainly was *not* a "dark and bloody ground." The name had been gained and perhaps deserved long before John Finley encamped at Eskippakithiki.

Equally important toward securing peace for Kentucky was the cession by Virginia to the Confederation of all her territory north of the Ohio River. The Continental Congress had found the claim of Virginia to the Northwest too shadowy for recognition but real enough for transfer. The cession was completed in 1783 and the Ohio made the northern limit of Virginia's sovereignty beyond the mountains. The treaty of Paris had withdrawn from the Indians the aid of the British; the action of Virginia left them for a care to the central government. This power in a series of treaties with the separate tribes took up energetically and, for the most part, successfully the task of appeasing the wrath and alienating the territory of the red men. The transfer of sovereignty redounded to the benefit of Kentucky. Virginia had not been able to prevent the depredations of the Ohio tribes; now they were forced to live in comparative quiet and Kentucky benefited by the change.

It would be far from the truth, however, to believe that the Kentuckians of 1783 realized that there would be no further danger from the Indians. To their minds the peril was as great as ever. They were slow to forget the carnage of the Licks and persistent in thinking that it could have been prevented had Virginia built the much-desired forts in northern Kentucky. The failure to protect Kentucky had not been entirely due to indifference on the part of Virginia; Clarke, the ranking officer in the west, had neglected, through sloth or disobedience, to carry out his instructions. From 1780 until 1786 the question of fortifying northern Kentucky was the most vital topic that the Kentuckians had to consider; it occupied a much larger share of their attention than did the Statehood movement or the agitation for the free navigation of the Mississippi. For this reason it is necessary to consider somewhat in detail the entire question of how the demand arose for the erecting of these forts, at what places they were designed to be placed and the reason for the failure to construct them. The movement for building a fort at the mouth of the Licking originated soon after the great siege of Boonesborough and was founded on the belief that such a post would do much toward preventing similar invasions for the future. Representations were made to the Virginia authorities to this effect, and in June, 1780, as has been related, the Virginia Council ordered the erection of the fort on the Licking as well as one on the Big Sandy. She ordered a regiment of Virginia troops under Colonel Crockett to proceed westward and garrison the fort. But Clarke was obsessed with the idea of fortifying Louisville and did not build the fort at the mouth of the Licking. After Byrd's invasion the Kentuckians became more than ever convinced that such a fort at the Licking was necessary if Kentucky wished to prevent Indian attacks. But Clarke continued to work on the fortifications at Louisville and to neglect the building of the posts desired by the Kentuckians. The consequence was that Clarke soon became very unpopular with the Kentuckians and a feeling sprang up against Louisville in Kentucky that has not disappeared even today. The feeling arose that, in addition to the fort on the Licking, one ought to be erected at the mouth of the Kentucky and another at Limestone. On September 5, 1781, Clarke, after the failure to make a campaign against Detroit, called the three county-lieutenants [1] together at Louisville and requested them to

---

[1] *Clarke MSS.*, Vol. LI, September 5, 1781, p. 84.

suggest a plan for action against the Indians. In reply, Logan advised that no expedition should be made, but that the forts should be built; if only one fort could be erected, it should be placed at the mouth of the Kentucky. Floyd wished to have a campaign made up the Miami, but also insisted on building the two forts on the Licking and Kentucky. The advice of Todd was of similar tenor. Finding that Clarke was yet inclined to fortify Louisville, the three men set forth their reasons for thinking the Falls an unsuitable place.[2] First, it was not on the Indian road to central Kentucky as were the other two places. In the second place, the transportation of provisions was much more difficult to Louisville than to the other places. Finally, Louisville was an unhealthful location for a fort. They further recommended that the fort at the Kentucky, if built, should be garrisoned by regular troops. The entire matter, it was agreed, should be laid before the Virginia Assembly. In December Governor Harrison wrote to Clarke, instructing him to build the three posts at the Licking, the Kentucky and at Limestone, and that sixty-eight militia should be assigned to each post.[3] In February, 1782, Clarke wrote to Harrison in a very surly letter that he was intending to establish the fort at the Licking immediately.[4] The announcement of his intention, however, seemed to consume his entire energy and the fort remained unbuilt. The dissatisfaction with Clarke and with Virginia was increasing daily; the people, of course, had no way of knowing that Virginia was sincerely try-

---

[2] *Cal. Va. St. Papers*, Vol. II, p. 562.
[3] *Clarke MSS.*, Vol. LI, Harrison to Clarke, December 20, 1781, p. 101.
[4] *Cal. Va. St. Papers*, Vol. III, p. 68.

ing to get the forts built. The feeling against Clarke was not allayed by the fact that he was persisting in his old plan of patrolling the Ohio by rowboats. By June, 1782, he had, as he stated in a letter to Harrison, completed two gondolas and a galley.[5] The latter craft was seventy-three feet long, possessed forty-six oars and carried one hundred and ten men. It possessed a respectable armament of six four-pounders and one two-pounder.[6] However, the men objected as strenuously as ever to doing naval work and a mutiny broke out on the galley in July. The larger boat was commonly referred to as the Miami galley and strove to attract a crew by the liberal terms of ten dollars a month and a suit of clothes.[7] Before fall came, Clarke had been compelled to give up the light armed gondolas because the men they carried were not sufficiently protected against the Indians,[8] but the sides of the galley had been made four feet high and it continued to patrol the Ohio and terrify the Indians for several years.[9] After the battle of the Lower Licks in August, Logan, Todd, Boone and others wrote vigorous letters to Governor Harrison, condemning Clarke's policy in fortifying Louisville and demanding that the forts be built on the Licking and at Limestone. This drew from Harrison a letter to Clarke, sternly reprimanding him for his failure.[10] Clarke, in reply, excused himself by saying that Indian troubles had prevented the erections of the forts before the battle and that he had tried to have them built as

[5] *Ibid.*, p. 121.
[6] *Ibid.*, p. 150.
[7] *Clarke MSS.*, Vol. LII, p. 29.
[8] *Ibid.*, p. 25.
[9] *Cal. Va. St. Papers*, Vol. III, p. 275.
[10] *Clarke MSS.*, Vol. LII, Harrison to Clarke, October 17, 1782, p. 50.

he returned from the Miami campaign in the autumn, but the militia would not enlist.[11] In the last days of the year outcast Cherokees [12] began to molest the travelers along the Wilderness Road, and a demand arose for a fort to be built at Cumberland Gap.[13] In February Harrison instructed Clarke to build the fort at the mouth of the Kentucky and give up the other two,[14] and Clarke, a little later, called on the three counties of Kentucky to deliver their taxes into his hands in order to pay the cost of construction; Lincoln was ordered to contribute sixty-five militia, Jefferson, twenty-five, and Fayette, ten.[15] All these things the counties promptly neglected to do and the forts remained unbuilt. In the summer of 1783 Clarke was relieved of his commission, and with the cession of the Ohio country to the Confederation the same year, Virginia definitely abandoned the long and vain attempt to fortify northern Kentucky.[16] But the discontent of the Kentuckians was a permanent thing. Mutterings were heard and men began to say that if Virginia were unwilling to protect them they were entitled to a government that would. The idea of separate Statehood became more current, and although the fear of the Indians gradually died away, the movement for autonomy, once begun, did not decrease. The beginnings of Kentucky's struggle for autonomy lay in Clarke's failure to build the forts for defending the exposed frontier.

---

[11] *Cal. Va. St. Papers*, Vol. III, p. 345.
[12] *Ibid.*, p. 384.
[13] *Ibid.*, p. 406.
[14] *Clarke MSS.*, Vol. LII, Harrison to Clarke, February 27, 1783, p. 76.
[15] *Cal. Va. St. Papers*, Vol. III, p. 476.
[16] *Clarke MSS.*, Vol. LII, Harrison to Clarke, July 2, 1783, p. 88.

Meanwhile, in March, 1783, the name Kentucky had been revived in the creation of the Judicial District of Kentucky. This district comprised the three counties of Jefferson, Fayette and Lincoln, and was called into existence by the need of a Court of Appellate Jurisdiction nearer than Richmond. By the provision of the act the District of Kentucky was to have a Supreme Court with one chief justice and two associate justices. There was to be, also, a clerk and an attorney-general. To the last-named position Walker Daniel was appointed. John May became clerk, John Floyd, Samuel McDowell and George Muter, judges. Near Crow's Station a new town was established for the place of holding court, and became, in effect, the capital of the District. It was christened Danville in honor of the attorney general.

The inhabitants of Kentucky at this time numbered 30,000 and increasing immigration was fast filling the land. With such a population, a fertile soil and a well-ordered government, Kentucky, it would seem, might well feel secure of its future. There were, however, two ills that were none the less potent that they were largely imaginary. One was the dread of the Indian invasion, the other, the lack of a market for the Kentucky products. The fear of another Indian invasion was kept alive by constantly occurring depredations. The Indians, in small bands, numbering oftentimes not more than a half dozen, stole in and out of the land, stealing the horses, carrying off provisions and occasionally murdering the settlers. One such marauding band killed John Floyd in March, 1783, and the pioneers were kept constantly alarmed by minor outrages. The evil was increased by the action of the land speculators who, in order to force down the price of land, did their utmost to keep the country in a turmoil.

That Kentucky in 1783 had no products to send to market did not at all deter the Kentuckians from clamoring loudly for a place in which to market them. To anyone acquainted with the inherent western characteristic of imagining greatly and talking at length, this condition will not appear anomalous. Kentucky was not producing enough even for home consumption, and if she had possessed a market could not have utilized it without supernatural assistance. Yet the speeches of her orators and politicians, numerous then as now, were weighted with reference to her enormous exports and marvelous commerce. But the only markets to which their produce could have gone was New Orleans, and New Orleans was a Spanish post closed as completely against western trade as were the ears of His Most Christian Majesty to all the allurements of the Evil One. To the Kentuckians the closing of the New Orleans as a market showed conclusively that their commerce was important and a market necessary. To the Spanish the desire of Kentuckians for a market showed conclusively the duty of the elect to make New Orleans a closed port. The entire absence of commerce neither prevented the regulations of Spain nor tempered the wrath of the Kentuckians. Pressure was brought to bear on Virginia that she demand through the central government that Spain should open up both New Orleans and the Mississippi to western trade. The failure of Virginia to secure this and the refusal of Spain to grant it inflamed the wrath of the Kentuckians against both. This took the shape against Spain in an open threat of violence and against Virginia in an increased desire for separation.

How long it would have taken the separation movement to mature under normal conditions there are no means of conjecturing; Indian troubles brought it swiftly to a crisis. Since 1776 over eight hundred and fifty men had been killed by the Indians in Kentucky, and as far as the settlers could see, things were in danger of getting worse instead of better.[17] The pay of the militia was withheld for indefinite periods according to the financial condition of Virginia;[18] the men were distrustful of their leaders and the leaders of their men; since the retirement of George Rogers Clarke there was no officer in Kentucky with authority to call out the troops from the entire District; finally, the Cherokees on the south began to be troublesome.[19] Shawnese and Cherokees were accustomed to steal in and out of the country, stealing the horses and murdering the settlers. Warfare of this kind was more irritating, if not more deadly, than wholesale invasions. Formerly the Kentuckians had been able to relieve their feeling and punish their tormentors by invading the Indian towns, but now the Shawnese territory was the property of the Confederation and the Cherokees were dwellers in the domain of North Carolina. There was nothing the Kentuckians could in legality do, and they chafed under the inactivity. As was natural, they ascribed all their evils to the policy of the Virginia government and the desire for separation that had been originated by Clarke's failure to construct the forts in northern Kentucky was

---
[17] *Cal. Va. St. Papers,* Vol. III, Steele to Harrison, September 12, 1782, p. 303.
[18] *Ibid.,* Vol II, Montgomery to Nelson, August 10, 1781, p. 315.
[19] *Ibid.,* Vol. III, Logan to Harrison, August 11, 1783, p. 522.

increased by Virginia's inability to protect them from Indian marauders. In 1784 the feeling came to a head and resulted in one of the ringleaders in the separation movement being summoned before the District Court and punished.[20] There was no Virginia statute that fitted such a crime, but the judges applied an obsolete law against a bearer of false news and fined the delinquent, Pomeroy, two thousand pounds of tobacco. James Wilkinson exerted himself vigorously at this time to stem the Statehood movement and was very active against Pomeroy. The Court expected that by this example the agitation might be suppressed, but it had no such effect, and it was not long before Wilkinson himself was uttering words more seditious than he had condemned in Pomeroy. A great part of the inhabitants of Kentucky, in fact, were not native Virginians, but had come in from Carolina or Pennsylvania and were by nature inclined to opposition to the parent State.[21]

In the autumn of 1784 a report reached Colonel Logan, the senior officer in Kentucky, that the Cherokees were meditating an invasion of Kentucky. The report was a canard and in all probability the work of the land speculators; it is not to Logan's credit that he believed it. That officer, however, straightway called a meeting of the militia officers in November to formulate plans for protection. The officers once assembled were strongly in favor of making an expedition southward before the Cherokees could invade Kentucky. Upon reflection it occurred to them that the law of Virginia made no provision for the invasion of a sister State by a colonel of

---

[20] *Ibid.,* Vol. III, Daniel to Harrison, May 21, 1784, p. 584.
[21] *Ibid.,* Vol. III, Speed to Harrison, May 22, 1784, p. 588.

militia, and the expedition perforce had to be abandoned. Moved by this irritating defect in the Virginia statutes, the officers decided to request Virginia to agree to a separation and give the Kentuckians an opportunity to deal with the Indians as the exigencies and their own fine sense of justice should determine. They called on each militia company to send one delegate to Danville in December and formulate plans for action.[22] This second meeting took place December 27th, with Charles Fleming, chairman, and Thomas Todd, clerk. The delegates to this meeting deliberated at length for ten days, and, in addition to asserting the necessity for a separation from Virginia, they issued an address to the people of Kentucky, suggesting that at the time of the regular election for the Assembly next April they should, also, select delegates to meet in May at Danville and take further steps toward separation. Twenty-five delegates were to be chosen by the three counties in proportion to their population.[23]

One or two things need to be noted in regard to this meeting of the militia officers. In the first place their action in deciding for a separation from Virginia was evidently not necessitated by any exigency then existing. The militia officers were all men who had seen active service against the Indians and who were well acquainted with Indian conditions north and south. They could hardly have escaped knowing that the reported Cherokee invasion was a myth; even if the invasion occurred, Logan had full authority to direct a defensive campaign within the limits of the District. With proper vigilance such

---
[22] Littell, *Political Transactions In and Concerning Kentucky*, p. 15.
[23] *Lettres d'un Cultivateur Americain*, Vol. III, p. 438.

a campaign would have effected quite as much as the contemplated invasion. The fear of the Cherokees was evidently not a reason but an excuse for their action; the military officers had made up their minds that they were going to have autonomy. The people were not by any means so decided. The second fact to be noticed is the action of the meeting in calling for delegates to be elected in proportion to the population instead of by the legal Virginia method of giving each county equal representation. By this ingenious plan Lincoln County, where the feeling against Virginia was the strongest, secured more representatives than she otherwise would have done. Much capital has been made of this action by Kentucky historians; it has been cited as a remarkable example of the inherent desire that animates all Kentuckians for social justice. It is, however, rather an indication that the art of politics rose early and flourished greatly in Kentucky.

The "Second" Convention, as it is usually termed, met in Danville May 23, 1785,[24] and organized by electing Samuel McDowell, president. After a week of deliberation they prepared a petition to Virginia, asking for Statehood and issued a call for another convention to be held, to which the delegates were to be chosen in proportion to the population. The petition to Virginia, after being prepared, was prudently left for the next convention to deliver. It never saw the light of day. The address, however, was made to the people and is even today not without interest in composition and subject-matter.[25] After summing up in terms of faultless rhetoric the principles of philosophy as enunciated by

---
[24] Littell, *Political Transactions*, Appendix I.
[25] *Ibid.*, p. 18.

Thomas Jefferson, the author proceeded to give seven reasons why Kentucky should separate from Virginia. The inability to call out the militia, the lack of executive power in the District, the disadvantage of government from Richmond and the absence of proper protection from the Indians were the chief complaints. As an afterthought allusion was made to the increase of taxes now at hand. James Wilkinson was the supposed author of both the petitions and the address to the people.

Meanwhile Nelson County had been formed out of Jefferson and was given representation in the "Third" Convention.[26] This convention met August 8th and was composed of thirty members. It is significant of the new era that Benjamin Logan was the only one of the old pioneers elected as a member. The name of James Wilkinson appears now for the first time prominently in Kentucky affairs, destined in the next few years to loom large in the life of the District. The two men are typical; Logan of the old regime now rapidly passing, and Wilkinson of the new just now being ushered in.

Logan had come to Kentucky in 1775 and had enjoyed undisputed leadership from the first. Physically he was a giant and possessed enormous strength. His courage was on a par with his strength, and in pioneer times there were current innumerable stories of his daring deeds. He was a Presbyterian in faith, and no man throughout a long life more sturdily lived up to his religion than he. Simple-hearted, fearless and straightforward, he deserves his place as the first among the Kentucky pioneers. His name inspired confidence among his contemporaries. If an Indian expedition was under

---

[26] Hening, *Statutes*, Vol. II, p. 469.

consideration, it was Logan who gathered the men and led the charge; if there was need of counsel or advice, everyone waited for Logan to speak. Loved and esteemed by the Kentuckians from the time he entered the land until his death, he deserves the tribute given him by a Kentucky historian: "Mentally and physically Logan was great."

Wilkinson had but one trait in common with Logan—fearlessness. Whereas Logan towered over six feet, Wilkinson was below medium height. Logan was simple and homely in speech, Wilkinson was suave and adroit. Of pleasing manners and acute intellect, he was in his time the most popular man in Kentucky. He was above all things else a politician. He had been born in Maryland and had seen much service in the Revolution and was suspected of complicity in the Gates embroglio.[27] He had displayed considerable military capacity and had been raised to the rank of brigadier-general. After the Revolution he had entered the service of Pennsylvania and had come to Louisville as a merchant in the autumn of 1784. His peculiar talents soon brought him into prominence in the District and he played a great part in Kentucky's struggle for Statehood. As was to be expected, he made many and powerful enemies, one of whom in his character of historian has done much to blacken his name. The character of Wilkinson is a most fascinating study. He has for the most part been depicted as base and unscrupulous. He has been branded as a traitor prepared to serve Spain while pretending to labor zealously for his own country.[28] That he received money from the Spanish treasury is not to be

---

[27] Wilkinson, *Memoirs*, Chap. I.
[28] McCaleb, *Aaron Burr*.

doubted. To one unacquainted with frontier life in the west the actions of Wilkinson will appear inexplicable or hopelessly base. But Wilkinson was but one of many; Kentucky contained hundreds of men of the type. Nor was the type considered then either extraordinary or bad. The rule of action for such men was to look keenly after the interests of their individual selves. They considered it none the less meritorious that this fascinating occupation sometimes led them to the brink of treason. According to their ethical standards it was no wrong to treat with an enemy, if the promises were not meant to be kept. It was not base to accept bribes, if the bribe-labor was not performed. It was no disgrace to be a pensioner of Spain, if the pensioner continued to serve his country. This dallying with Spain was common and was considered good conduct, inasmuch as it "fooled" Spain and resulted in the accumulating of many shekels by the individual Kentuckians. In such light must Wilkinson be considered. That he sold himself to Spain is indisputable; that he never did the work for which he received the pay is equally indisputable; that he ever purposed or intended to do such work, no one that understands the Kentucky of 1785 will for a moment believe. His entire life was a continued and exclusive looking after himself, and if in the course of it he received money from the enemy, neither the enemy was benefited nor Kentucky hurt.

The "Third" Convention met in August with twenty-six of the thirty delegates in attendance.[29] After

---

[29] The proceedings of the numerous conventions in the 80's are given and discussed at large in John Mason Brown's Political Beginnings of Kentucky, in Littell's Political Transactions in and Concerning Kentucky and in Green's Spanish Conspiracy.

making McDowell president of the convention, they took up the petition to Virginia left over to them from the preceding convention. In a committee headed by Mr. Muter the petition received some amendments and alterations, after which it was reported to the convention and unanimously adopted. It is noticeable that Virginia was petitioned to acknowledge the independence and sovereignty of Kentucky; admission to the Union was not suggested. Admission to the Union, in fact, could not be considered as an advantage by any people in the year of grace, 1785. An address was also made to the Kentucky people by the customary frontier method of mailing it in manuscript to the doors of the courthouses. Chief Justice George Muter and the District Attorney, Harry Innes, were delegated to bear the petition to the Virginia Assembly.

These two delegates reached Richmond in November, 1785, and at once began work toward having their petition granted. They found the Virginia lawmakers surprisingly pliable as far as separation was concerned. On January 6, 1786, they passed the first Enabling Act providing for the separation of Kentucky on certain conditions.[30] These conditions were that there should be no change in the boundary; that Kentucky assume a part of the State debt; that land rights remain unchanged; that residents and nonresidents be equal in the matter of taxation; that the Ohio be open to navigation; and that all disputes between Virginia and Kentucky be settled by arbitration. For the accepting or rejecting of these conditions, a convention should be held at Danville on the first Monday in September, and, if accepting, Kentucky should become a State at some date prior

---

[30] Hening, Vol. XII, p. 37. Madison's letters during this period reflect the entire willingness of Virginia to grant a separation to Kentucky.

to September 1, 1787, *provided that Congress, before June, 1787, had admitted her to the Union.*

This last provision aroused the ire of the Kentucky politicians, of whom Wilkinson was deservedly the leader. They did not desire admission to the Union, but immediate and unconditional independence. Wilkinson and others announced themselves as candidates for the "Fourth" Convention on a platform calling for immediate independence. Wilkinson was opposed by John Marshall in a heated campaign, but was elected; his enemies asserted that his election was secured only by illegal acts on the part of the militia officers at the ballot box. But when the convention was called together in Danville on the twenty-sixth of September, it was speedily discovered that there was no quorum present for the transaction of business. The cause of such a condition of things was to be found in Indian troubles.

The Indians north of the Ohio River had never ceased to be troublesome. After the Northwest territory had been ceded by Virginia to the Confederation, the latter government had appointed Clarke, Butler and Lee as commissioners to make treaties with the Indians within its bounds.[31] In January, 1785, at Fort McIntosh, they made a treaty with the Wyandots, Delawares, Chippewas and Ottawas; one year later at Fort Finney peace was made with the Shawnese. For the moment, however, the making of peace seemed to increase the virulence of Indian hostilities. They literally swarmed over the land, stealing the horses and cattle, murdering the settlers and exasperating the Kentuckians beyond measure. In the spring of 1786, a band of seventy outcast Cherokees,

---

[31] Butterfield, *Clarke's Conquest of the Illinois,* p. 497.

called Chickamaugas, moved north and settled beyond the Ohio River, whence they gave their entire energies to the harassing of the Kentucky settlements.[32] In April of this year Logan wrote to Governor Henry of Virginia, complaining bitterly of the Indian depredations and suggesting that a campaign be made against them. He gave his opinion that Clarke, then residing at Louisville, was the proper man to lead the campaign. Clarke was just then recovering from a sickness, the origin of which Logan charitably refrained from mentioning. Governor Henry thereupon instructed Logan to call a meeting of the field officers and take such measures as were necessary to protect themselves from the Indians.[33] These instructions were given in May, and as the suggestion to make Clarke leader had not been disapproved by the Governor, Logan called a meeting of the officers for the second of August, with the avowed intention of placing Clarke in charge of the militia.[34] Henry had told them to do what was necessary to protect themselves, and to their minds this authorized them to lead an expedition across the Ohio if they thought best. While the officers were waiting for the time of meeting, there came to their hands a petition from Jefferson County that the militia of the entire district be called out to aid her against the Indians.[35] This appeal was signed by fifty-four original settlers of the county and George Rogers Clarke's name was in the number. The entire district, in fact, was demanding that something be done, and when the meeting was finally called to order at Harrodsburg on the second of August

---

[32] *Cal. Va. St. Papers,* Vol. IV, p. 119.
[33] *Ibid.,* p. 120.
[34] *Ibid.,* p. 155.
[35] *Cal. Va. St. Papers,* Vol. IV, p. 160.

no time was lost in placing Clarke in control and deciding upon a campaign against the northern Indians.[36] Whatever scruples the officers may have had in regard to leading a Virginia army into foreign territory were easily overcome by an opinion of the District Court that such an expedition was legal.[37] That Clarke had been dismissed from the Virginia line, had become a notorious drunkard and an object of suspicion to the Kentuckians did not at all prevent them from selecting him as their leader.

The invading army was to consist of two thousand men and they were ordered to rendezvous at Clarkesville opposite Louisville. Yet when the time came to go not more than half that number could be persuaded to march and these went reluctantly, having no confidence in Clarke. From the beginning disaster and mismanagement attended the undertaking.[38] The troops marched overland to Vincennes and awaited there the arrival of the provisions. These had been loaded on nine keel boats and started to Vincennes by way of the Ohio and the Wabash. But low water on the latter stream delayed them nine days and when they arrived at Vincennes the discontented army found that half of the provisions were spoiled. Logan had been left behind in Kentucky to lead a force against the Shawnese. Clarke's open intemperance had alienated the loyalty of officers and men, and a rumor that he had proposed terms to the Indians spread through the rank and file and brought the fermenting rebellion to a crisis. Three hundred men deserted and returned to Kentucky. Clarke had to content himself with remaining at Vincennes where his high-handed conduct of affairs soon brought down upon him the wrath

---
[36] *Ibid.*, p. 166.
[37] *Ibid.*, p. 195.
[38] Butterfield, *Clarke's Conquest of the Illinois*, p. 505.

of Virginia and the Confederation. Meanwhile Logan had collected seven hundred and ninety men and led them against the Shawnese with his customary skill and good fortune.[39] He was gone twenty days, burned the Shawnese towns, killed a number of warriors, took numerous prisoners and returned rapidly and successfully. Logan's success, however, was as unpopular as was Clarke's failure. While Logan himself was doubtless guiltless of misconduct, his lieutenants, and notably Patterson, aroused the ire of the Kentuckians by their assumption of authority.[40] It was charged and proven that there was much impressing of private property for the campaign and that even some of the militia had been sold into slavery. In a letter to Henry, Colonel Todd asked for an investigation into the non-success of Clarke's army.[41] Altogether it was a long time before the Kentuckians forgot the animosities of this unhappy campaign.

The "Fourth" Convention had all this time been sitting at Danville without a quorum. The members present were far from idle. They had prepared and sent to the Virginia Assembly in the care of John Marshall a memorial setting forth their discontent with the Enabling Act and the impossibility now of fulfilling its conditions regarding the time of separation; they requested a modification. The Virginia Assembly thereupon passed the second Enabling Act. By the provisions of this act Kentucky was to become a separate State in January, 1789, if Congress admitted it to the Union before July 4, 1788. It also called for another convention to be held in Danville on the third Monday in September. When the militia of Logan's and

---
[39] *Cal. Va. St. Papers,* Vol. IV, p. 204.
[40] *Ibid.,* p. 186.
[41] *Ibid.,* p. 182.

Clarke's armies returned to Kentucky, a quorum was obtained in the convention only in time, according to the second Enabling Act, to adjourn.

The land was already fermenting with discontent over the luckless expedition of Clarke and this fresh delay in the Statehood movement added to the irritation. Wilkinson and his friends declared for immediate independence without regard to membership in the Union. To make matters worse a "Committee of Correspondence" made up of Pittsburg gentlemen, sent a communication to Kentucky declaring that John Jay, the secretary of state, and Don Gardoqui, the Spanish minister, were negotiating for the surrender to Spain of the Mississippi. This truthful rumor Wilkinson with ready oratory transmuted into a reality. A convention was called to protest against the outrage, but the delegates when they came to meet found that the said outrage had entirely failed to materialize.[42]

The "Fifth" Convention met in September and again went through the solemn form of petitioning Virginia for separation.[43] They also sent a petition to Congress asking for admission to the Union and prevailed on Virginia to send one of the Kentucky delegation, John Brown, to Congress as district representative. But when Brown reached Philadelphia he found the old Confederation already moribund. Congress was willing to do nothing but wait for the new government to go into effect. The time named in the second Enabling Act for the admission of Kentucky passed without the Kentucky memorial being acted upon. Meanwhile the Kentuckians had elected a convention to frame a Constitution. This convention assembled at Dan-

---

[42] Littell, *Political Transactions,* Appendix VIII.
[43] *Ibid.,* p. 32.

ville July 28, 1788, with Samuel McDowell as president. Hardly were they organized for business before a letter was received from Brown reporting his failure and ascribing it to the efforts of the New England representatives who were influenced by jealousy of the rapidly growing West. He mentioned an interview he had had with Don Gardoqui in which the Spanish minister had offered many privileges to Kentucky if she would set up an independent government. The convention after a debate of five days issued a call for another convention to be held in November at Danville.

The election that followed was bitterly contested between the Court party headed by members of the District Court and the Country party which was in favor of conservative action. The result was a victory for the latter and when the Convention—the "Seventh"—met in November, the Court party found itself in the minority. Wilkinson and Brown were both members of the convention and did their utmost to secure an immediate declaration of independence. Their influence was great. Brown had long been a member of the Virginia Assembly and possessed deservedly the confidence of his people. Wilkinson was now more popular than ever. He had taken a cargo of ham, flour and tobacco on flat boats to New Orleans in June, 1787, and sold it for a great advance over Kentucky prices.[44] There can be no doubt but that he made arrangements with the Spanish Governor Miro to detach Kentucky from the Union in return for a pension and liberal trading privileges for himself. There can, likewise, be no doubt in the minds of those who understand western character that Wilkinson had not the slightest intention of keeping faith. He was, as he later termed it, "bluffing" for his own financial gain. He

---
[44] Collins, Vol. I, p. 21.

remained in July and August at New Orleans and started home in September. Like most travelers of that time, he came by sea to Baltimore and then overland to Kentucky where he made his appearance in February, 1788, riding in a coach drawn by six horses, possessed of great funds and a signed pass from Miro that he could bring any cargo he wished to New Orleans without paying duty. He soon interested Innes, the district attorney, and Sebastian, one of the district judges, in his plans and the evidence seems to show that they also became pensioners of Spain with the same motives as Wilkinson.

The various conventions and their efforts to achieve Statehood were not the only matters that claimed the attention of the Kentuckians at this period; in fact, the entire movement for autonomy occupied but a minor place in the thoughts of the people. It was a movement in which the politicians of the district were keenly interested, but the Kentucky people then, as now, were little disposed to be guided by their politicians and remained for the most part passive, notwithstanding the great efforts to arouse their interest and their passions. No greater misconception could possibly be had of the true state of affairs in Kentucky at this time than to represent the people as being in a state of constant excitement over the Statehood movement; it interested them only intermittently and their attention and thoughts were commonly directed to other things. Kentucky was beginning to develop a commerce of her own and her people were fast spreading over the entire district. As the people scattered and trade grew greater a demand arose that the rivers should be provided with ferries and that roads should be established over which goods might be transported. In October, 1785, the Virginia Assembly passed an act establishing three additional ferries over the Kentucky River and two over the Ohio in Jefferson County.[45] The provision for ferries over the Ohio indicate that population and trade were beginning to extend from Kentucky northward into the Indian territory. One year later the Assembly passed an act providing for a State road to be built from Lexington to the falls of the Great Kanawha and to be completed in three years.[46] As provision had already been made for a road from the Kanawha to Richmond, Kentucky was to be given direct communication with the Virginia capital.[47]

As the population of Kentucky continued to increase, Virginia met the need for closer government by a multiplication of the counties. In October, 1785, Bourbon was formed from Fayette County and Lincoln was subdivided into Lincoln, Madison and Mercer. The next year a still further division was made by forming Mason from Bourbon and Woodford from Fayette. The creation of these new county governments made it possible to organize more effectively the militia of the district and to provide for a better maintenance of order and distribution of justice.[48] Another important step was taken in October, 1788, when the Assembly formed the Kentucky counties into a district with one representative in Congress.

Military affairs also occupied no little part of the attention of the Kentuckians during 1786 and 1787. In March, 1787, while Colonel Logan was absent in Richmond, Captain John Logan[49] raised a company of one hundred and thirty men and led them into Tennessee on

---
[45] Hening, Vol. XII, p. 83.
[46] Ibid., p. 282.
[47] Ibid., p. 218.
[48] Ibid., pp. 658, 658, 668.
[49] Cal. Va. St. Papers, Vol. IV, p. 256.

the trail of a band of marauding Cherokees. He aimed to attack the Cherokee town of Crow Town, but missed his way and fell in with a band of Chickamaugas. To the Kentuckians in their present temper this seemed a special dispensation of Providence, and they promptly made use of it. Seven of the Indians were killed. Then the Kentuckians returned home, leaving a trail of furious Indians behind them. Hardly were they gone when some forty of the Chickamaugas set out for Kentucky to avenge the death of their kinsmen.[50] Happily they were met by the Indian trader Martin and were persuaded to abandon the warpath. This expedition of Logan's was like that of Clarke's in the preceding year in that it had been an illegal invasion of foreign territory. As it was, Virginia was prompt to frown upon such measures, and in May the Governor sent positive instructions to the Kentucky officers that the militia under no conditions was to be led out of the district. After that the militia officers contented themselves with plans for defense and did not again cross the boundary.[51] In February, 1787, they called out two companies of militia for permanent service, one to guard Limestone, which had become a great landing place for the immigrants to Kentucky, and another to range the frontier of Fayette in a search of prowling Indians. Muter and Innes recommended to the Governor in the early spring that he should appoint four Indian commissioners to give their entire time to the management of Indian affairs in Kentucky. Randolph did not take the advice, but contented himself with a message to Congress, asking that Virginia be given permission to chastise the Indians that

---

[50] *Ibid.*, p. 261.
[51] *Cal. Va. St. Papers*, Vol. IV, pp. 237-427. *Passim.*

were harassing Kentucky, but nothing came of the request. In the midst of these exasperations there came instructions from Virginia for the punishment of Clarke and Logan for undertaking the campaign of 1786, and the district attorney, Innes, contributed toward the feeling the military had for Virginia by refusing to execute the order. In April, 1788, the Indians again became troublesome and a meeting of the field officers was called at Danville. They called out three hundred and sixty-six of the militia for permanent duty and enlisted a special force of sixty-six scouts to hunt for Indians. As a result of these vigorous measures, Kentucky enjoyed a degree of peace for the next few months that she had not known for many years.

Mention must be made of two events that were subjects of interest to the Kentuckians of this period. One was the settlement of Ohio and the other was the formation of the State of Franklin by the people of Tennessee, who were living under much the same conditions as were the Kentuckians. Ohio had acquired a quasi-Constitution by the Ordinance of 1787, and the activities of the Ohio Land Company and its subsidiary, the Scioto Company, soon resulted in bringing settlers into the land. This was a two-fold advantage to Kentucky: it interposed a barrier between the Indians and the Kentuckians and it placed a line of settlers along the route that their trade took in going to Philadelphia. It would have been no more than natural if Kentucky had been influenced by the example of Tennessee to declare its independence. Virginia, whose wish it was that Kentucky should not have separation until provision had been made for taking her into the Union, feared for the effect that the example of Franklin might have. Pressure was brought to bear on the infant State and Virginia received assurances from the *de facto* Franklin government that Kentucky would not be supported by her in a course that Virginia feared. That there ever was any danger that Kentucky would allow herself to be influenced by the example of Franklin is not credible to anyone who understands the nature of the genus Kentuckian. It was much more likely that the Kentuckians would be influenced by Spanish promises.

In the "Seventh" Convention Brown declared that Spain stood ready to extend various commercial privileges to Kentucky if she were independent. Wilkinson told of his trip to New Orleans in the summer of 1787 and read a lengthy memorial on the subject of trade with that city. Wilkinson was given a vote of thanks by the convention, which, after drafting an address to Virginia and another to the people of Kentucky, adjourned. Virginia in the meantime had heard of the inaction of Congress in admitting Kentucky and had passed the third Enabling Act, December 29, 1788.[52] The act, after calling for another convention to meet in July, 1789, had provided that Kentucky, in becoming a separate State, should assume a part of the domestic debt of Virginia and should continue dependent on her as to the lands given by Virginia to her soldiers in Kentucky.

To these two provisions the Kentuckians had no intention of submitting, and when the "Eighth" Convention met, July 20, 1789, its first act was to send a protest to Virginia and ask for a modification of the terms. Virginia readily complied, passed a fourth Enabling Act omitting the obnoxious provisions and called a convention for July 26, 1790. Kentucky was to become independent of

---

[52] Hening, Vol. XII, p. 788.

Virginia on a day to be fixed by the "Ninth" Convention provided Congress had previously admitted her to the Union. It was to be the duty of the "Ninth" Convention to call another for the purpose of framing a Constitution for the new State.

The "Ninth" Convention named June 1, 1792, as the date of separation, issued a call for the Constitutional Convention and adjourned after sending a memorial to the new Federal government, asking for admission to the Union. Washington, now president, recommended the admission of the new State. February 1st, Congress passed the requisite act, and on June 1, 1792, having framed a Constitution and elected Isaac Shelby as first governor, Kentucky passed from a district into a State and became a member of the Union.

During the last two or three years preceding the separation of Kentucky from Virginia the district had lived in comparative peace as far as the Indians were concerned. The Indians had now even ceased to penetrate into the interior of Kentucky at all, even for horse stealing, and confined their activities to harassing travelers on the two main routes into Kentucky, the Wilderness Road and the Ohio River. A summary stop was put to the Wilderness Road depredations in December, 1790, when the county-lieutenants of Mercer, Madison and Lincoln were instructed to order out a guard of thirty men alternately to take their station at Cumberland Gap and protect the travelers. The efforts to prevent the marauding on the Ohio River or to avenge it was more protracted. In September, 1790, the Federal government placed General Harmar in command of an expedition against the Miami villages. A detachment of three hundred militia under Colonel Hardin joined him at Fort Washington at the mouth of the Licking and the army marched northward, only to meet with a disastrous defeat at the hands of the Indians led by Big Turtle. The conduct of the Kentucky militia in this battle was disgraceful, and was exceeded only by the rashness of their leader, Hardin. But with characteristic western disposition they refused to take the blame and insisted that Harmar had been the cause of the defeat.

The Federal government now appointed a Board of War to reside in Kentucky, with authority to call out the Kentuckians for service against the Indians. In May, 1791, this Board ordered an expedition against the Wabash Indians and gave the command of it to General Charles Scott, with Wilkinson as second in command. Seven hundred mounted men composed this army, and they met with complete success. But the expedition of St. Clair in November, 1791, had a far different ending. The Kentuckians were distrustful of regular officers and went with St. Clair reluctantly. Before the day of the battle three-fourths of the one thousand men that had started with him had deserted and the remaining were far from distinguishing themselves in the battle. But the various expeditions, successful or not, were all beneficial to Kentucky, inasmuch as they kept the attention of the Indians distracted from her borders. Within a few months a leader was to be found whose success would wipe out all memory of these defeats.

ECONOMIC AND SOCIAL.

THE economic beginnings of Kentucky are to be found almost as far back in the past as the foundations of its political history. At the beginning of the French and Indian war, the Governor of Virginia gave to the militia of his State a specific reason for enlistment in the promise of western lands. According to the terms of his proclamation, 200,000 acres of land were to be surveyed on or near the south bank of the Ohio River and divided among the militia.[1] The terms were liberal, as was appropriate in the case of men who in all probability would not live to demand their execution. For reasons which do not require explanation, these lands were not surveyed till the close of the struggle, and in 1763 the proclamation of King George in regard to his newly won territory again took up the land question. The land was to be surveyed for the veterans in amounts proportionate to their rank. Field officers were to receive 5,000 acres; captains, 3,000; subalterns or staff officers, 2,000; non-commissioned officers, 200; and the lowly private, 50.[2]

But the same proclamation that set forth these terms likewise closed the Kentucky lands to settlements, reserving them to the Indians. Not until 1770 did the Virginians obtain the legal sanction to settle in Kentucky. In October of that year the treaty of Lochaber with the Cherokees placed the western boundary at the Kanawha, and Colonel Donelson in surveying ran it along the Kentucky instead. This action, acquiesced in by all parties, opened

---
[1] Hening, Vol. VII, p. 669.
[2] *Ibid.*

up Kentucky for the Virginians. The English shortly announced a new policy, to survey the lands in tracts of from fifty to one thousand acres and sell them at auction.[3] But the Virginia House of Burgesses showed itself rebellious, and Governor Dunmore, in fulfillment of his promises, sent the Virginia surveyors out in 1773 and 1774 to locate the lands for the veterans.[4] These surveyors did not pay strict attention to boundary lines, but did considerable surveying west of the Kentucky River. Most of the surveys, however, had been made east of the Kentucky, when in 1774 Dunmore's war put an end to all surveying, legal and illegal.

In the spring of 1775 the Transylvania Company began its settlement of Kentucky lands. The company offered to each man making the initial trip with Boone or Henderson tracts of 500 acres at a cost per hundred of 20 shillings.[5] At the same time it reserved the right to increase the price to those coming in later. In October, 1775, the company changed the terms of land grants; for a price of 50 shillings each settler was to receive 640 acrees with an additional 320 for each taxable settler he brought in.[6] By January, 1776, 900 claims had been recorded and 560,000 acres surveyed.

It will be remembered that one of the grievances of the Harrodsburg men, as set forth in their remonstrance, was this increased price of land. In point of fact, it was altogether to the advantage of the settlers that Virginia should assert jurisdiction over Kentucky, inasmuch as under Transylvania land cost 50 shillings per hundred acres and

---

[3] Dunmore's Proclamation, *Cal. Va. St. Papers.*
[4] *Supra,* Chap. V.
[5] *Journal of Virginia Convention,* p. 51.
[6] *American Archives,* Vol. IV, p. 554.

under Virginia cost nothing at all. The fall of Transylvania put an end to her land system, though the land warrants issued by her were legalized.

In the meantime, during 1775 and 1776, the Virginians continued to take up lands in Kentucky. So in 1776 there were three kinds of land claims in Kentucky: the claims based on military service, the claims taken out under Transylvania, and a great multitude of claims taken out without any warrant or title whatever. June 24, 1776, the Virginia Convention passed a resolution that all men then actually settled in Kentucky should be given preference to their lands, and the General Assembly, in October, 1777, followed up this resolution with an act providing that all who had taken up lands in Kentucky prior to June 24, 1776, should have title to 400 acres.[7] A law passed two years later, October, 1779, gave to each settler who had been in Kentucky a year prior to January, 1778, or had raised a crop of corn, 400 acres as a settlement right and a pre-emption of 1,000 acres.[8] A cabin had to be erected to secure this pre-emption. Lands taken up after January, 1778, were to be passed on by a Court of Land Commissioners named in a law of the same year.

By the provisions of the land law of 1779, future titles to Kentucky land were to be secured only through treasury warrants.[9] A land office was provided for and a Register was appointed by the Assembly. Henceforth land was to cost 40 pounds per 100 acres and the method of securing the title was an intricate one. A prospective land owner was required to deposit at Richmond the necessary money and receive a land warrant. This warrant

---

[7] Hening, Vol. IX, p. 355.
[8] *Ibid.*, Vol. X, p. 38.
[9] *Ibid.*, p. 50.

merely named the quantity of land and authorized its survey. In each county of Kentucky was an official surveyor, and by him, or his deputies, the survey was made *wherever the holder of the warrant desired.* Trees, rocks, water courses, etc., were used to mark the boundaries. Plat and certificate of survey went on the surveyor's record and had to be returned to Richmond within one year. Within six to nine months later a deed was given.

The defects of this law are apparent. In issuing warrants for amounts without specifying locations, opening was left for great confusion; the same ground was quite likely to be surveyed several times. The power of the owner to place his survey in any shape he desired resulted in many unsurveyed fragments and scraps of farms being enclosed by surveyed land. "Blanket" surveys were common in which the holder of the warrant ran his lines around great territories, being, of course, guaranteed only such lands as were not already surveyed. By these means the fragments and scraps were secured, but in most cases they were occupied by settlers without title and dispossession entailed litigation and often bloodshed. The provisions of the law were so involved that many settlers never completed their titles and were eventually dispossessed. The litigation has vexed the State to this day, and even now there are thousands of acres whose occupants have no other title than that of continued possession.

Yet in this law Virginia probably did the very best she was able. Nothing but a public survey of all Kentucky prior to settlement could have prevented the evil. Such a survey was impossible for several reasons. In the first place, many settlers had come into the frontier in the confusion of early Revolutionary times and taken up claims before Virginia could formulate any actual land law. Moreover, physical conditions in Kentucky made such a survey impossible; Virginia had no surveyor at that time able to conduct a survey of Kentucky on a large scale in the mountains or even in the Bluegrass.

The Court of Claims provided for in this law has already been described. The law remained in force, with minor changes, until 1792. In May, 1781, a law was passed authorizing the County Courts of Kentucky to direct surveys for the poor people of the land.[10] Each family was granted 400 acres at a price of 20 shillings per 100 acres. Credit was given for two and one-half years. The law was to be in force until May, 1783, but when the time arrived a law was passed extending it for six months and reducing the price to 13 shillings.[11] In November, 1781, a deputy land-register was provided for to reside in Kentucky.[12]

Of the actual size of the farms taken up by the settlers prior to 1792, little that is definite can be learned. Under Transylvania rules 960 acres could be secured in one grant and by Virginia settlement and pre-emption rights, 1,400 acres. After 1779 the size of a grant was limited by the paying capacity of the settler. It is not unlikely that up to 1780 the average size and the maximum size was the same. After that there was a tendency to reduce the size, and by 1792 in all probability the farms were less than 1,000 acres, being larger in the Bluegrass and much smaller in the mountains.[13]

---
[10] Hening, Vol. X, p. 431.
[11] Hening, Vol. XI, p. 296.
[12] *Ibid.,* Vol. X, p. 445.
[13] Hughes, *Lands in Dispute.*

The productivity of the Kentucky land in pioneer times is indicated by the following figures: Hemp, 800 cwt. per acre; maize, 60 bushels; wheat, 30 bushels; barley, 40 bushels; oats, 50 bushels; clover, 25 cwt.[14] According to the same authority unimproved land in Kentucky cost from 1 to 8 shillings; improved, 12 to 15 shillings, and if there was an orchard the price rose to 1½ pounds sterling.[15]

In 1792 the three leading crops in Kentucky were corn, hemp and tobacco. As was natural, Indian corn was always the first crop to be planted by the new settler, since for the first few years his family, as well as his cattle, depended on it for subsistence. In early Kentucky the ground, after being plowed, was harrowed with large brush from the trees and was then laid off in furrows "both ways."[16] The corn was planted by dropping it by hand; when it matured both blades and ears were stripped from the stalk and stored away. For the most part only yellow corn was raised in early days, and in 1792 this was selling for twenty-five cents per bushel. The corn was plowed but once and no sort of fertilizer was used to repair the soil for the next crop. In fact, it was not poor ground the settler had to fear, but excessive fertility; if wheat was sown on new ground, it grew so rank as to be useless. Wheat crops could be raised only after four or five corn crops.[17]

In early Kentucky, hemp was considered superior to tobacco as a staple crop.[18] It was first raised near Danville by Archibald McNeill in 1775, and continued until the Civil war to be a principal product of Kentucky. In early times hemp served as the standard of exchange in Ken-

---
[14] Imlay, *Kentucky*, Letter IV.
[15] *Ibid.*, Letter VII.
[16] A. Michaux, Travels, *Early Western Travels*, Vol. III.
[17] Filson, *Description of Kentucky*, p. 23.
[18] Moore, *Hemp Industry in Kentucky*.

tucky, and in 1786 Virginia made it receivable for taxes at 30 shillings per hundred weight.[19] In 1792 the usual price was 25 shillings.

Tobacco did not become an important crop in Kentucky till after 1787. Since it is a crop that can not be largely consumed by the producers and it was practically impossible to get it to market because of distance and poor transportation, the necessary result was that little was raised and that for a very low price—two cents per pound. The mode of cultivation followed that in use in Virginia, which meant stripping the leaves from the stalk when the plant matured and leaving the stalk standing in the field. After the opening of the New Orleans market to Wilkinson, the growing of tobacco took on new life, and it soon became the principal crop of export in the State. This increased demand for tobacco naturally raised the price, and in 1786 a Virginia law made it receivable in taxes at 20 shillings per hundred weight.[20] One year later the rate was raised to 23 shillings.[21] The market for the tobacco was found in New Orleans. Tobacco, however, in early Kentucky had to be delivered to warehouses established by State license and there inspected by State officers.[22] When the tobacco was delivered at these places certificates were given to its owner and these naturally enough passed current as money in the primitive economic life of the time.

The present road system of Kentucky is founded on the traces of pioneer times, and those, in turn, were based on the Indian and buffalo trails. There was an essential difference between the two, since the Indian paths were nar-

---

[19] Hening, Vol. XI, p. 30.
[20] Hening, Vol. XI, p. 259.
[21] *Ibid.*, p. 455.
[22] *Ibid.*, Vol. X, p. 205.

row, while the buffalo trails were many rods wide. Lewis Evans' map of 1755 indicates the most important of the Indian roads in Kentucky. These have already been described. There were, however, numerous offshoots and branches of these roads and many of them were afterwards adopted as routes for county highways.[23] The buffalo trails led from all directions to the "Licks"; they were more numerous by far than the Indian roads, and like them were often adopted as highways.

Filson's map of 1793 shows the road system of Kentucky in pioneer times. Lexington was the converging point of nine roads, Danville, of four. The four most important roads were the Wilderness Road, the Nashville Road, the Lexington-Limestone Road, and the Louisville roads. All these were made of the same material: viz., dirt. They were of unequal width along their course and had no grading. A road in pioneer Kentucky was simply a strip of land over which the trail passed. The Virginia Assembly, in 1779, appointed Calloway and Shelby to mark out a way for pack horses over the Wilderness trail. This did not mean that before this time the trail was not in use for pack horses, but merely that the trail was to be improved and the best branches indicated.[24] Though little was done at this time in the way of improvement, the road continued to be used in increasing measure for immigration and trade. It was the custom for people going from Kentucky to Virginia to travel in companies under guard, and these trips were advertised long ahead so that all travelers might take advantage of them. The Lexington-Limestone road was never a subject for State action before 1792. Its

---

[23] Verhoeff, *The Kentucky Mountains.*
[24] Hening, Vol. X, p. 143.

origin lay in the Indian-buffalo trail that connected both places with the Lower Blue Licks. It came into prominence first as an immigrant road to central Kentucky for those coming down the Ohio, and later as a trade route by which the Pennsylvania merchandise reached the Bluegrass. The first wagon was taken over it in 1783. The course of the road was the present Maysville and Lexington pike. At Lexington began the road to Nashville; it made with the Limestone Road a continuous highway across the land and was a famous route for travelers, and, later, for trade. Its course is shown on the Filson map; it passed through the "Barrens" of Kentucky, where a traveler in 1792 might go forty miles without seeing a house. Because of the nature of the ground over which it passed, it formed an easier road than the two already mentioned. It was not improved before 1792. The Louisville roads were also modified trails connecting that town with Lexington and Danville. At these towns they connected with the roads already mentioned. The Louisville roads were free from obstruction, for most of their course, and could be traveled by wagons from the first. All the Kentucky roads, however, had to cross numerous rivers and these were seldom fordable. Due to this fact the Virginia government early authorized the establishment of ferries at the necessary places. The Boonesborough ferry in 1779 was the first of these and was followed by many others. In 1787 the authority to establish ferries was given to the County Courts of Kentucky.[25] In 1786 Virginia authorized the building by private subscriptions of a "New Road" from Lexington to the Kanawha.[26] It was unfinished in 1792.

---

[25] Hening, Vol. XI, p. 500.
[26] *Ibid.*, p. 196.

The settlement of Kentucky crept out from the central Bluegrass along these four great roads. Indeed, pioneer Kentucky may well be likened to a wheel of which the Bluegrass was the hub and these roads the spokes. Washington, Mayslick, Lower Blue Lick, Millersburg and Paris grew up along the Limestone Road, while Frankfort, Shelbyville, Midway and many others were founded on the roads to Louisville. The road through the "Barrens" did not at first induce settlement, but after 1792 settlers began to take up farms along the road and towns came into existence at the usual halting places of the travelers.

From the time Kentucky County was formed in 1776 until the day of its admission in 1792, the life of its inhabitants was one of turmoil if not of danger. There was much fighting and more talk of fighting with the Indians, and one of the most essential facts in the early history of Kentucky was the organization of the militia on which Kentucky depended for protection.

It was the Virginia law that all free male citizens between the ages of eighteen and fifty should be a part of the militia and subject to military service at the will of the State.[27] The usual exceptions were made of the feeble-minded and the incapacitated, etc. The militia was to be organized by counties with the county-lieutenant at the head with the title of colonel. Under him were the majors and captains in order, all of whom received their commissions from the Virginia authorities. Among the county-lieutenants he was the ranking officer who had been longest in command, and in case two or more received their appointment at the same time, the seniority was determined by lot. The county-lieutenants had the authority to call out the

---

[27] Hening, Vol. XI, p. 476.

troops in case of invasion, but otherwise this power was reserved to the Governor of Virginia. In Kentucky, the settlers were furnished with rifles by the Virginia government, and these rifles were understood to belong to the settlers as long as they remained in Kentucky. As a matter of fact, the arms seldom returned to the government, no matter where the pioneer removed. The militia privates only received pay when they were actually called out by the officers in the service of Virginia. Then they were compensated munificently at the rate of five dollars a month, with one ration a day additional.

It was the custom of Virginia from time to time to send troops from the older counties to those in the more exposed west. These were enlisted for a definite period of time, and if much trouble was brewing, remained constantly under arms until their time expired. For these, regular commissaries were established and maintained at each fort. These had in their employ "hunters" whose business it was to see that the troops were supplied with meat. At stated times the militia accounts were audited and the men paid.[28]

Ammunition for the use of the Kentucky militia was of course furnished by Virginia. It was kept in the various forts and doled out by the sparing hand of the militia officers. This official ammunition, of course, was only used when the militia was called out; on forays and hunts the pioneers had to shift for themselves. Often the ammunition trains on their way to Kentucky were attacked by Indians, who boasted that the kind-hearted Virginians kept them as well supplied with powder as the Kentuckians did with horses.

---

[28] *Autobiography of Daniel Trabue.*

By the law of 1784 the Kentucky militia was to have a private muster every three months, a regimental muster in March or April and a general muster in October or November. They were to be drilled in the discipine that Von Steuben had introduced into the Revolutionary army. But the law was never enforced and the militia remained in 1792 little more than a a rabble on the parade ground, but on an Indian raid a thing of terror from the North Carolina line to the Great Lakes; they went into service ununiformed and highly regardless of rank and discipline, but they fought none the less valorously for that, and theirs is the credit that Kentucky was enabled to live through the strenuous days of Indian warfare and finally come into Statehood.

In military as well as other affairs, the unit of government in Kentucky was the county. Until 1783, when the District Court was established, the county governments were the only forms of control of which the Kentuckians had any experience. At the time of separation from Virginia, Kentucky was composed of nine counties: Jefferson, Lincoln and Fayette created in 1780; Nelson, 1784; Bourbon, Madison and Mercer, 1785; Woodford and Mason, in 1788. Each of these had its usual quota of justices of the peace and a Court of Quarterly Sessions. Each county, too, was given representation in the Virginia Assembly. It is of interest that the different counties were not given representation in proportion to their population, but each had the same number of delegates—two each. When, in 1788, the Kentucky counties were given a Congressional representative, John Brown was chosen and remained in office until Statehood.

When the District of Kentucky was created in 1783, a District Court was established, consisting of a judge, two assistant judges and an attorney.[29] The Court was to meet quarterly and was to sit for eighteen days at each session. The salary of the judge was fixed at 250 pounds, of the assistants at 200 pounds, and the attorney at 150 pounds.[30] In 1784 the salaries of the judges were increased to 300 pounds.[31] John Floyd was the first judge, with McDowell and Muter as assistants and Walker Daniel, attorney. On the death of Floyd, Muter became judge, with McDowell and Sebastian as assistants; Innes became attorney when Daniel died.

The counties each had a sheriff and a surveyor appointed by the Governor. The seat of government was Louisville, for Jefferson; for Fayette, Lexington, and for Lincoln, Harrodsburg. When these three counties were created, James Thompson was appointed surveyor for Lincoln; George May for Jefferson, and Thomas Marshall for Fayette. George May had been the surveyor of Kentucky County.

It must be admitted that the early Kentuckians were not distinguished for religious piety. There were many denominations among them, of which the Catholic, the Methodist, the Baptist and the Presbyterian were the most considerable, but they scarcely affected the current of Kentucky life. Contemporary writers noted with amazement the absence of piety in the land, and were not slow in predicting a fitting retribution.

There were three hundred Catholics in 1792, and they merited and secured a reputation for good citizenship and

---

[29] Hening, Vol. XI, p. 85.
[30] *Ibid.*, p. 398.
[31] *Ibid.*, p. 499.

godly character, such as had distinguished the early Quakers in Pennsylvania. The Kentucky Catholics came almost entirely from Maryland.[32] In their old homes they were poor, and the prospect of good land in Kentucky attracted them. Until 1785 the members of the church were few; Hart and Combs were at Harrodstown in 1776, and there were a few others at the various stations. In 1785 a considerable number of Catholics from St. Marys, Charles and Prince George's counties moved to Kentucky and settled on Pattinger's Creek. The land was poor there and the prospect uninviting, but the congregation made the best of it. By 1787 there were fifty Catholic families in Kentucky, but no priest. They encountered fierce opposition from the Protestants. Father Wheelan ministered to the small flock from 1787 to 1790, at which time he returned to Maryland. From 1790 till 1793 William DeRohan, from South Carolina, labored as an irregular priest in Kentucky.

The early history of the Presbyterians in Kentucky centers around the Reverend David Rice.[33] He came to Kentucky from Virginia in 1783 and gathered the members of his church into three congregations. They were located at Danville, Cane Run and Dick's River. In 1786 the first synod was held at Danville, and in 1792 there were twelve organizations of Presbyterians in Kentucky.

Between Presbyterian and Methodist in early days there was more co-operation than rivalry. In 1783 the Reverend Francis Clark came to Kentucky and establised a church at Danville. The church was of slow growth and had a membership of but ninety in 1787. Daw and Ogden were appointed itinerant preachers in 1786, and by their efforts

---

[32] Spalding, *Sketches;* Badin, *Mission du Kentucky.*
[33] Rice, *Memoirs.*

HISTORY OF PIONEER KENTUCKY 243

Methodism soon became a vital force in the district. In 1788 two circuits were formed, Lexington and Danville. In 1700, Bishop Asbury came to Kentucky and a Methodist Church was built at Masterson's Station. A conference was held, 300 pounds was subscribed for a school and two new circuits made, Limestone and Madison. In 1790, there were nine ministers among the Kentucky Methodists and the church membership numbered 1,400.[34]

By far the largest denomination in early Kentucky was the Baptist. The majority of the settlers from the Yadkin region were Baptists and they from the beginning more than outnumbered all the other denominations. Squire Boone himself was an itinerant Baptist preacher, as was also William Hickman, who came to Kentucky in 1776. In 1790 there were forty-two Baptist churches in Kentucky and the membership numbered over 3,000. No other denomination could show such results.[35]

Kentucky in 1792 had a population in excess of 100,000. Of these not more than 10,000 were members of the four churches that have been named. There were, in fact, a goodly part of the people that belonged to minor organizations. It might be said of the religions of Kentucky, as of its currency, that every civilized country contributed something. Yet, after the most liberal estimate is made, the admission must still be made that two-thirds of the population of Kentucky in 1792 were content to live without the fold of the church.

The increase of population in Kentucky was an object of wonder and even jealousy to the eastern States. In seventeen years it had leaped from nothing to over 100,000;

---

[34] Redford, *Methodism in Kentucky.*
[35] Marshall, *History of Kentucky,* Vol. I, p. 446.

no other State in the Union had experienced such growth. Up to 1780 the population had not numbered more than a few hundred, but in that year beegan the great migration from Virginia, and three years later it was estimated that Kentucky contained 12,000 people; by 1784 the number had become 20,000; by 1785, 30,000; by 1790, 73,000, and by 1792, 100,000. This population was confined almost wholly to the Bluegrass and was composed of rural communities. Settlement was going on all the time in the mountains along the roads that led to the Bluegrass, but in 1792 it was yet inconsiderable. There was no town in Kentucky numbering more than 1,000 inhabitants. In 1790 Lexington contained 834 inhabitants; Washington, 462; Louisville, 350, and Danville, 150. Boonesborough was still one of the thriving towns in Kentucky and Maysville was bidding fair to become the metropolis of the west. Most of the population of Kentucky was Virginian, with Maryland second and North Carolina a close third. The people were almost entirely of English blood, with a small per cent. of Germans.

The subject of the mountain population of Kentucky has always been a fertile field for speculation on the part of the sociologists. They have been said to be the descendants of the younger children of the Virginian aristocracy; to be the Scotch-Irish of a later immigration than those settling in the Bluegrass; to be Bluegrass settlers whom accident or stress of circumstance forced to settle in the mountains. A minute study of history will show that the beginning of settlement in the mountain was along the roads that ran through the to the Bluegrass. Taverns and hostelries for the accommodation of travelers formed the nucleus from which the settlements expanded. The

Wilderness Road was the first region to be settled. As for the settlers, they were essentially of the same rank and class as those in the Bluegrass. Early Kentucky recognized no difference between mountain population and that of central Kentucky. Whatever difference exists today is due to the fact that the two sections have developed differently economically since their settlement.

Kentucky being settled from the frontier regions of the eastern States, did not display so much difference in classes as did the older States. The patrician element in the population was submerged in the overwhelming flood of the so-called plebians. Free land and the equal opportunity for wealth soon leveled any imported distinctions, and Kentucky, instead of imitating the social systems of the south, originated a social structure of the west—where the wealth and power reposed in the hands of the middle class with the upper and lower classes conspicuously absent. The Maryland and many of the Virginian settlers brought slaves to Kentucky, and in 1790, out of a population of 73,000, 12,000 were slaves. Yet slavery in Kentucky was far different from what it was in South Carolina or even in Virginia. Negroes and white men, master and slave, worked together in the fields, marched together against the Indians, and after death slept side by side in the family cemetery. It would be no exaggeration to say that slavery as it existed in Kentucky was the mildest form of servitude mankind has witnessed.

Primitive Kentuckians, whether plebe or patrician, bond or free, lived very much the same kind of life. The houses were all of logs prepared by the very adequate method of felling trees, lopping off the branches and notching the ends of the logs so they would fit together when the house was raised.[36] The logs were sometimes hewn square, but were quite often left round. The chinks between the logs were daubed with clay, making the house, for all its rough appearance, a place thoroughly impervious to the weather. Sometimes a stone chimney was built, but more often the chimney was of sticks lined with clay. They were, of course, always built on the outside. The floor of the cabin was commonly earthern and the roofs were made of boards rived, generally, of ash. The furniture and utensils within the house were as rude as the house itself. The bed consisted of slabs laid across a number of poles and the chairs were slabs supported by legs made of sticks. The tables were of similar manufacture to the chairs and the eating apparatus that graced them was not inharmonious. Knives and forks were rare; two or three was the ordinary quota to a family. The plates, etc., were wooden and the introduction of delft ware was seriously opposed on the ground that it would dull the knives. Cooking was done in the great fireplace which formed the most prominent part of the room.

The bill of fare was by no means unlimited; it consisted for the most part of "hog and hominy," and varied little throughout the year. Johnnycake was at first the only kind of bread known to the Kentuckians; milk and mush was the usual supper—the latter often eaten with sweetened water. Game of different kinds was sometimes obtained and bear meat was regarded as a great delicacy. Tea and coffee were reserved for the sick and were considered as a mark of effeminacy if taken by people in good health.

---

[36] Doddridge, *Notes;* Butler, *Valley of the Ohio.*

Considering the nature of the remedies given for the various diseases which affected the early Kentuckians, it would seem that there was much inducement to remain well. All the diseases common to children were imputed to worms, and the remedies were heroic indeed. Salt, pewter, sulphate of iron or green copperas in huge doses was the prescription in all such cases. The bark of the white walnut tree peeled upward constituted a powerful emetic; peeled downword, it formed a cathartic of wonderful power. If anyone was bitten by a snake, the flesh of the snake, if applied to the wound, was supposed to neutralize the poison. A fluid made of boiling chestnut leaves was also a favorite remedy. The great number of cures effected by these remedies may have been somewhat influenced by the fact that the Kentucky snakes (the copperhead excepted) are entirely harmless. Gun shots were treated with slippery elm bark, while erysipelas, or Saint Anthony's fire, was assuaged by the blood of a black cat. It is a matter of record that black cats were remarkably scarce in early Kentucky.

Domestic animals of any kind were not numerous in Kentucky. They were slain year after year by the Indians on their raids. Prior to 1780, when the population of Kentucky for the most part lived in forts, the horses and cattle were necessarily allowed to wander through the forests and were taken into the fort only in case of siege. The hogs thus running wild soon acquired a fierceness so great that the panthers and wild cats hesitated to attack them. It may also be observed that they developed a speed which, if properly directed, would have rendered them formidable competitors in the Derby. After the settlers left the forts and erected farmhouses the hogs and sheep were quite commonly kept under the house if it were provided with a floor. Uneasiness on the part of the cattle was always regarded as an indication that Indians were near, and many a fort was saved in this way from destruction at the hands of its foes. For food the stock depended on the fruits of the forest or the cane and Indian corn raised by the settlers.

The clothing worn by the Kentuckians was almost altogether of home manufacture. Each household possessed a rude tannery where the hides used in the making of shoes were tanned. Moccasins were commonly made of deer skins, and in winter were stuffed with grass and leaves to keep out the cold. The clothing, consisting of long trousers and a hunting shirt, was home spun and "store" clothing was practically unknown before 1780. A coonskin cap completed the outfit. It must not be thought, however, that the dress of the pioneers was uniform; there were as many variations as there were inhabitants of Kentucky. The young men sometimes adopted Indian attire and appeared in public clad only in breech-clouts and paint. Quite commonly, too, the women and children went barefooted, wearing shoes only on special occasions.

Early Kentucky was as distinguished for its lack of schools as for its disregard of religion. There were, of course, no public schools in Kentucky and such private ones as there were could boast of little but the name.[37] The teachers were generally Irish, and their principal qualification seemed to be a capacity for consuming "moonshine" in indefinite quantities. The alphabet was commonly learned from characters painted on a shingle and other knowledge was acquired in similar ways. Books were scarce, and, as a

---

[37] E. A. Venable, in *National Educational Association Report* for 1889; Lewis, *History of Higher Education in Kentucky*.

consequence, there was much studying together—a state of things resulting in much confusion, inasmuch as everyone studied aloud. The good students were often rewarded by the teacher passing around a bottle of whiskey or a "plug" of tobacco. Unremitting application of the rod was relied upon to remedy all defects physical, mental or moral. These schools were designated as Old Field Schools for the reason that the school building was erected on ground that had been exhausted and thrown out.

Kentucky was, in 1792, in appearance far different from the land of fifteen years before. The forests were fast disappearing from the Bluegrass. Fields of hemp, corn and tobacco dotted the face of the land. Settlement was spreading to the mountains and the Barrens. Indian fighting was rapidly becoming but a memory and of the old leaders only two or three were left. Logan was living quietly on his farm in Lincoln County, full of age and honors. Harrod was dead, treacherously murdered, it was whispered. Clarke was at Louisville, amusing an intemperate old age with fancies of future greatness in the service of France. Land sharks had compelled Boone to leave Kentucky. Henderson was dead; Todd was dead; Floyd was dead. The Pioneer Age of Kentucky history was at an end.

INDEX

A.

Adventure, a motive for settlement, 27.
Allegewi, 30, 31, 32.
Animals, domestic, 247.
Ancient forts, 36.
Assembly, Transylvania, 91, 100.

B.

Baptists, 243.
Barboursville, 44.
Barrens, 8.
Battle Run, 184.
Bedinger, Maj., 154.
Big Bone Lick, 9, 45.
Big Sandy, 6.
Black Hoof, 13.
Bledsoe, 56.
Board of War, 228.
Boone, Daniel, comes to Kentucky, 50; capture, 52; meets Long Hunters, 55; with family to Kentucky, 62; with Stoner, 67; in Dunmore's War, 74; opens road to Kentucky, 86; returns to North Carolina, 98; returns to Kentucky, 99; recaptures girls, 104; a captain, 112; saved by Kenton, 115; captured at Lower Blue Licks, 132; life among the Indians, 135, 136; returns to Boonesborough, 136; court-martialed, 148; major, 149; at Lower Blue Licks, 190.
Boonesborough, building, 89; description of, 94; attack upon, 115; great siege, 139.
Boundaries, of Kentucky, 2, 170.
Bowman, J., 112, 117, 119.
Bowman Expedition, 153.
Bourbon County, 223.
Brown, John, 220.
Bryant's Station, 152; siege, 184.
Buffaloes, 9.
Bullitt, Captain, 59.

Bullock, Leonard, 74.
Byrd's Invasion, 163.

C.

Calloway, Richard, 86, 112, 114, 119, 137, 140, 142.
Cane, 4.
Carter's Valley Settlement, 69.
Carolina, Western, 24.
Catawa, 7.
Catawba, 7.
Catholics, 241.
Census, Harrodstown, 120.
Chartier, 11.
Chatteraway, R., 6.
Chenoa, 6.
Chenoka, 6.
Cherokees, 19, 32, 56, 75, 83.
Chickamauga Expedition, 224.
Chickasaws, 13, 162.
Chillicothe, 17, 133, 153.
Clarke, G. R., at Harrodstown, 97, 101; goes to Virginia, 103; secures powder, 105; major, 112; sends men to Illinois, 114; drafts militia accounts, 121; plans Illinois campaign, 122; raises troops, 124; builds blockhouse at Louisville, 127; builds Ft. Jefferson, 163; against Shawnese, 166; brigadier-general, 172; campaign against Detroit, 173; relieves Ft. Jefferson, 174; reprimanded by governor, 183; conduct in 1782, 196; dissatisfaction with, 205; expedition of 1787, 217.
Clothing, in early Kentucky, 248.
Cool, Wm., 50.
Convention, "second" for statehood, 211; "third," 212, 214; "fourth," 216, 219; "fifth," 220; "sixth," 221; "seventh," 221, 226; "eighth," 226; "ninth," 227.
Corn, raising of, 234.

Crops, in early Kentucky, 234.
County Government, 240.
Court of Quarter Sessions, 119.
Court, District, 241.
Cresap, Captain, 66.
Croghan, Geo., 49.
Cumberland, gap, 28; river, 6; mountains, 5.
Cuttawa, 7.

D.

Danville, 206.
Dark and Bloody Ground, 78.
Delawares, 17.
Delegates, to Virginia, about statehood, 215; to Congress, 220.
District, judicial, 206.
District Court, 241.
Dick, Captain, 55.
Douglass, Jas., 63.
Drennon's Lick, 61.
Dunmore's War, 66.

E.

Education in Kentucky, 248.
Election, first in Kentucky, 114.
Enabling Act, first, 215; second, 219; third, 226; fourth, 226.
Eskippakithiki, 11, 47, 50, 51.
Estill's defeat, 180.
Exploration of Kentucky, by Walker, 43; by Gist, 44.
Evans, Lewis, 46.

F.

Farms, size of, 233.
Fayette County, 170.
Ferry, on Ohio, 129; on Kentucky, 158; on Kentucky and Ohio, 223.
Finley, John, 46, 50.
Floyd, John, 63, 90, 99, 119, 170, 209.
Food, pioneer, 246.
Forts, frontier, 175, 201; ancient, 36.
Ft. Jefferson, 162, 174.
Ft. Massac, 127.
Ft. Pitt, 65, 110.
Ft. Stanwix, 59, 82.

Franklin, State of, 225.
French and Indian War, 47.

G.

Girty, Simon, 187, 195.
Gist, Christopher, 44.
Great Salt Creek, 8.
Greathouse, 66.

H.

Hamilton, Henry, 109, 111, 117.
Hancock, Stephen, 137, 143.
Hard Labor Treaty, 83.
Harmar's Expedition, 288.
Harrod, James, 59, 92, 104.
Harrodstown, built, 63; reoccupied, 90; convention at, 102; memorial to Virginia, 103; siege, 113; county seat, 119; census, 120.
Hart, brothers, 74.
Henderson, Richard, 72; Wataga treaty, 80; to Kentucky, 88; holds convention, 92; returns to North Carolina, 98; grant from Virginia and North Carolina, 106; at Boonesborough, 166; runs boundary, 171.
Henry, Patrick, 73.
Hite, A., 60.
Hite, I., 64.
Hogg, James, 74, 99, 101.
Holder, Joseph, 50, 105, 120, 153, 184.
Houses, in early Kentucky, 245.
Hoy's Station, 184.

I.

Indian Fields, 2, 12.
Indian Expedition of 1787, 217.
Indians, title to Kentucky, 82; English feeling toward, 28; northern, 16, 178; use by England, 200; take side of English, 72, 108; officers, 110.
Iroquois, 10, 82.

J.

Jefferson County, 170.
Jefferson, Fort, 162, 174.

INDEX

K.

Kenton, 95, 99, 114, 115, 138, 167.
Kentucky, forests, 2; mountains, 5; rivers, 6; "licks," 8; game, 9; name, 15; origin of population, 21; roads into, 28; in 1792, 249.
Kentucky County, 104.
Kentucky River, 7.
Knox, James, 55.

L.

Land, Proclamation of 1754, 229; Dunmore's Proclamation, 230; Transylvania policy, 85, 230; Act of 1776, 231; of 1777, 231; of 1779, 231; of 1781, 233; warrants, 169
Land Court, 159.
Laughrey's Defeat, 173.
Leestown, 102.
Lexington, 96, 151.
Limestone Creek, 60, 105.
Lincoln County, 170.
Lochaber, Treaty of, 83.
Logan's Speech, 67.
Logan, Benj., 91, 112, 116, 119, 153, 167, 170, 192, 203, 209, 212, 218, 219.
Long Hunters, 54.
Louisa River, 7.
Louisville, 61, 100; blockhouse, 127; fort, 151, 161; fortified, 202.
Lower Blue Licks, 130, 189.
Loyal Land Company, 43.

M.

Madison County, 223.
Martin's Station, 165.
May, John, 120, 161, 206.
Mammoth Cave, 7.
McAfee Bros., 59; Robt., 60, 90.
McBride, Jas., 46, 47.
McDowell, Samuel, 211.
McGary, Hugh, 99, 189, 191, 193.
Medicine, early, 247.
Mercer County, 223.
Methodists, 242.
Miami Indians, 19.

Miami Expedition, 196.
Militia, 112, 158, 161, 183, 209, 224, 227, 238.
Millewakane River, 7.
Mingoes, 9.
Mooney, James, 50.
Moundbuilders, 30, 33, 34, 35, 36, 37.
Mount Sterling, 180.
Mountain, population, 247.

N.

Neely, Alexander, 53.
Nelson County, 212.
Nepernine River, 6.
New England and Kentucky, 221.
New Orleans, 207.
Northwest, 109.

O.

Ohio Company, 43.
Ouasiotos Mountains, 5.

P.

Paint Creek Expedition, 138.
"Path" Treaty, 79.
Patrol boats, 173, 204.
Pigeon River, 6.
Pilot Knob, 45.
Piqua, 17.
Point Pleasant, 68.
Pontiac, 48.
Presbyterians, 242.
Preston, 63.

R.

Red River, 51.
Roads, in Kentucky, 236.
Rockcastle River, 44.
Roger's Defeat, 160.
Ruddle's Station, 164.

S.

Saint Asaph's, built, 91; attacked, 115.
Sandy Island, 32.
Scott's Expedition, 228.
Sedition, 209.
Settlement, Motives of, 26.

Shannoah, 13.
Shannopin Town, 45.
Shelby, Isaac, 77.
Shawnese, 6; at Indian Fields, 12; in Ohio, 16; capture Boone and Stewart, 52; attack Boone, 62; title to Kentucky, 81; attack Boonesborough, 101; capture girls, 104; capture Boone, 130; besiege Boonesborough, 135.
Shenandoah Valley, 24.
Slavery, 245.
Statehood, 227.
Stewart, 50, 52.
Stoner, Michael, 67, 89, 99.
Strode's Station, 152, 179.
Supreme Court of Kentucky, 206.
Surveyors, Early, 58.
Sycamore Shoals, 76.

T.

Taylor, Hancock, 59, 63.
Tennessee River, 6.
Title to Kentucky, 81.
Tobacco, 235.
Todd, John, 105, 114, 119, 162, 170, 189.
Totteroy River, 6.
Trails, Indian, 3.
Transylvania Company, 75.

Transylvania Colony, boundaries, 78; land laws, 85; Assembly, 91; name, 92; population in 1775, 95; land office, 96; meeting of proprietors, 98; memorial against, 102; dissolution, 106.
Treaty of 1783, 199.
Twetty, Capt., 87.
Twigtees, 19.

U.

Upper Blue Licks, 184.

V.

Virginia, title to Kentucky, 81; aristocracy, 22; economics, 21.

W.

Walker, Dr. Thomas, 43, 171.
War Road, 14.
Wataga, settlements, 69; treaty, 76.
Wilderness Road, 158.
Wilkinson, James, 209, 212, 213, 216, 221, 226.
Williams, John, 98, 99.
Winter, hard, 1779, 157.
Wyandots, 18, 179, 180.

Y.

Yadkin, 24.

www.ingramcontent.com/pod-product-compliance
Lightning Source LLC
Chambersburg PA
CBHW071705160426
43195CB00012B/1577